T0320830

Bribery and Corruption in Weak Institutional Environments

Drawing on twenty years of research and observations, Li explains how bribery and corruption are carried out in countries with weak institutional environments, and how these activities become globalized. By distinguishing rule-based, relation-based and clan-based governance, this book offers a novel explanation to the age-old puzzle of why some countries thrive despite corruption. It also sheds light on the symbiotic roles corruption and anticorruption campaigns play in maintaining dictatorships. Applying cost–benefit analysis to different governance environments, Li argues that as non-rule-based economies expand, the transition from relying on private relationships to relying on public rules is inevitable. However, by highlighting the globalization of corruption by non-rule-based countries, this book warns against the potential threats and consequences of bribery by powerful dictatorial governments. This book will appeal to scholars, analysts and graduate students studying corruption, as well as policymakers, business professionals and executives seeking insights into the characteristics of bribery and corruption within different institutional settings.

SHAOMIN LI is Eminent Scholar and Professor of International Business at Old Dominion University. His research has appeared in *Journal of International Business Studies, Harvard Business Review, The Economist, The Wall Street Journal,* and *The Financial Times,* amongst others. In 2008 the Governor of Virginia presented him with the Outstanding Faculty Award.

Bribery and Corruption in Weak Institutional Environments

Connecting the Dots from a Comparative Perspective

SHAOMIN LI

Old Dominion University, Virginia

CAMBRIDGE
UNIVERSITY PRESS

University Printing House, Cambridge CB2 8BS, United Kingdom

One Liberty Plaza, 20th Floor, New York, NY 10006, USA

477 Williamstown Road, Port Melbourne, VIC 3207, Australia

314–321, 3rd Floor, Plot 3, Splendor Forum, Jasola District Centre,
New Delhi – 110025, India

79 Anson Road, #06–04/06, Singapore 079906

Cambridge University Press is part of the University of Cambridge.

It furthers the University's mission by disseminating knowledge in the pursuit of
education, learning, and research at the highest international levels of excellence.

www.cambridge.org
Information on this title: www.cambridge.org/9781108492898
DOI: 10.1017/9781108631440

First published 2019

Printed and bound in Great Britain by Clays Ltd, Elcograf S.p.A.

A catalogue record for this publication is available from the British Library.

ISBN 978-1-108-49289-8 Hardback

In memory of my father, Honglin Li (1925–2016), who inspired me to conduct research that impacts society

Contents

Figures

Tables

Acknowledgments

I would like to thank the Department of Management at Old Dominion University's Strome College of Business for providing an open and supportive environment. I am grateful to the following people who provided help and advice on the project: Anil Nair, Alison Schoew, David Selover, Johannes Wendt and Jun Wu.

At Cambridge University Press, I would like to thank my editor, Valerie Appleby, for her guidance and advice. It was Valerie's enthusiastic encouragement and support that enabled me to develop this project into a book and to find a great home for it. I am also indebted to Podhumai Anban, Toby Ginsberg and Matt Sweeney, who guided me through the manuscript preparation and production process at the Press. Finally, I thank the anonymous referees for their constructive comments and suggestions.

As always, my deepest gratitude goes to my family: my wife, Amy, whose unwavering support allowed me to concentrate on writing my book; and our daughter Diana, whose witty, humorous (and occasionally sarcastic) comments were like a fresh breeze in the hot summer days of writing. Thank you.

I Introduction: Why Study Corruption in Countries with Weak Institutional Environments?

TUNISIA. The country was ruled by the dictator Ben Ali from 1987 to 2011. While he was known to be corrupt, the public did not know the extent of his corruption. Needless to say, Ben Ali was beyond the law and no one could investigate him for corruption. After Ben Ali's fall in 2011, the new government seized the following illegal gains by him and his family and friends: "550 properties, 48 boats and yachts, 40 stock portfolios, 367 bank accounts, and 400 enterprises at an estimated value of $13 billion (the equivalent of 25 percent of the 2011 Tunisian gross domestic product), as well as $28.8 million held in a Lebanese bank account" (Yerkes & Muasher, 2017, p19).

VIRGINIA, the United States. From the early to the mid-2010s, there was a high-profile corruption case that mesmerized Virginians, and also shocked the whole nation, because the person charged in the case, Bob McDonnell, was the state's governor and a 2016 presidential hopeful. In 2011, while he was still in office, Bob McDonnell and his wife were investigated by the Virginia State Police for corruption: receiving from a businessman gifts and loans totaling $177,000 to promote the businessman's product. It turned out that the governor did not even have the power to do so: his call to the University of Virginia to study the product was ignored by the scientists at the university (Walker, 2013). McDonnell and his wife were indicted for and convicted of corruption though the conviction was overturned by a higher court for a retrial which never happened.

MALAYSIA. This country is currently mired in a large corruption scandal involving billions of dollars. The corruption scandal revolves around two focal points: the Malaysian state-owned fund, 1MDB, and the family of the former prime minister, Najib Razak. What is interesting is that this scandal is not confined to Malaysia; it affects many countries and international organizations. As of July 2018, the following countries or foreign entities were known to be affected by the scandal: Switzerland (especially Swiss banks), Hong Kong, Scotland, the United States (including several major financial institutions and a film studio), Singapore, Luxembourg, the United Arab Emirates, the Seychelles, China, and Australia (Wikipedia, 2018a).

1

CHINA. The country's economy has enjoyed high growth in the past thirty years or so. Its export-driven economy has earned China a large trade surplus and a huge reserve in US dollars. The Chinese Communist Party controls the country's resources and decides how to use them. One of the ways it has been spending the country's resources is to embark on a global philanthropic effort of unrivaled scope and scale. From 2000 to 2014, China provided aid, totaling $350 billion, in various forms to 140 countries and territories. Since 2009, China has been the largest provider of foreign aid. In addition, the Chinese government provides funding to about 150 countries to teach Chinese language and culture. It has also set aside $5.1 billion for scholarships for foreigners to study in China (AIDDATA, 2017; Radio Free Asia, 2018; Wikipedia, 2015b).

While these facts may, in themselves, be intriguing in different ways (depending on the perspective or the background of the reader), it may not be obvious why I have listed them here. How do they relate to what we will discuss in this book? As I will explain in this chapter briefly, and in the following chapters in greater detail, they are closely related to the reasons why we want to study bribery and corruption in countries with weak institutional environments, and how such bribery and corruption affect the world. Before we delve into our main topics, though, let us review the general background to the study of corruption.

1.1   CORRUPTION: A GLOBAL EPIDEMIC

Corruption is a major problem across the globe. If we take a glance at the map developed by Transparency International (TI), the leading international corruption watchdog, based in Germany, which monitors corruption in the world, and we note, on the map, the use of shading to indicate the level of corruption in each country, we find ourselves overwhelmed by a huge shadowy globe! Countries that are very clean (lightly shaded) are far outnumbered by countries that are corrupt (heavily shaded) (see Figure 1.1). Specifically, Transparency International created a "Corruption Perception Index," based on survey data, that uses a scale of 0 (highly corrupt) to 100 (very clean) to measure the level of corruption in each country (see Table 1.A.1 in the Appendix to this chapter). In 2017, the year in which the latest survey results were released, the global average score was 43, below the mid-point of 50. Only 23 out of 176 countries have achieved a score of 67 (two-thirds of the full 100) or higher. Fifty percent of all countries have a score of 38 or lower! These numbers indicate that, unfortunately, being corrupt is the norm among many of the countries of the world. Most people live in countries in which corruption and paying bribes are part of their daily lives. Furthermore, there is no sign that the situation is improving. According to Transparency International, there were more countries witnessing a worsening of corruption in 2017 than there were countries that had seen an improvement. Even with the caution that the TI's corruption scores are based on the perceptions of the people surveyed, we can still safely say that corruption, worldwide, is persistent and is not getting better. This not-so-optimistic trajectory has prompted TI to emphasize that the global community has "the urgent need for committed action to thwart corruption" (Transparency International, 2017).

The realization that corruption is deeply rooted and that it has spread widely throughout so many countries is not new; numerous scholars in the fields of political science, economics, sociology, and management have produced voluminous studies about it (see, e.g., Fishman & Golden, 2017 for a review on the study of corruption). However, corruption is a complicated and multi-faceted phenomenon that infiltrates the different dimensions of societies across geography and time, so that there are many aspects of corruption that have not been carefully studied in detail; consequently, there are many gaps in the literature of corruption studies. One of them is the lack of new and insightful perspectives to explain the various types and effects of corruption across societies with different institutional environments, especially among countries that are more infected by rampant corruption. For example, while Peru and China are both ranked as highly corrupt by Transparency International, with a corruption score of 35 for Peru and 40 for China (Transparency International, 2017), the effect of corruption on the two countries'

#cpi2017

www.transparency.org/cpi

FIGURE 1.1 Map of Corruption Perception Index, 2017
Source: Transparency International, 2017

economic development seems to be quite different. A Western business executive traveling in Peru and seeing the poverty and the poor infrastructure could easily conclude that corruption has hurt the country badly; however, the same executive traveling in China and seeing the abundance of consumer goods and first-rate infrastructure would be puzzled as to why corruption does not seem to slow China's rapid economic development. Thus, there is a need for what sociologist Robert Merton would call "a middle range theory" (Merton, 1968), which can integrate theory and empirical observation and provide an insightful explanation of certain aspects of corruption and its effect on a society.

In this book, from the perspective of institutional theory, I will examine the bribery–corruption relationship in countries with weak institutional environments and how this relationship interacts with and affects the economic development in these countries and in the international political economy. In doing so, I will propose several new arguments, including an explanation of why some of these countries thrive despite corruption, and the emergence of a new form of corruption in which a national government bribes the rest of the world.

I will draw on the research and frameworks that I have developed or co-developed with my colleagues during the past fifteen years or so (Alon, Li, & Wu, 2016; Li, 2004, 2017; Li & Ouyang, 2007; Li, Park, & Li, 2004; Li & Wu, 2010), and will add my new thoughts and observations. To support my arguments in the book, I will use evidence that I have accumulated, both from observations and from interviews that I have made on the differences between the East and West.

The basic premise of my arguments in this book is that the likelihood of acts of corruption and bribery, which are the individual-level behaviors of a government official or of a business executive (or of a citizen), is, to a great extent, determined by the institutional environment of the society. This environment will not only determine an intention to pay and/or to take bribes, but it will also determine the consequences for the economy of someone's doing so. In other words, differences in institutional environments lead to diverging outcomes of corruption. Specifically, I will focus on the antecedents and the consequences of corruption in societies in which the governance institutions, such as the rule of law and the free flow of information, are weak, because, after all, these societies suffer the most from the adverse effects of corruption, and therefore urgently need help to fight it.

In this introduction, I will provide the background necessary for the study of corruption and will briefly describe the theoretical framework and the major topics to be covered in the book.

1.1.1 What Is Corruption?

In this book, I focus on corruption by government officials and I adopt the definition of corruption offered by Shleifer and Vishny (1993), which describes corruption as the sales of government goods or services by government officials for private gains. Those "private gains" can go directly to the official or to the relatives, friends, or any collaborators of the official. The government goods or public goods can range from huge projects worth billions of dollars (such as approval of government procurement), to public infrastructure projects, public goods and services vital to citizens (such as quotas of public schools, public hospital beds, or firefighting services), to routine services (such as obtaining a passport, visa, permit, or driver's license). For example, when a citizen applies for a passport at a government passport office, instead of processing the application according to government rules, a corrupt passport officer may first threaten to reject the application and then may extort extra payments to process it.

Sometimes the public goods or services can be eliminations of bads (the opposite of goods in economic terms), such as prison terms. For example, a warden may furnish an overly positive report for a prisoner's parole request if the prisoner pays a bribe, or an official may simply create a new fee for all firms without delivering any corresponding service, and then punish any firms that refuse to pay.

I.I.2 The Negative Effect of Corruption on the Economy

Figure 1.2 shows the relationship between the corruption level and the level of per capita income across countries. The trend is very clear: poor countries tend to have a high level of corruption.

Theoretically, there is a consensus among the scholars of corruption that, in general, corruption has a negative effect on economic development (see, e.g., summary reviews by Fishman & Golden, 2017; Holmes, 2015; and Rose-Ackerman and Palifka, 2016). The reason that corruption hurts economic development is two-fold: misallocation of resources, and loss of economic resources.[1]

More specifically, the reasons why corruption adversely affects economic development can be understood from the following perspectives. First, the country's citizens and firms are the ones that have to pay for the corruption, and those payments will be displaced from productive use by those citizens and firms. As a result, corruption takes much-needed economic resources, such as capital investment funds or funds for education, away from economic development and puts them into corrupt officials' pockets.

Second, in order to increase their opportunities to take bribes or to steal from public funds, corrupt officials tend to increase governmental approval processes to make them more powerful so that, at each approval step, the official in charge can ask for bribes, wasting both time and capital for people and businesses. The corrupt officials can also create new, one-of-a-kind projects or projects with complicated and opaque cost structures, so that they can easily steal funds from them. These behaviors can cause a misallocation of resources, both for the economy and for society. An example of these projects is real estate development in many countries, which requires many approvals in land zoning and acquisition, building codes and inspections, financing approvals, and so on. Each step in this long and complicated process provides an opportunity for the approving official to extort payment. Another kind of resource-distortion project is the expensive, custom-designed project that cannot be easily

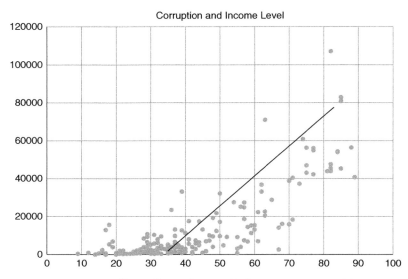

FIGURE 1.2 Corruption and per capita income across countries
Vertical axis: three-year (2014–2016) average income (GDP) per capita (US
$); horizontal axis: Corruption Perception Index (CPI) score (2017) (1 =
most corrupt, 100 = least corrupt).
Sources: Transparency International and World Bank. The chart includes
180 countries with non-missing data of CPI and income per capital.

benchmarked, so that the corrupt official and the briber can collude to
jack up the total cost and split the illegal gains. Projects of this sort
include nuclear power plants and mega construction projects such as
airports and highways. Corruption-induced distortion has plagued
many underdeveloped countries. For instance, traveling in poverty-
ridden African countries, one would see underfunded and rundown
elementary schools but one would also notice expensive highways
that could be used for landing airplanes. A possible reason for this
disparity is that the cost of building new schools can be relatively easy
to calculate on a per-student basis and thus has little room for squeez-
ing out bribery to pay officials, whereas the construction of an expensive highway is a more lucrative project for stealing funds.

Since corruption is illegal, even in the most corrupt countries
(Fishman & Golden, 2017, p. 27) offenders risk being caught and punished. This leads to the third way in which corruption hurts economic

development. In order to avoid detection, corrupt officials tend to create more secret projects and to hide their ill-gotten gains away from their own societies in foreign banks, further exacerbating the negative effects caused by the first and second reasons. Furthermore, the grim prospective of being caught – or even shot – forces the corrupt officials to ask for a huge amount of money to make the effort worth their while (or life). As Shleifer and Vishny (1993) show, giving harsh punishment to corrupt officials does not stop corruption, as it does not address the root cause of it; it merely increases the price of corruption. The effect of corruption on the economy and on corrupt officials is a vicious circle. More corruption makes an economy poorer; a poorer economy makes the per capita income lower, and thus the corrupt officials' paychecks smaller, which prompts the corrupt officials to extort more bribes, increasing their chance of being caught.[2] From this perspective, we can argue that cleaning up corruption is beneficial for the corrupt officials because, as the society has more resources freed from corruption to invest in the economy, the per capita income will rise and so will that of the officials. This reduces the drive for extorting bribes, which reduces the chance of being caught. The success stories of Hong Kong and Singapore in fighting corruption are cases in point (see Chapter 7 and Quah, 2017).

The above reasons can also explain why corruption is so difficult to eradicate: First, the official, such as the head of state, who has the power to clean up the corruption, is often the one behind it. Obviously, he or she has no incentive to expose his or her own activities. In general, a government full of corrupt officials tends to lack effective mechanisms to monitor and prosecute those corrupt officials (in effect, themselves). Second, the secrecy of corruption makes detection difficult. This is especially the case when the briber is not a victim of the corruption (see Chapter 2, Table 2.1.1) so that the briber, like the corrupt official, wants to hide the corrupt transaction. In general, the property right of the state is fuzzy and impersonal, so for corruption that involves stealing state properties, the incentive for other officials to detect and turn in the culprit is low.

Third, the very nature of the bribery–corruption relationship requires that there be a built-in positive feedback mechanism that ensures that it never stops and that it increases in scale and scope. For example, in many highly corrupt governments, in order to become an official and to get promoted, one must bribe the officials who control the personnel and promotion decisions. Thus, it is not difficult for bribers to figure out that, once they get the new position, they need to collect more than they paid for it in order to make the risk-taking endeavor worthwhile.

I.2 MY APPROACH TO EXAMINING CORRUPTION IN THIS BOOK

I.2.I *An Institutional Approach to Studying Corruption*

Corruption is not randomly or sporadically spread across all of the countries in the world. It has a fairly clear pattern, and it systematically affects some countries more than others. A number of theoretical frameworks have been developed to explain cross-country patterns in corruption (see reviews by Fishman & Golden, 2017; Rose-Ackerman & Palifka, 2016; and Holmes, 2015). While these frameworks differ in many aspects, they converge on the common, systematic features that are present in societies suffering rampant corruption.

A good way to understand the features of highly corrupt societies is to look at the features of *very clean* societies. Research shows that all of the very clean societies share the following features (Shleifer & Vishny, 1993; Tanzi, 1998):

1. **A political system that ensures fair and effective political competition.** Pressure from opposition parties is an effective way to keep incumbent officials more honest and less corrupt. In contrast, in highly corrupt societies, the political power tends to be exclusively controlled by one political group, such as a party, a family, or a military dictator.
2. **A limited government.** Reducing the government's role in the economy and the society mitigates corruption. In highly corrupt societies,

government control over the economy and the society tends to be extensive, and, in many cases, the government owns and operates economic activities and competes with private businesses.

3. **The rule of law.** To effectively fight and eradicate corruption, a society must have a well-established legal system that is fair and efficient. Hardly any highly corrupt societies have this crucial feature. In these societies, the legal system tends to be underdeveloped, and an independent and non-political judiciary system tends to be missing.

4. **Free and competitive media.** A free press has proven to be a highly effective way to expose and fight corruption. In highly corrupt societies, the state usually controls the flow of information, effectively preventing the exposure of corrupt officials by the media.

5. **Development of a civil society** (the political participation of citizens). The participation of ordinary people in battling official misconduct and embezzlement is necessary to change a corrupt culture, to develop social trust, and to make the government accountable. However, most highly corrupt governments fear and stifle the development of a civil society.

6. **An adequately paid workforce in the government.** Government employees in highly corrupt societies tend to be poorly paid, and can make extorting payment from people and businesses a necessary part of their regular income. This is a vicious cycle: the extortion by poorly paid officials from people and from firms slows the economic development; then, the slowed economic development makes the officials more poorly paid, which forces them to extort more from the people and the firms, which, in turn, further slows the economic development. A key measure in Hong Kong and Singapore's successful experience in eradicating corruption is that they raised the salary level of government employees close to the market level in order to reduce their incentive to ask for bribes (Berlinger, 2012; De Speville, 1997). This reduction in extortion by officials helps economic development, and faster economic development affords them higher raises, which further reduces the incentive to resort to corruption. A by-product is that the less corruption committed by officials, the less the chance that they will get caught, which makes their lives safer. Thus, in the long run, eradicating corruption is beneficial, even for corrupt officials.

All of these six features are systems or arrangements at the societal level; some are legal, political, and economic in nature, while others are social and cultural. A common term used by social scientists to describe them is *institutions*. The institutional arrangement of a society plays perhaps the most important role in determining how prevalent corruption is in that society.

This book addresses the pattern of corruption across countries by using an institutional approach (North, 1990). According to North, institutions are the rules of the game that govern the socioeconomic exchanges in a society, whereas individuals and organizations are the players in the game who are trying to use the rules to maximize their welfare (North, 1990). North's framework not only offers a theoretical understanding of socioeconomic behaviors, but also provides a useful analytical tool to examine the interplay between the macro social environment (the institutions) and the micro behaviors (by the players). At the macro level, the institutions are rules that either constrain or facilitate certain behaviors of individuals or of organizations. These rules can be formal rules (or hard constraints) explicitly set by a government, such as economic and political policies, regulations, or laws. Rules can also be informal (or soft constraints), such as social attitudes, social forms, and values. Key features of informal rules are that they tend to be implicit and unwritten, and based on social convention. Collectively, informal rules form an important part of the culture of a society. The interplay between formal and informal rules may help us to understand how institutions change and how those changes affect the behavior of the players: the individuals and organizations. The causal relationship between the formal and the informal is two-way. Cultural beliefs may be formalized into laws, and a newly codified law can change a culture. In general, formal rules can be changed rather quickly (e.g., a government can promulgate a new law overnight); whereas informal rules – culture – tend to change slowly. A common phenomenon in almost all societies is that, after the elimination of a law, the social attitude (culture) supporting the eliminated law will linger for many years.

Based on institutional theory, I argue that it is the macro institutional environment of a society, which consists of political and economic systems and national cultural norms, that shapes the bribery and corruption behaviors at the individual level of the officials and the business people in that society. This perspective enables us to understand why corruption is more prevalent in some societies than in others, under which institutional settings corruption can be less harmful, and which institutional factors determine the success and failure of anticorruption campaigns.

I.2.2 Putting Bribery–Corruption under a Microscope: Dissecting the Briber and the Bribee

After I set corruption in the context of a macro institutional environment, I will further examine the bribery–corruption relationship from the perspective of both the bribe payer (the briber) and the bribe taker (the bribee, or the corrupt official).

The act of corruption, based on the definition given earlier in this chapter, implies that it involves at least two players: the bribe taker and the bribe payer, and the exchange between them (see Figure 1.3). However, most of the existing studies on corruption have used the term "corruption" to implicitly include the bribery side without explicitly discussing it. In this book, I will discuss the bribee and the briber separately, and in more detail.

I.2.3 A Focus on Corruption in Societies with Weak Institutions

From the short cases presented at the beginning of the chapter, we may make several interesting observations that will help us understand how they are related to the topics of the book. First, the cases of Tunisia and Virginia are in a stark contrast: the GDP of Tunisia is about one-tenth that of Virginia ($40 billion for Tunisia and $393 billion for Virginia in 2017). However, the ratio of the size of the corrupt gains by the heads of Virginia

FIGURE 1.3 An anatomy of a bribery–corruption act
Source: Author

and Tunisia is less than 1 to 10,000. Tunisian ruler Ben Ali's loot of billions of dollars dwarfs the Virginia governor's improper take of $177,000 – by a large margin. Furthermore, the Virginia governor was investigated by the police in the state he governed, signifying the ability of the political system to handle corruption even by the head of a state, whereas in Tunisia, the only way to investigate Ben Ali was when he was overthrown by a violent revolution. The case of Malaysia shows that corruption in a country with a weak institutional environment is not contained in that country; instead, it can spread to countries with strong institutions and to international organizations that uphold high ethical standards. The case of China, which is a country with a weak institutional environment, presents a new form of corruption, as I will argue in the book, in which a national government bribes the rest of the world.

In general, corruption is not a major social problem in an advanced democracy with a mature market economy, since it offers an institutional setting that includes all of the six features that we briefly reviewed earlier in this chapter – features that are necessary and sufficient to maintain a very clean governance environment and to systematically, fairly, and effectively expose and correct corruption when it occurs. By contrast, corruption is one of the biggest issues in countries in which some – or generally all – of the six features are missing. Most fundamentally, many of the countries with weak institutional environments tend to be ruled by a dictator or an authoritarian government that bans political participation by the people and that disregards the rule of law, making corruption, often rampant corruption, an inherent part of their political and economic systems.

As the world is increasingly globalized due to international trade and investment, corruption has been exported from these countries to the entire world. This includes the mature democracies.

Based on these facts and considerations, I will, in this book, focus on bribery and corruption in those countries with weak institutions and I will note how this corruption affects the world. Below, I will briefly review the contents of my book.

3. Organization of the Book

In Chapters 2 and 3, we will examine the act of corruption from the viewpoint of the two parties involved: the bribe taker and the bribe payer. Chapter 2 looks at corruption from the bribe taker's perspective. It first reviews the types of the bribery–corruption relationship from the industrial organizational perspective, and it specifies three types of relationships: the big mafia model, the many small mafias model, and the competitive model. It then discusses how the bribee's claim and tenure affect economic development. It reviews the effect of corruption in three types of political regime: autocracy (dictatorship), anocracy (countries undergoing transition), and mature democracy. I will show that, in general, mature democracies with sound legal systems can effectively curb corruption, while in non-democracies (including ill-developed and dysfunctional democracies), corruption is a chronic and persistent phenomenon.

In Chapter 3, I will examine corruption from the bribe payer's perspective. I will first discuss the motivations for people or firms paying bribes to officials. Two types of bribery behaviors are identified: bribery out of necessity and bribery for profit. I will review studies on how much bribers pay and what they get out of it. I will also illustrate what I call "the food chain of bribery and corruption."

The chapter then will shift attention to the bribery–corruption relationship and will examine how the micro environment affects the relationship. I will first examine how multinational firms deal with a highly corrupt macro environment in a country. I will review different approaches by multinational firms in responding to the demand for bribes in a host country from a business ethics perspective, and I will elaborate upon the imperialist approach, the universalist approach, and the relativist approach. After this discussion, I will introduce a dynamic model to explain the bribery behavior of firms by considering three factors: the macro institutional environment that either encourages or punishes bribery, firm bribery or anti-bribery behavior, and inter-firm competition in bribing. Using the model, I will show that, first, if the overall institutional environment is highly corrupt, regardless of how clean (anti-bribing) a firm is, its environment will force the firm to bribe. Second, I will show that, if the combined self-restraint from bribing by all firms is greater than the combined motivation to bribe by all firms, the level of corruption will be manageable; otherwise, the level of corruption will escalate rapidly. Third, I will explain that a firm's effort to bribe or refrain from bribery may have a multiplicative effect and may significantly change the bribing momentum in a society.

In Chapter 4, I will introduce a framework of rule-based versus relation-based governance environments, and will discuss the ways in which the governance environment can help us to understand corruption. A widely held view is that certain cultures are more tolerant of, or even encourage, corruption (see reviews on the cultural explanation of corruption by Fishman & Golden, 2017; Rose-Ackerman & Palifka, 2016; Holmes, 2015). In such cultures, bribery is viewed as a necessary catalyst in cultivating a close relationship between the briber and the bribee, which in turn enables the briber to receive services from the bribee. A problem with this view is that it fails to recognize what has shaped such a corruption-prone culture, which itself is not exogenous and is therefore influenced by political and economic institutions (such as the economic development level and the legal system).

I will present a framework of rule-based versus relation-based governance environments to address the weakness of the cultural argument. The governance environment is the set of social, political, and economic rules (institutions) that, together, facilitate or constrain the choices of a governance mechanism by individuals and organizations in order to protect their interest in social and economic exchanges. For example, in a society with a fair and efficient legal system, people and firms tend to rely on the court to resolve disputes. This is the "rule-based" way. However, in a society in which the public laws are unfair and the judges are corrupt, people and firms tend to rely on private relations in a "relation-based" way (such as asking powerful people to mediate) in order to settle their differences. For a rule-based governance system to work, a society must invest in building an effective legal system that includes rule-setting, as well as rule-enforcing and rule-interpreting bodies. This is costly. But once such a system is well established, whether it enforces one transaction or billions of transactions, the sunk (or fixed) costs do not change. So a rule-based system, with its high fixed costs and low incremental (marginal) costs, favors large-scale market exchanges. In contrast, a relation-based system has few fixed costs (since people tend to deal with their family members and friends and do not rely on public enforcement), but it also has high and often rising marginal costs (since, when a relation-based business grows, it eventually has to deal with strangers, and private enforcement of strangers can be

difficult and costly). In sum, relation-based governance can be efficient when the scale of an economy is small. As the economy expands
from a small locality to national and international markets, it has to
adopt the rule-based system in order to be competitive.

I will show that a society's reliance on a relation-based governance system is not primarily due to its culture, but rather to its stage of
political and economic development. When the state is not able to
enforce rules impartially, people rely on private relations. If a firm or
an individual circumvents public rules and uses private relations to
obtain public goods (such as government approvals or contracts), or to
dispute resolutions, this implies that the official who provides the
favor to their friend is corrupt. Corruption is built into relation-based
societies.

In Chapter 5, I will discuss perhaps the biggest puzzle in the
study of corruption, which is why some economies thrive despite
corruption. The relation-based governance framework can help
solve the puzzle. In a society that is covered by many close-knit
and overlapping private networks, particularized trust (as opposed
to generalized trust) is established through the effective punishment of the members in a network who breach a commitment.
In such a governance environment, a business person who wants to
obtain a lucrative public project but does not know the official who
controls the project can always get to know the official through
a series of overlapping networks. In such a relation-based environment, there is an effective reward and punishment mechanism
within each network, which can be transferred between networks
by members who belong to connecting networks. This means that
the corrupt official does not have to award the project to his or her
relatives, who may not know how to complete the project; rather,
the official can give the project to the bidder offering the highest
bribe, who, *ceteris paribus*, tends to be the most efficient contractor. Thus, ironically, due to the particularized trust nurtured by the
relation-based system, corruption can become less predatory (or
relatively more "efficiency enhancing"), allowing some relation-

based countries to thrive despite corruption. Leff (1964) speculated that if corrupt bureaucrats were to auction off public projects to the highest business bidder, corruption could be efficient. But he did not address the risk of being caught for corruption, which makes such an auction impossible. I will further show that, in non-rule-based societies that do not have extensive close-knit relational networks, corruption tends to be a deadweight loss, and is, thus, most detrimental.

By the end of this chapter, I will have developed the central theme of the book: that it is the macro institutional environment that, to a great extent, determines corruption and bribing behavior at the micro, the individual, or the organizational level. All of these items point to the importance of the political system of a society and how it deals with corruption, which will be the focus of the next chapter.

In Chapter 6, I will focus on corruption in one of the most important types of society with a weak institutional environment: the dictatorship. First, based on "the iron triangle" of dictatorship argument proposed by Rodrick MacFarquhar (MacFarquhar, 2016), I will make my argument as to why corruption and anticorruption campaigns are necessary and inseparable institutional arrangements under dictatorships. Second, I will evaluate whether anticorruption campaigns are ineffective in curbing corruption in authoritarian societies.

In societies ruled by an authoritarian regime that controls vast political, social, and economic resources, corruption is not only inevitable, it is also necessary – in the sense that the ruler needs to give the privilege to extort bribes to his or her cadre of officials as an incentive for them to efficiently and effectively perform their duties. However, if this is left unchecked, the insatiable demand for bribes by those corrupt officials will get out of control and may incite a social revolt. Thus, while allowing corruption, the ruler must keep it under control and must appease any social discontent about rampant corruption. A clever and effective way to achieve this balance is by using anticorruption campaigns. Since authoritarian societies do not have the rule of law, such campaigns are not conducted according to the laws of independent law enforcement bodies; rather, they are conducted by the ruler, without checks and balances and without impartiality. As a result, those campaigns can achieve two goals: first, they can quench citizens' anger towards corrupt officials; second, they can be used selectively by the ruler to purge his or her political rivals and enemies. Thus, the opportunity to corrupt and the selective anticorruption campaigns form the two legs that support the iron triangle of dictatorship. Due to the inherent lack of legitimacy and the inability to fairly and effectively clean up corruption, dictatorships tend to be locked in a boom-and-bust cycle of corruption and anticorruption campaigns.

Chapter 7 discusses the paths of transition from a highly corrupt society to a highly clean society. I will first argue why the transition is necessary and inevitable, from a cost–benefit perspective derived from the framework of a rule-based versus a relation-based governance system. As the scale and scope of the economic exchanges in a society expand from local to national to international, relying on private relations (e.g., the bribery–corruption relationship) to govern the transition will become more and more expensive, and firms, and the society as a whole, must shift away from relying on private relations to relying on public rules such as laws and regulations. I will spotlight the process and the difficulty of the transition, using the cases of Hong Kong, South Korea, Tunisia, and China. Issues arising from transition include the danger of a governance vacuum during the transition, and the tendency to make too many new rules during the transition.

In Chapter 8, I will discuss the globalization of corruption by countries with weak institutional environments. This globalization has two dimensions. The first is the global spread of corruption by these countries. Using the cases of Brazil's "Operation Car Wash" and Malaysia's 1MDB, I will show that corruption spreads like a disease, worldwide, to other countries, including those with a mature democracy and a strong rule of law. In the process, the corrupt governments of countries with weak institutions and privilege-seeking multinational corporations from mature democracies band together, united by their common greed, to form a corrupt alliance.

The second dimension is new: when a national economy has become one of the largest economies in the world and its dictatorial government controls the vast resources of the nation, the government may embark on a global spree of bribing many countries and international organizations. Using China as a case, I will bring the reader's attention to this issue.

In the final chapter, Chapter 9, I will conclude by recapping my main arguments and the contributions in the book, including my effort to dissect corruption from both the briber and bribee's perspective; my new theoretical framework of corruption based on the governance environment; my explanation of the puzzle as to why some countries thrive despite corruption; my argument regarding the symbiotic relationship between corruption and anticorruption campaigns in dictatorships; my argument about the inevitability of the transition away from reliance on corruption from the stage of development perspective; and my call for attention to the globalization of corruption by countries with weak institutions, especially by large corrupt governments.

I will end the book by highlighting the hopes in the fight against the globalization of corruption. Specifically, I will discuss the fighting power of information, and the fighting power of businesses cooperating to oppose corruption, and I will discuss strategies for firms and policy considerations for governments to use during the transition. I will emphasize that, in spite of the difficulties and even the worsening of corruption during the transition, building a mature democracy with the rule of law is the ultimate solution to the corruption problem.

APPENDIX 1.A

Table 1.A.1 *Corruption Perception Index, 2017*

Country	CPI score 2017	Rank
Afghanistan	15	177
Albania	38	91
Algeria	33	112
Angola	19	167
Argentina	39	85
Armenia	35	107
Australia	77	13
Austria	75	16
Azerbaijan	31	122
Bahamas	65	28
Bahrain	36	103
Bangladesh	28	143
Barbados	68	25
Belarus	44	68
Belgium	75	16
Benin	39	85
Bhutan	67	26
Bolivia	33	112
Bosnia and Herzegovina	38	91
Botswana	61	34
Brazil	37	96
Brunei Darussalam	62	32
Bulgaria	43	71
Burkina Faso	42	74
Burundi	22	157
Cabo Verde	55	48
Cambodia	21	161
Cameroon	25	153
Canada	82	8
Central African Republic	23	156
Chad	20	165

Table 1.A.1 (*cont.*)

Country	CPI score 2017	Rank
Chile	67	26
China	41	77
Colombia	37	96
Comoros	27	148
Congo	21	161
Costa Rica	59	38
Côte D'Ivoire	36	103
Croatia	49	57
Cuba	47	62
Cyprus	57	42
Czech Republic	57	42
Democratic Republic of the Congo	21	161
Denmark	88	2
Djibouti	31	122
Dominica	57	42
Dominican Republic	29	135
Ecuador	32	117
Egypt	32	117
El Salvador	33	112
Equatorial Guinea	17	171
Eritrea	20	165
Estonia	71	21
Ethiopia	35	107
Finland	85	3
France	70	23
Gabon	32	117
Gambia	30	130
Georgia	56	46
Germany	81	12
Ghana	40	81
Greece	48	59
Grenada	52	52
Guatemala	28	143

Table 1.A.1 (*cont.*)

Country	CPI score 2017	Rank
Guinea	27	148
Guinea Bissau	17	171
Guyana	38	91
Haiti	22	157
Honduras	29	135
Hong Kong	77	13
Hungary	45	66
Iceland	77	13
India	40	81
Indonesia	37	96
Iran	30	130
Iraq	18	169
Ireland	74	19
Israel	62	32
Italy	50	54
Jamaica	44	68
Japan	73	20
Jordan	48	59
Kazakhstan	31	122
Kenya	28	143
Korea, North	17	171
Korea, South	54	51
Kosovo	39	85
Kuwait	39	85
Kyrgyzstan	29	135
Laos	29	135
Latvia	58	40
Lebanon	28	143
Lesotho	42	74
Liberia	31	122
Libya	17	171
Lithuania	59	38
Luxembourg	82	8
Macedonia	35	107

Table 1.A.1 (*cont.*)

Country	CPI score 2017	Rank
Madagascar	24	155
Malawi	31	122
Malaysia	47	62
Maldives	33	112
Mali	31	122
Malta	56	46
Mauritania	28	143
Mauritius	50	54
Mexico	29	135
Moldova	31	122
Mongolia	36	103
Montenegro	46	64
Morocco	40	81
Mozambique	25	153
Myanmar	30	130
Namibia	51	53
Nepal	31	122
Netherlands	82	8
New Zealand	89	1
Nicaragua	26	151
Niger	33	112
Nigeria	27	148
Norway	85	3
Oman	44	68
Pakistan	32	117
Panama	37	96
Papua New Guinea	29	135
Paraguay	29	135
Peru	37	96
Philippines	34	111
Poland	60	36
Portugal	63	29
Qatar	63	29
Romania	48	59

Table 1.A.1 (*cont.*)

Country	CPI score 2017	Rank
Russia	29	135
Rwanda	55	48
Saint Lucia	55	48
Saint Vincent and the Grenadines	58	40
Sao Tome and Principe	46	64
Saudi Arabia	49	57
Senegal	45	66
Serbia	41	77
Seychelles	60	36
Sierra Leone	30	130
Singapore	84	6
Slovakia	50	54
Slovenia	61	34
Solomon Islands	39	85
Somalia	9	180
South Africa	43	71
South Sudan	12	179
Spain	57	42
Sri Lanka	38	91
Sudan	16	175
Surinam	41	77
Swaziland	39	85
Sweden	84	6
Switzerland	85	3
Syria	14	178
Taiwan	63	29
Tajikistan	21	161
Tanzania	36	103
Thailand	37	96
Timor-Leste	38	91
Togo	32	117
Trinidad and Tobago	41	77

Table 1.A.1 (*cont.*)

Country	CPI score 2017	Rank
Tunisia	42	74
Turkey	40	81
Turkmenistan	19	167
Uganda	26	151
Ukraine	30	130
United Arab Emirates	71	21
United Kingdom	82	8
United States of America	75	16
Uruguay	70	23
Uzbekistan	22	157
Vanuatu	43	71
Venezuela	18	169
Vietnam	35	107
Yemen	16	175
Zambia	37	96
Zimbabwe	22	157
(global average:	43.07)	

Source: Transparency International, 2017

NOTES

1. We will not consider the social and political costs, for the time being.
2. Of course, in a rampantly corrupt society, corrupt officials use their power to protect themselves, so their chance of being caught and prosecuted tends to be low.

2   Bribe Takers: Types of Corruption and Their Effects on Efficiency

> A South African contractor reported the following to Corruption Watch, the South African branch of Transparency International: "We are contractors building RDP units on the West Rand for a certain construction company. After we have completed the units, the construction company staff tell us that in order for the inspectors to come out, we must pay the staff members and the inspectors bribes, which range from R100 to R1000 [about US $7.5 to US $75]. The units have all been completed successfully, but an inspection is refused unless we pay a bribe."
>
> –*Corruption Watch*[1]

2.1   TYPES OF BRIBERY–CORRUPTION RELATIONSHIP

Corruption, the sale of public goods by government officials for their private gain, is an exchange of political, economic, or social interests. As in all exchanges, some parties may benefit and others may be hurt. In other words, the game of corruption may be zero-sum or not zero-sum. Regarding winners and losers in economic exchanges, we can identify three types of relationships.

The first is what Shleifer and Vishny (1993) call "corruption without theft." Using the example of a passport application, let us assume that the official fee is $50; a passport issuing officer threatens to reject an applicant unless he pays the officer $30 in addition to the official fee. The applicant pays $80, and the officer pockets $30 and turns over the $50 official fee to the government. The corrupt officer does not steal from the state. As far as the state's revenue is concerned, the state is not hurt by this act of corruption. However, the applicant is forced to pay more and, thus, is hurt by the corruption. He is angry about the corruption and it is very likely that he will expose the corrupt officer if the opportunity to do so arises, as was the case of the South African contractor in the opening story of this chapter.

The second type is "corruption with theft" (Shleifer & Vishny, 1993), which is similar to "looting/rent-scraping" corruption in Wedeman's study (Wedeman, 1997). In this scenario, instead of charging $30 on top of the official fee of $50, the officer asks the applicant to pay a price lower than the state's price in cash with no receipt (say, $40) in order to get his passport. The applicant is more than happy to oblige, and the officer pockets the $40 without giving anything to the state. In this case, the corrupt officer is stealing from the state. However, the applicant gets what he needs at a lower cost and, thus, has little incentive to expose the corrupt officer.

The third type is what I call "victimless corruption," which is similar to "dividend-collecting corruption" in Wedeman's (1997) terminology. For example, let us assume that the mayor of a city has tremendous power and wants to benefit from it. Let us further assume that the mayor knows that if he or she forces businesses to pay or to steal from the state without delivering anything of value, the chance of being caught is high, since he or she will be hated by the victim, who may be the briber or the society (or its agent: the government). So, instead, the mayor tries to identify entirely new projects that do not use public funds, may benefit the society at large, and are profitable enough for him or her to take a cut. For example, he or she may propose to create an amusement park with local characteristics and then award the project to business friends to invest in and build. The park fills a market (and therefore, a social) need and it brings tax revenues to the city and profits to the mayor's business friends, who in turn pay him or her handsomely in private. In this scenario, all of the parties – the corrupt official, the bribers, and the society – win.[2] Table 2.1. summarizes the three types of the bribery–corruption relationship.

The different types of bribery–corruption relationships interact with the macro institutional environment to produce different patterns of corruption and different economic outcomes of corruption.

Table 2.1 *Winners and losers in different types of bribery–corruption relationships*

Party in the corruption game	(1) Corruption without theft	(2) Corruption with theft	(3) Corruption without victims
Briber	Lose	Win	Win
Corrupt official	Win	Win	Win
Society	Indifferent (No loss in state revenue)	Lose (State losing revenue)	Win

2.2 THE BRIBEE: TYPES OF CORRUPTION IN DIFFERENT POLITICAL–ECONOMIC SYSTEMS

The bribees, the receivers of bribes from the bribers, are the government officials who are corrupt. From the perspective of the bribery–corruption transactional relationship, a key question about the transaction is whether the exchange of goods can be completed as expected by both sides. Shleifer and Vishny (1993) examine the relationship from an industrial organization perspective and postulate three types of bribee: a monopolist (a single mafia) type, an independent monopolist type, and a competitive type (in which case the bribe reduces to zero).

2.2.1 *The Big Mafia Model*

The first type (Shleifer and Vishny's "monopolist"), which I call "the big mafia model" (see Figure 2. 1), exists in a society in which there is a ruler who controls the entire society, especially the entire government hierarchy and almost all of the economic resources. The dictator can be a single person, a clan, an armed force, or a political party. While forms vary, they share certain commonalties. First, they tend to exert absolute control over the executive branch of the government, which overshadows the legislative and judiciary branches, essentially nullifying the latter

FIGURE 2.1 The big mafia model: the briber pays, and the bribee delivers the goods (the approval)

Big Mafia

Firm

two. Second, dictators need to maintain an armed force that is loyal to them and thus can be used by them to crush any challenges. Third, these dictators tend to create an ideological foundation for their absolute rule. The ideology may be political, theological, or economic, such as communism, nationalism, religion, or fascism.

From the briber–bribee relationship perspective, the essence of the big mafia model is that the target for the bribery is clear: the ruler, who has the capacity to keep their promises and to deliver the promised goods. For example, a briber – perhaps a firm that wants to do business in a country and needs approval from several government ministries (such as the telecommunications, transportation, and trade ministries) to begin a project – would offer to pay the ruler, directly or indirectly, for help. The help takes the form of the ruler instructing their ministers to approve the project. The firm's objective is to limit the payment to an acceptable level and to make sure that the ruler delivers: namely, that the firm gets all the approvals from the relevant ministries.

From the ruler's perspective, they would set the price of each bribery–corruption transaction by their ministers to maximize the total amount of bribes that they could get during their tenure. In other words, the ruler should not kill the geese (all of the current and potential bribers) that lay those golden eggs. It is in their interests to set the bribe prices high enough but not so high as to stifle businesses in their kingdom. If the amount of the offer from the firm is satisfactory to the ruler, they would then instruct each of their ministers to charge a set bribery payment so that the total amount of bribes would not be so high as to scare the firm away but would be high enough for all ministers to have a healthy cut, with the ruler keeping the largest amount. The ruler would keep a close eye on their ministers, those who carry out the bribery–corruption transactions on their behalf, and who would, of course, take their "fair" (in the eyes of the ruler and the ministers' peers) share. In general, if the ruler discovers that a minister is greedy and charges more than their fair share, the ruler will get rid of the minister. So, in the long run, the ruler – if they are smart and able to take a long-term view – may achieve an optimal amount of bribes for themselves and for all the minsters so that investors will keep coming and so that their operations will be profitable.

In terms of organizational structure, the big mafia model can be seen as a centralized corruption model (Tella, 2013), in the sense that the decision and process of corruption are centralized in the hands of the head of state. Communist states (Shleifer & Vishny, 1993), such as the former Soviet Union, North Korea, and China, can be characterized as the big mafia model. Some highly centralized right-wing regimes, such as that of Indonesia under the rule of Suharto (who ruled 1967–1998), Taiwan under the rule of the Chiang family (Chiang Kai-shek and his son Chiang Ching-kuo, who together ruled 1949–1988), and South Korea under the rule of Park Chong Hee (who ruled 1963–1979) all loosely fit this model (Alon et al., 2016).

"MR. TEN PERCENT"

The late Indonesian president Suharto, who was well-known for being corrupt and for demanding bribes, had a nickname: "Mr. Ten Percent" (his wife was sometimes called "Madame Ten Percent"), referring to the bribes that he and his family allegedly demanded from the deals and projects that he approved (Lee, Oh, & Eden, 2010; Moreorless, 2018). According to the Australian manager of a software company, the purchasing official from a foreign government told him that "the going rate is ten percent" (Pedigo & Marshall, 2008, p. 63). A survey by the Vietnam Chamber of Commerce and Industry finds that 80 percent of the country's mining firms spent about 10 percent on "informal expenses" (GAN Integrity, 2017b). Studies also show that the return on bribes that firms pay is about 10 times (Cheung, Rau, & Stouraitis, 2012; Karpoff, Lee, & Martin, 2010), which is in line with the 10 percent figure discussed above.

2.2.2   *The Many Small Mafias Model*

The second type of bribery–corruption relationship is what I call the "many small mafias model" (see Figure 2.2), or decentralized corruption (Tella, 2013). It refers to the bribery–corruption relationship in countries in which many officials independently control a section of the political economy, so that a briber has to bribe all of them in order to obtain the necessary approvals. Shleifer and Vishny (1993) used the term "independent monopolists" to describe this type, since each monopolizes a particular government good that is needed by businesses – and there is no substitute good. For example, an investor who wants to build an automobile assembly line needs a water supply from the government public water agency, electricity from the state power grid, the permission to discharge wastes, a certificate of safety inspection, and many other approvals. Each of the approvals is independently controlled by a government agency. Since there is no single powerful big mafia with the authority to set the price of a bribe for

Many Small Mafias

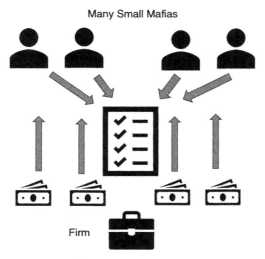

Firm

FIGURE 2.2 The many small mafias model: the briber has to pay all of the mafias to obtain the public good (which has to be approved by each member of the mafia jointly and independently)

each department or to coordinate all of the departments to get all of the necessary approvals for the investor, each department head has an incentive to ask for an exorbitant amount of bribe. As a result, the total amount of the bribes that the investor has to pay can be so high that they may not be able to afford it. If the investor fails to get approval from any one of the agencies, the assembly line will not be built.

In general, corruption under the many small mafias model is worse than that in the big mafia model, because the briber does not always know whom to bribe. Due to information asymmetry and to the secrecies shrouding the bribery–corruption relationship, it is difficult or impossible for the briber to check which small mafia's promise is credible. Successfully bribing and obtaining an approval from one minister does not guarantee that the briber can obtain the public good that they want, because the heads of other ministries need to be satisfied as well. Any of the gatekeepers may raise their price, ask that bribes be repeated, or breach their promises. As a result, the total amount of bribes is much higher, and there is no guarantee of success for the briber (Alon et al., 2016; Shleifer & Vishny, 1993).

Some of the highly corrupt African countries may fit the "many small mafias" model. According to Tella, "[d]ecentralized or disorganized corruption is a feature of most African countries" (Tella, 2013, p. 58). Corrupt officials from different departments may visit a firm separately multiple times, demanding payments. "In 2002, manufacturing firms in Kenya had an average of 21 visitors from different government bureaucracies, particularly the Kenya Revenue Authority, the Ministry of Labour and the National Social Security Fund" (Kimuyu, 2007, p. 205, quoted from Tella, 2013, p. 65).

In Indonesia, after "big mafia" Suharto was overthrown, it was widely expected that corruption would be drastically reduced. However, to the surprise and dismay of many observers, corruption did not decrease. Instead, the country is now experiencing "a different kind of corruption," according to a Gallup study, "During Suharto's rule, the government and corruption were highly centralized at the national level, and costs associated with corruption were predictable. But the fall of the dictatorship led to decentralization of authority throughout the country, giving more power to local authorities. Instead of eliminating corruption ..., decentralization broadened the number of individuals seeking bribes and kickbacks" (Gallup, 2016).

2.2.3 The Competitive Model

The third model of bribery–corruption relationship exists in countries in which a given public service can be obtained from more than one government official (see Figure 2.3). This is considered as the "competitive type" in Shleifer and Vishny's analysis (1993). In this model, the public service cannot be monopolized by any government official. Examples of such public goods or services include the issuance of passports or driver's licenses in the United States. A US citizen can apply for a passport in any passport issuance office in the USA. If a passport processing clerk demands a bribe, the citizen can simply move to the next service window or to a different office. Since it is

Multiple agents providing same services

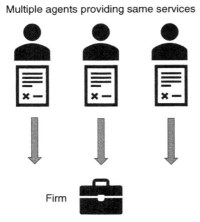

FIGURE 2.3 The competitive model: a given public good is offered by more than one government agency

Firm

virtually impossible for all of the passport processing clerks to collude, the citizen does not have to pay a bribe to apply for a passport, and, moreover, the citizen can easily report the bribe-demanding clerk to the law-enforcement authorities, further deterring such a corrupt attempt.

2.3 HOW BRIBEES' CLAIMS AND TENURE AFFECT ECONOMIC DEVELOPMENT

From the principal–agent perspective, corruption is viewed as the act in which a good owned by the principal (the government) is sold by the agent (an official) for private gain (Rose-Ackerman, 1978). Given the principal–agent problem, implicitly, the corrupt official has some "effective property rights over the government good he is allocating" (Shleifer & Vishny, 1993, p. 600). This "effective property right" can be viewed as a *de facto*, not *de jure*, claim. This is key to understanding the corrupt behavior, because the official does not officially own the public good, and therefore cannot officially claim the proceeds from selling the good. But their position in the government gives them the control rights over the good. The *de facto* nature of the claim, which is insecure because it is illegal and temporary since the official may lose their position, greatly influences the corruption behavior of the official. For example, they may sell the good at a price below its value, if it is safer to do so (a good example of "corruption with theft"), or they may sell the good at an exorbitantly high price if the official senses that their tenure is about to end. This is analogous to Mancur Olson's example of roving bandits versus stationary bandits (Olson, 1993). According to Olson, roving bandits have no long-term interests in the areas that they rob, so they do not invest in the infrastructure of the areas. They tend to steal the maximum that they can take, making it impossible to develop the areas. In contrast, stationary bandits can monopolize the claim over the areas and are, therefore, committed to the areas they rob. In order to enjoy the long-term benefit of their claim, they will refrain from bleeding the areas dry, and will even put some of their loot back into the area for development in order to receive a steady or even an increasing stream of income.

In a study comparing the economic consequences of corruption in Africa and East Asia, Oluwaseun Tella observed that, while corruption has been high in both Africa and East Asia, the latter tends to have stable governments and to be ruled by rulers who hold power for extended periods. Under these rulers, corruption is centralized or even nationalized. According to Tella, East Asian rulers "monopolize corruption, orchestrate graduate stealing and provide public goods in order not to impede subjects' investment" (Tella, 2013, p. 56). For example, in South Korea during the dictatorial rule of Park Chung Hee, "the state set the parameters within which corruption took place, and as a result corruption functioned as a dynamic part of the development process" (Moran, 1999, p. 571). The regime's stability and its implicit approval of corruption encouraged corrupt officials to keep their proceeds in their countries to be reinvested rather than hiding them in Swiss banks, which contributed to economic growth.

I once interviewed a successful businessman who had first-hand experience of dealing with corrupt officials in China. After he told me that corruption is necessary in the current business environment in China and that there are some successful corrupt officials, I asked him what constituted a successful corrupt official. He summarized that a "successful" corrupt official is someone who can sustain their corrupt behavior long-term and is liked by everyone, including both their superior and their subordinates. To achieve this, the official must be able to "balance the relationship between the state, the collective, and the individual." I chuckled at this quotation because it is a well-known slogan coined by Mao Zedong (Mao, 1986, p. 727). Ironically, Mao coined the phrase to urge his cadres to work honestly for the state. My interviewee was mocking Mao and telling me that corrupt officials have found a new meaning in Mao's phrase that guides them to success in corruption. Essentially, according to my interviewee, a corrupt official should not and cannot just loot the state coffers, even if they have the power to do so. If they do that, they will end up in prison in no time. Instead, the corrupt official should use their power to enlarge the pie (i.e., to grow the economy of the locality of which they are in charge). After achieving this, they should first make sure that the state gets its share of the enlargement (which also can be used to reinvest for further growth); second, they should give all who work for or with them their fair shares of the growth; and lastly, they should reward themselves. In other words, they must be a stationary bandit, not a roving bandit.

Contrary to the stationary bandit environment, a roving bandit environment would mean that the regime is not stable or that the top rulers are changed frequently or unpredictably, often through bloodshed such as a military coup or violent revolution. Since terms in post are uncertain or short, corrupt officials will be more greedy in taking bribes, and will tend to keep the loot out of the country. All of these tend to exacerbate the negative effect of corruption on the economic development of the country. In his comparative study of Africa and East Asia, Tella characterizes corruption in Africa as a roving bandit environment (Tella, 2013).

Somalia provides a vivid example of rampant corruption under a highly fragmented national government. In 1991, the authoritarian regime of Somalia collapsed. Since then, Somalia has been ruled by a "clan-based power-sharing formula," which makes the society extremely unstable. Different clans and religious forces rule different regions and are semi-autonomous, which enables these independent rulers to demand bribes. As a result, "[c]orruption is endemic in the country" (Rahman, 2017, p. 3). Since 2006, Somalia has been consistently ranked at the bottom of the Corruption Perceptions Index (Transparency International, 2017). The officials who control the state bank simply steal from the bank. For example, from 2013 to 2014, 80 percent of withdrawals from the state accounts at the Central Bank of Somalia "were made by individuals and not used to fund government operations or the provision of public services" (Bertelsmann Stiftung, 2016, quoted from Rahman, 2017, p. 4). Public employees are not paid from time to time, which, in turn, forces them to seek bribes in order to survive. Citizens and businesses, after being forced to pay unbearable amounts of bribes, lose their incentive to work and to produce, completing the vicious circle of top officials stealing directly from the state coffers, low-ranking public employees being forced to extort bribes to survive, and citizens and firms no longer wanting to work, making the country poorer and the officials loot more.

2.4   THE TYPE OF BRIBEES AND THEIR EFFECTS ON ECONOMIC DEVELOPMENT

Parallel to the analysis of bribe types, my coauthors and I conducted a study on how regime type moderates the effects of corruption on economic growth (Alon et al., 2016). Like the scholars who were both puzzled and motivated by the rapid economic growth under corruption in East Asia, we were intrigued by the contrast between the phenomenal economic performance of China under a dictatorship with rampant corruption versus the apparent economic chaos in some countries undergoing democratic transition, which has cast a serious doubt on the established belief that democracy provides a better tool in both fighting corruption and developing the economy.

In an attempt to shed light on this issue, we conducted a study on the relationship between corruption, regime type, and economic growth, using data from more than 100 countries between 2008 and 2012. What we found actually reconfirmed the well-established notion that democracy is, after all, a better tool in fighting against corruption and in developing the economy, with two twists: the democracy has to be mature, and the developmental trajectory is not a straight line. During an infant democracy, corruption may become worse. Below is a summary of our study (Li, Alon, & Wu, 2017).

We first distinguished three types of political regime, in order to examine how the corruption–economic development relationship varies across them.

Type 1. Autocracy: This is a totalitarian/authoritarian regime or a dictatorship, such as Suharto's Indonesia before the late 1990s or today's China under the rule of the Chinese Communist Party. It is characterized by a strong dictator or a ruling party that wields an iron-fisted control over the society. This type of government controls economic activities and uses its control to maximize total bribes, which in turn provides incentives for the officials to facilitate business and thus increases GDP. Under such a regime, the bribery target is clear, and the delivery of goods to the briber is secure. This corresponds to the "big mafia" corruption model mentioned earlier in this chapter. For example, if a developer bribed Suharto to get his construction project going, Suharto would instruct all of the relevant government departments to approve the project, allowing them to take reasonable amounts of bribes in the process. There are about 20 countries in our sample that are ruled by autocracy.

Type 2. Anocracy: This is a regime type in which autocracy begins to crack, due to the social pressure to democratize. The absolute rule of the "one big mafia" disintegrates, while an efficient and effective democracy has yet to be fully established, creating opportunities for bureaucrats, or the "many small mafias" as mentioned earlier in this chapter, to monopolize power in the regions or the markets that they control. For example, immediately after Suharto was overthrown, there was no dictator to order and coordinate all of the departments to give the green light to a project, and each department head had a strong incentive to extort as much payment from the developer as possible, making the cost of a bribe much higher and the probability of getting approvals from all of the departments much lower. Newly established infant democracies, such as Russia in the 1990s or Egypt after the Arab Spring, fit this model. In anocracy, turf wars among government agencies worsen, and hinder economic development, until the countries in question become mature democracies. In our study, 44 countries exist in anocracy.

Type 3. Mature democracy: This regime type is characterized by governmental checks and balances that substantially reduce or minimize monopolies over key government services, and is what Shleifer and Vishny call the "competitive type" (1993). As an example, in a mature democracy there are at least two government agencies that offer key government services (recall the US passport application example used earlier in this chapter). While North America and Western Europe have long been mature democracies, the type has also emerged in other parts of the world (e.g., Botswana, Israel, Japan, Mauritius, and Uruguay). Compared to the other two regime types, it has the highest economic development level and income, and the lowest level of corruption. Given the high development and income level, the growth rate inevitably will slow down. This regime type covers the largest number of countries in our research: 94 countries are mature democracies.

Our statistical analyses provide some interesting insights into how regime type, corruption, and economic growth interact. Using the World Bank's measure on control of corruption, we found that the levels of corruption in autocracies, anocracies, and mature democracies are 0.41, 0.66, and –0.21, respectively (a high, positive number means high corruption). The five-year average economic growth rates are 5.42%, 4.35%, and 2.70% for autocracies (with a per capita income of US $8,523), anocracies (with a per capita income of US $5,312), and mature democracies (with a per capita income of US $16,160), respectively.

Putting the two statistics together, an interesting picture emerges: both autocracies and anocracies have a high level of corruption. However, autocracies have a high level of economic growth, despite their high level of corruption. Furthermore, their corruption level is not the highest; that distinction belongs to anocracies. Mature democracies have the lowest level of corruption and the lowest economic growth rate (due to their highest level of per capita income), as expected.

Using multiple regression analysis, which allows us to examine how the interaction between regime type and corruption affects economic growth while controlling for other factors that may affect economic growth, we found that the interaction between anocracy and corruption exerts a strong negative effect on economic growth. In other words, corruption is the main culprit that hurts the economies undergoing a democratic transition. In contrast, we find that the interaction between autocracy and corruption is strongly positive, rather than negative, as in anocracies. Corruption seems to enhance economic growth in autocracy.

Anecdotal evidence supports our statistical findings. In China, a clear case of autocracy, the economy has been growing at a fast pace, accompanied by a high level of corruption (an important issue that we will discuss at length later in this book). In Russia, right after the fall of communism, many small mafias emerged and independently demanded payments from business people seeking approvals, making corruption worse and less efficient, as no one small mafia could deliver what the business people wanted without the consent of other small mafias.

From the late 1980s to 2008, we witnessed the chaos into which Russia and its satellite countries descended after the fall of the Berlin

Wall; we saw the strengthening of communist rule after the Tiananmen Square crackdown, which was followed by rapid economic expansion in China; and we suffered the financial meltdown in the advanced democracies and the free markets. These events seem to have contributed to the rise in popularity of the idea that a dictatorship is superior to a democracy in terms of economic growth.

Our study shows that this view fails to consider the relationship between regime type and corruption, and thus it does not help us understand why infant democracies tend to experience economic difficulties. This failure makes its conclusion that dictatorship is a superior political system in terms of delivering economic growth not only misleading but also incorrect. The surge in corruption during transition is a by-product, and thus should not be used as a reason for not undergoing transition. This is merely a convenient excuse for dictators to suppress democratization.

Our regime type and corruption study provides further support to the typology of the bribee that we discussed earlier in this chapter. Autocracy corresponds to the "big mafia" model or the stationary bandits, anocracy is equivalent to the "many small mafia" model (roving bandits), and mature democracy can be viewed as the competitive model, in which a public good is offered by more than one government source.

NOTES

1. Corruption Watch. 2012.
2. We should note that corruption without victims only exists as relative to the other two types; we may argue that if there is no corruption, and if the market is completely competitive and efficient, then the amusement park would be built in the long run by private developers without their having to pay bribes. Thus, the social benefit would be greater than with corruption.

3 Bribe Payers: Why Do People Pay? What Do They Get? Can They Refuse to Pay?

Mr. Oscar Centeno was a driver working for the Argentine government, a job that would have been unexciting, routinely transporting officials and running errands, except that he was secretly ferrying millions of dollars of cash in bags from bribe payers to his bosses. What is more unusual is that he took notes about the bribe money he drove: "the times, value and even the weight of the bags of money he said he delivered as he drove around Buenos Aires." He also listed the people involved, the addresses he visited, and various other details. From 2003 to 2015, he faithfully wrote down these activities and filled eight notebooks. It is estimated that the total amount of cash he had delivered is about US $56 million.[1]

We now turn to examine the bribery–corruption relationship from the briber's side. Why do people and firms bribe government officials? What is the benefit of doing so? In a society with rampant corruption, can people and firms refuse to pay bribes to officials in order to change the corrupt environment? In this chapter, we will first examine this issue from the bribe payer's perspective (why they pay bribes), and we will then review how the institutional environment affects bribing behavior.

3.1 WHY DO PEOPLE AND FIRMS BRIBE?

Paying bribes is costly for the briber, whether an individual person or an organization, such as a firm. The costs can be multi-dimensional.

Financially, bribing has the following costs. First, it reduces one's cash flow. Second, there is a risk that the bribee will fail to deliver the goods that the briber paid for, incurring further financial costs. From a legal perspective, bribing is illegal in virtually all countries, at least *de jure*, including the countries in which corruption is rampant. Thus, engaging in a bribery–corruption relationship carries the risk of being caught and punished. From the cultural perspective, the people or firms that pay bribes to corrupt officials may feel that doing so violates their moral principles and, thus, they are psychologically distressed by their own behavior. In general, people and firms do not want to pay bribes to government officials unless they have to (Lee et al., 2010). So logically, there must be some perceived benefits for people and firms to bribe government officials. What can people and firms get from bribing government officials?

In the literature on corruption, most studies focus on the corrupt officials, addressing the reasons why officials engage in corruption. Fewer studies consider the question: "Why do bribers bribe?" Part of the reason, in my view, is that the government, or the government officials, are the source of the corruption (more exogenous), whereas people and firms' bribing (which is more endogenous) is merely a response to the demand from the corrupt officials. Another part of the reason for the focus of the studies is the lack of quantitative data (Cheung et al., 2012). For example, the global corruption watchdog Transparency International (2017) publishes a "Corruption Perception Index" every year, which is a popular data source for, and is frequently used by, scholars of corruption for their studies. Transparency International also publishes a "Bribe Payers Index," though less frequently and including fewer countries. Its most recent Bribe Payers Index was published in 2011 and covered only 28 countries (Transparency International, 2011); Transparency International asked business executives in these countries how often firms headquartered there engaged in bribery in that country. Table 3.1 presents the survey results from 2011 and 2008.

As can be seen from Table 3.1, bribery by foreign firms in a host country (the country where the foreign investment is from) is perceived to occur in all home countries (those receiving the foreign investment) surveyed, including in the home countries that are the least corrupt, such as the countries at the top of Table 3.1. Comparing the BPI scores of 2011 and 2008, the average is the same, suggesting

Table 3.1 *Bribe Payers Index by country, 2011 and 2008*

Country	2011 score	2008 score
Netherlands	8.8	8.7
Switzerland	8.8	8.7
Belgium	8.7	8.8
Germany	8.6	8.6
Japan	8.6	8.6
Australia	8.5	8.5
Canada	8.5	8.8
Singapore	8.3	8.1
United Kingdom	8.3	8.6
United States	8.1	8.1
France	8.0	8.1
Spain	8.0	7.9
Korea, South	7.9	7.5
Brazil	7.7	7.4
Hong Kong	7.6	7.6
Italy	7.6	7.4
Malaysia	7.6	No data
South Africa	7.6	7.5
Taiwan	7.5	7.5
India	7.5	6.8
Turkey	7.5	No data
Saudi Arabia	7.4	No data
United Arab Emirates	7.3	No data
Indonesia	7.1	No data
Mexico	7.0	6.6
China	6.5	6.5
Russia	6.1	5.9
Average	7.8	7.8

Countries are scored on a scale of 0–10, where a maximum score of 10 corresponds with the view that companies from that country never bribe abroad and a 0 corresponds with the view that they always do.
Source: Transparency International, 2011

that perceptions of the level of foreign bribery by country show little improvement over time.

According to the BPI, Chinese and Russian companies have the highest tendency to engage in bribery when they conduct business in other countries. "It is of particular concern," Transparency International warns, because the Chinese and Russian economies are the major economies and they are expanding with a faster pace in the global market. "The countries at the receiving end of Chinese and Russian investment feel the effects not just of the financial flows, but also of the associated business operations and activities" (Transparency International, 2011, p. 12), such as their habit of engaging in bribery.

The high bribery frequency of firms from China and Russia, countries whose governments are also highly corrupt, indicates that the governance environment of the home country influences the bribery behavior of its firms abroad. As Transparency International reports, "the perceived likelihood of companies from a given country to bribe abroad is strongly related to perceptions of corruption in the public sector of that country" (Transparency International, 2011, p. 3). Figure 3.1 shows the correlation between BPI and CPI.

Recently, there have been more studies that focus on bribe payers (e.g., Cheung et al., 2012; Karpoff et al., 2010; Lee et al., 2010; Svensson, 2003). From studies on bribe payers, we learn that most bribe payers bribe for the following two reasons: (1) to overcome the often-complicated bureaucracy or other governmental barriers so that they can live a normal life or conduct daily business, or (2) to obtain lucrative business opportunities controlled by the government. Below, we will discuss each type in more detail.

3.1.1   Bribery Out of Necessity

This is a common type of bribery that exists in societies that suffer the following deficiencies. First, the government is bureaucratic and controlling. It imposes many complicated procedures and levels of approvals on people and businesses, covering many aspects of daily

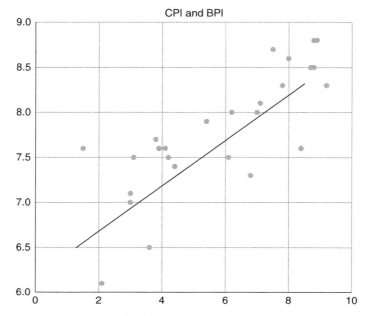

FIGURE 3.1 Relationship between CPI and BPI
Horizontal axis: CPI 2011 (1 = most corrupt, 10 = least corrupt)
Vertical axis: BPI 2011 (1 = most corrupt, 10 = least corrupt)
The correlation coefficient between CPI 2011 and BPI 2011 is 0.80
Source: Transparency International (2011)

life and business practices. For example, in Uganda, firms are often forced to pay government officials so that they can export or import goods and obtain public services (Svensson, 2003). Another example is how complicated it is to register a new business in different societies. India's bureaucracy is known to be cumbersome and stifling (BBC, 2012; Morris, 2010). According to wikiHow, a leading "how to do things" website, to register a business in India, one needs to go through many steps (the website listed nineteen), fill out three applications, write and submit two documents which need to be publicly notarized and approved by the government, and submit information about one's passport, proof of address, educational qualifications, and current occupation. One also needs a passport-sized photograph.

The registration fee is based on the company's capital assets (wikiHow, 2018b).

In contrast, in most states in the USA, registering a company is very simple: no passport or any identification document is needed, and no capital assets are required. For example, in Virginia, to register a limited liability company, one need only apply for the company name with the State Corporation Commission, and get an Employee Identification Number from the Internal Revenue Service for tax purposes (wikiHow, 2018a).

Second, the government bureaucracy is inefficient due to low morale and incompetence, which is usually due to the low rate of pay for government employees. Thailand is a good example, in this regard. Thailand's police officers, while powerful, are poorly paid by the government, which is an ideal combination for extorting bribes. According to a *Bangkok Post* article, "Thai police officers are paid around 14,760 baht per month (6,800–8,340 baht for entry level) [about $200–$250, note by author] and have to buy their own guns and even office supplies" (Kamnuansilpa, 2015). As a result, "facilitation payments and gifts are common in practice ... Corruption is pervasive in Thailand's police force" (GAN Integrity, 2017c).

Third, there is a shortage of basic public services such as hospital beds, public schools, or electricity and water supplies. The shortage of government services and the surge in bribery in Hong Kong from the 1950s to the 1960s is a case in point. In 1945, Hong Kong's population was about 600,000 to one million. After the 1949 victory of the communist revolution in China, a large number of people fled China to Hong Kong. By the late 1960s to early 1970s, the population had quadrupled, to about 4.3 million. The rapid population growth put a huge strain on Hong Kong's public services. "Everything was in short supply: food, housing, water, schools, health care, services of every kind" (De Speville, 1997, p. 13). This, plus the hands-off, laissez-faire British rule that relied on the market for everything, caused a huge surge in bribery and corruption.

The bribee of this type of bribe tends to be a low- or middle-level official who just carries out government procedures and stamps "Approved" or "Rejected" on people's or firms' application forms. Usually, this type of payment is an extra cost and is forced upon the payer, and thus is a dead weight on the bribe payer. As result, people and firms that are forced to pay bribes out of necessity hate it.

Bribe payment out of necessity fits the classical argument that to bribe is to "grease the wheels of bureaucracy." Compared to the type of bribe for obtaining a lucrative project (which we will discuss later), amounts paid in bribes out of necessity are relatively small. For example, in Uganda, the median graft payment by firms is about US $1,800 (Svensson, 2003). According to Svensson's study, for the same public good or service, the official who controls it may demand very different amounts of bribe payments from different firms. Svensson postulates that the corrupt official bases their price on the firm's ability to pay (which is often unknown to the official). He suggests that the official does not price the good based on their own costs, and that there is no objective criteria for them to calculate the cost, so the amount of bribe that the corrupt official asks is arbitrary.

Transparency International calls this type of bribe those "paid to low-level public officials," or "petty corruption" (as opposed to "grand corruption") (Transparency International, 2011, p. 18; Sartor & Beamish, 2018). This type also corresponds to what Wedeman calls "looting/rent-scraping corruption" (Wedeman, 1997).

3.1.2   Bribery for Profit

The second reason to bribe is to profit from it, as opposed merely to greasing the wheels of bureaucracy (Cheung et al., 2012). For instance, an individual may bribe a high-level official in order to get a well-paid job in the government; a foreign firm may bribe a head of state in the hope of being awarded a multibillion-dollar contract. The fundamental reason for this type of bribery is that (1) the government controls vast amounts of political, economic, and social resources, and (2) there is no fair, open, and efficient public rule in distributing and awarding the resources.

There are many examples of firms bribing governments to get preferential treatment or lucrative government contrasts, public assets, or exclusive licenses for extraction, mining, or distribution rights (Cheung et al., 2012). For example, "several oil companies (including Mobil Oil, Texaco)" were alleged in the early 2000s to have paid "bribes to the Kazak government in return for oilfield development rights." Telecom Italia was accused of bribing the former Yugoslavian president, Slobodan Milosevic, "for the sale of 29% of state-owned Telecom Serbia in 1997" (Cheung et al., 2012, Panel A.3).

The need and, thus, the frequency of paying bribes varies across industries, as can be expected. The more control over an industry by the government, the greater the need and the frequency of paying bribes by firms to the controlling officials. Table 3.2 depicts the level of bribery by industry, estimated by Transparency International.

The agricultural and light manufacturing sectors are the least susceptible to bribery. The industries that are most heavily affected by bribery are public works, utilities, real estate, oil and gas and mining. Based on this pattern, we can conjecture that industries that are more regulated, more lucrative, and that use natural resources tend to be more bribery-prone.

In addition to using the terms "grand corruption" and "petty corruption" to loosely correspond to bribery out of necessity and bribery for profits, scholars also use the term "passive" (out of necessity) versus "active" (for profit) briberies to correspond to the two types (GAN Integrity, 2017b).

It is important to note that the line between bribery from necessity and bribery for profit can sometimes be fuzzy. While in many cases, bribery can be clearly seen as one or the other, there are situations in which a bribe cannot be easily categorized. For example, a firm may bribe a tax officer to reduce or to eliminate its share of the contributions to education and city construction imposed on businesses by the local government. Since these contributions are

Table 3.2 *Bribe Payers Index by industry in 30 countries, 2011*

Industry	BPI score
Agriculture	2.9
Light manufacturing	2.9
Civilian aerospace	3.0
Information technology	3.0
Banking and finance	3.1
Forestry	3.1
Consumer services	3.2
Telecommunications	3.3
Transportation and storage	3.3
Arms, defense and military	3.4
Fisheries	3.4
Heavy manufacturing	3.5
Pharmaceutical and healthcare	3.6
Power generation and transmission	3.6
Mining	3.7
Oil and gas	3.8
Real estate, property, legal and business services	3.9
Utilities	3.9
Public works contracts and construction	4.7

0 = lowest bribery frequency, 10 = highest bribery frequency

additional burdens on the firm, this can be viewed as petty corruption to "grease the wheels" out of necessity. However, eliminating these contributions may enable the firm to reduce costs and, therefore, to gain a competitive advantage over its rivals, achieving higher profits. In this sense, this can be viewed as bribery for profit.

How Much Do Firms Pay?
Since this type of bribe is for profit, what is the magnitude of the "investment"? And how much return do bribe payers get, on average? Several studies have attempted to answer these questions. In the study

by Cheung et al. (2012), which uses a sample of 166 prominent bribery cases worldwide in the period 1971–2007, the authors estimate that the median bribe in their sample is $2.5 million, which is much higher than the median bribe paid out of necessity ($1,800) that we cited earlier (Svensson, 2003).

According to a study by Karpoff et al. (2010), the US Department of Justice and the Securities and Exchange Commission estimated that, based on the bribery cases that they had prosecuted, on average, for each dollar of bribe, the gain for the bribing firm is about $11. In the Cheung et al. study (2012), the authors estimate that the return on bribes, measured by market capitalization increase, is $10–$11 per dollar of bribe.

If these estimates are accurate, the return on this type of bribe is quite handsome. Unlike bribes out of necessity, bribes for profit are not forced, but voluntary. In one of my interviews on bribery in China, an interviewee who was well educated made the following comment:

> When I read the history of England before the Magna Carta [made in 1215 to limit the power of the monarch, author note] which shows a pattern that the king is always in debt and asks money from business people and the business people are so fed up with the king's borrowing that they try to avoid him, I was like: "God, the English king must be powerless!" If [Chinese] President Jiang Zemin wanted to borrow from me, I would give *all* I have to him and tell him "Don't worry about paying me back," because his blessing would send many lucrative deals in my direction and make me a billionaire in no time!

The contrast between the reluctance of English businessmen to give money to the English king and the willingness of Chinese business people to bribe the Chinese president is, as the interviewee puts it, due to the lack of power by the English king, so bribing him would be a poor investment.

However, it seems that, in today's world, politicians in power have a lot to deliver to bribers, even in countries with absolute poverty. In Somalia, the central government is highly fragmented, weak, inefficient, and ineffective. The country is extremely poor, and, due to the high corruption and insecurity, economic productivity is extremely low. All of these facts suggest that bribery payoff is low and, logically, that people do not want to pay high prices to get elected to such a fractured and ineffective government. However, reports show the opposite. According to various reports, the going rate for a parliament seat is $1 million, and votes are sold for up to $30,000 per head. The rampant vote sales have prompted an anticorruption group to call a recent election in Somalia "the most expensive election, per vote, in history" (BBC News 2017, quoted from Rahman, 2017, p. 4). Furthermore, this occurred in a country in which half of the people live on less than $1.90 a day. The case of Somalia adds to the main point of this subsection: that bribery pays well, even in one of the poorest countries.

Which Type Is More Prevalent, Petty Corruption or Grand Corruption?

Earlier, we described two types of corruption: grand corruption (bribes paid to high-ranking officials to profit from getting lucrative projects and other preferential treatment), and petty corruption (bribes paid to low-level officials to facilitate or expedite the bureaucratic process). Of the two types of bribes, which is the more prevalent? While comprehensive data are yet to be collected, a Transparency International survey shows that grand corruption is more prevalent than petty corruption. According to Transparency International, "companies using improper contributions to high-ranking officials intended to secure influence over policy, regulatory and/or legislative decisions" is more common in 16 of the 19 business sectors that it surveyed, across 28 countries (Transparency International, 2011).

As can be seen from Figure 3.2, in most industries, grand corruption outranks petty corruption. The industries that governments deem important, lucrative, and that relate to national security, and

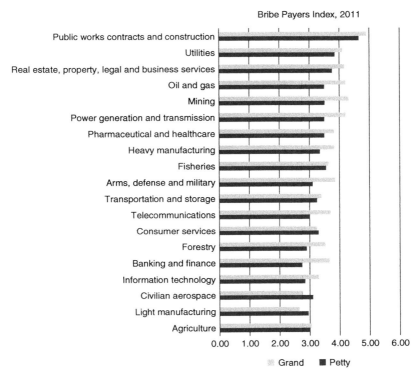

FIGURE 3.2 Bribe Payers Index, petty versus grand corruption, by industry in 30 countries, 2011
0 = lowest bribery frequency, 10 = highest bribery frequency

the industries that use scarce natural resources, have the highest frequency of grand corruption. These include banking, forestry, telecommunications, defense, oil, and gas.

Grand corruption is closely related to corruption with theft and corruption without victims (see Chapter 2, Table 2.1). Bribers are eager to pay, and bribees are happy to accept. In the process, the corrupt officials are enriched, and the bribing firms receive a nice return – usually ten times what they paid. In such a bribery–corruption relationship, the briber is not a victim, and therefore has no incentive to turn the bribee in, making grand corruption difficult to catch.

FIGURE 3.3   The (food) chain of bribery and corruption

3.1.3   The (Food) Chain of Bribery and Corruption

A briber can also be a bribee, as shown in Figure 3.3. In my lecture on corruption, I ask my students to tell a story about the relationship between the figures illustrated in Figure 3.3. While their stories are imaginative and fun to read, they tell me that the picture pushes them to think deeply about bribery–corruption relationships.

Some of my students have described the bribery–corruption relationship as between employees and company management such as the CEO. This is incorrect in the context of bribery and corruption relationships. In my lecture (and in this book), "corruption" refers to corruption by government officials. It is "the sales of government goods or services for the corrupt official's private gains." What I want my students to learn is that the bribery–corruption relationship in a society with rampant corruption is not about kickbacks between private firms, which are dealt in corporate governance.

In Figure 3. 3, the figure on the right represents citizens or the firms, the payers of bribes. They either pay out of necessity (the majority of cases) or they pay for profits. The middle person represents the mid-level government officials or power brokers who take bribes from below and bribe the people above them for the privilege of selling public goods for private gains. They are both briber and bribee. They most likely bribe for profits. The figure on the left is the highest official in the government, the big mafia, who does not have to bribe anyone (which implies that he maintains his rule by terror and force). The setting can be expanded by adding many mid-level officials and far more bribe-paying-only citizens and firms.

3.2   THE BRIBERY–CORRUPTION RELATIONSHIP AND THE MACRO ENVIRONMENT

Most scholars of corruption have agreed that the macro institutional environment, to a great extent, determines the propensity of people and firms to pay bribes. If most government officials are viewed as highly corrupt, and especially if the top leaders of a government are known to be corrupt, then ordinary citizens and business people are also highly likely to pay bribes to the officials that they have to deal with in their lives or their business operations. For example, "Corruption is a serious problem for businesses in Peru, with irregular payments, bribes and favoritism of government officials in awarding contracts being particularly common. In fact, a very weak judiciary, inefficient government bureaucracy and high levels of favoritism have culminated in high corruption levels in almost all sectors of the Peruvian economy" (GAN Integrity, 2016). Scholars also refer to a systematically corrupt environment as "pervasive corruption" (Lee et al., 2010).

3.2.1   *What Are the Responses by Multinational Firms to a Pervasively Corrupt Environment?*

When a firm operates in a society in which most government officials are corrupt, how does it cope with such an environment? Should it bribe, or should it refuse to bribe? While this question applies to all of the firms in the society, it is especially acute for foreign firms whose home countries have a low level of corruption and do not tolerate it. Should these firms do as locals do, or do as they would at home?

Scholars of business ethics have been debating this and have not reached any consensus on how to deal with the dilemma of whether or not to bribe. Pedigo and Marshall conducted a survey on the practice and attitude of managers from Australia (a country with a low level of and low tolerance for corruption) doing business in corrupt countries, and identified the following five approaches taken by Australian managers in dealing with local corruption (Pedigo & Marshall, 2008).

Imperialist approach. By this, Pedigo and Marshall refer to an ethnocentric view (i.e., a home-country-centered view) that the managers should "do as you would at home" (Pedigo & Marshall, 2008, p. 65). Implicitly, this approach assumes that the home country has a much higher standard with regard to bribery than the host country (and this is why it is called "imperialist," presumably). Since the interviewees' home country, Australia, has little tolerance for paying bribes, they do not bribe. The responses that the authors received from the managers interviewed are unequivocal in vivid language: "But no, we won't do that," "I would say forget it," "I would turn a deaf ear to it" (Pedigo & Marshall, 2008, pp. 65–66). The bases for this approach are (1) the home country's law and standards, and (2) personal values and judgments. The business consequences are that they will lose the business in the country. But to a moral imperialist, that is a price worth paying. As one respondent put it, when the local official hinted that if there were no bribe there would be no deal: "Then so be it" (Pedigo & Marshall, 2008, p. 66).

Universalist approach. Universalists follow the rules and standards set up by international organizations such as the World Trade Organization or the established guidelines followed by global trade groups or by global industries (Pedigo & Marshall, 2008). In general, these rules and standards are more stringent than those of the home country in curbing bribery. So we may argue that the universalists are close to imperialist in their attitudes toward bribery.

Relativist approach. Relativists follow the maxim "when in Rome, do as the Romans do." As one of the authors' interviewees put it succinctly: "if you are not willing to take that [i.e., to bribe] then you should never try to do the business in those countries" (Pedigo & Marshall, 2008, p. 66). A function of the relativist approach is that it helps in building relationships with local officials (Pedigo and Marshall call this the "relationship-building approach").

3.2.2   The Interaction between Firms and the Environment

The relationship between the bribe payers – the ordinary citizens and firms – and the macro environment is one of the most important areas for the study of the bribery–corruption relationship, in both the academic/theoretical sense and the practical sense. Academically, we do not have well-established theories based on commonly accepted assumptions or axioms about bribery–corruption behavior. For example, while there is more or less a consensus that corruption is bad for economic development, views diverge on why some countries thrive despite corruption. Another disputed issue is whether or not multinational corporations should bribe in a highly corrupt environment. In additional to the lack of consensus in theories, we do not have statistically solid evidence about the relationship between bribery, corruption, and economic development, due to the difficulty of collecting bribery and corruption data. Practically, the need for a better understanding of bribery and corruption behavior at both the micro (individuals and firms) and the macro (the institutional environment) levels has never been greater, as corruption is not only deeply rooted in many counties; it transcends national borders. Policy makers and business executives worldwide need good knowledge about bribery and corruption in order to fight against them.

Bribery: The Tragedy of the Commons

From a game-theoretical perspective, when a multinational corporation with high moral standards, opposed to bribery and corruption, enters a foreign country in which corruption is rampant and bribery is a common practice, it faces a situation observed by Garret Hardin half a century ago in his well-known essay, "The Tragedy of the Commons" (Hardin, 1968). Since paying bribes is costly for all firms, it is in their best interest that no firm pays bribes. However, most firms know that if others do not pay bribes, yet one firm does, the bribe-paying firm will receive preferential treatment from the corrupt official and therefore will gain competitive advantages in the market. Furthermore, realizing that its rivals think the same way, a firm's rational choice is to bribe. When most or all firms follow this logic and pay bribes, all of the competitive advantages disappear, because they have collectively raised the prices of bribes, resulting in the tragedy of the commons (or "the prisoner's dilemma," as game theorists call it).

Fortunately, the evolution and the development of human societies since Hardin have proven that the tragedy of the commons can be avoided, as evidenced in the social consensus of most mature democracies, in which the overwhelming majority of the citizens voluntarily nurture, obey, and protect public rules and common interests in the political, economic, and social systems. Platteau (1994) lays out the following cultural conditions (generalized morality) that are necessary for a society to maintain law and order and therefore avoid the tragedy of the commons. First, a sufficiently large number of people must choose to be honest; second, they must have faith in others to be honest; third, their commitment to be honest must be strong enough not to be tarnished by some dishonest members of the society (cheaters); fourth, cheaters (free riders of the system maintained by honest people) must have a strong feeling of guilt; fifth, honest people must be "willing to sanction breaches of honesty conventions even when their own interests have not been harmed by the observed breach (and despite the fact that private sanctioning activities will probably not bring them any direct reward in the future)" (Platteau, 1994, p. 765). Considering these conditions, my coauthor and I developed a model of bribery.

A Dynamic Model of Bribery

In order to further understand how the bribery behavior of a firm in a highly corrupt society interacts with other firms and with the overall social environment, my coauthor and I developed a dynamic model of bribery behavior of firms that takes the following factors into consideration: the macro institutional environment; a firm's attitude toward bribery and its bribery behavior; and the inter-firm competition in bribing government officials (Li & Ouyang, 2007). Below, I will briefly describe the model, which I have slightly modified here (for more details, please see Li & Ouyang, 2007).

Our model depicts a large number of firms (n firms) that operate in a country in which corruption exists. In other words, firms bribe government officials to gain competitive advantages over their rival firms.

$$R_i = dB_i/dt = G_i - \alpha_i B_i + \beta_i B_j$$
$$Where\ i = 1, 2, \ldots n; j = 1, 2, \ldots n, i \neq j$$

Equation (1) is a dynamic model that examines how a firm's bribing activities change over time. The firm in question is denoted by a subscript i; the rate of change in firm i's bribing activities is denoted by R_i, which is determined by the change in the amount of bribing activities of firm i, denoted by B_i. Taking the derivative of B_i over time t, or dB_i/dt, we obtain the rate of change in bribing activities for firm i.

B_i represents the amount of bribes that firm i pays to government officials. In a pervasively corrupt environment, it is necessary for firms to pay bribes in order to conduct business. As a rational player, the decision maker of the firm must believe that the benefit from bribing the government officials, which may be permissions to conduct business or preferential treatment in getting projects, must be greater than, or at least equal to, the amount of the bribes paid. In this sense, B_i can be viewed as the minimum gain from bribing for firm i.

The rate of change in bribing activities is further determined by three factors, G_i, α_i and β_i. G_i measures the aggregate level of corruption in the government of the society in which firm i does business. G_i can be approximated by the total gains from corruption by all of the corrupt officials in the society, including all of the bribes that they receive from people and firms (such as B_i), and outright theft from the state coffers. If no official is corrupt in the society, G_i approaches zero; if most officials are corrupt, it becomes a large positive number.

a_i and β_i are the two opposite forces in the firm, determining its tendency to bribe or not to bribe. a_i is the anti-bribery force, which can be based on the moral beliefs of the managers (or on the organizational culture of the firm) and the anticorruption laws of the home country of the firm (Pedigo & Marshall, 2008). β_i, the bribing tendency, can be based on relativism, relationship-building incentives (Pedigo & Marshall, 2008), or the desire of the firm to make more money in the (corrupt) local market.

In plain English, Equation 3 says that over time, whether a firm will increase or decrease its bribing activities is determined by three factors. First, the more corrupt the government (G_i), the more likely it is that firm i will increase its bribery activities. Second, its own tendency to not bribe (a_i) exerts a check on its own bribery activities (B_i). The third factor is its own tendency to bribe (β_i), which is influenced by how much its rival firms (all the B_j's for $i \neq j$) bribe.

Our interest is to see under what conditions the bribery levels of all firms do not escalate to such an uncontrollably high level that they simply cannot operate in the society. We assume that there exists an equilibrium, $E^* = (B_i{}^*, B_j{}^*)$, for all of the firms in the society at which their bribery activities are under control or can remain at an optimal level so that no firm wants to increase its bribery activities. Using a two-firm example, we can achieve this equilibrium under the following conditions:

$$\begin{aligned}
B_1{}^* &= (\beta_1 G_2 + a_2 G_1)/(a_1 a_2 - \beta_1 \beta_2); \\
B_2{}^* &= (\beta_2 G_1 + a_1 G_2)/(a_1 a_2 - \beta_1 \beta_2);
\end{aligned} \qquad (2)$$

Equation system 2 says that all firms will have to bribe more if (1) the competitive pressure (β) is higher, or (2) if the general environment (G_i) is getting worse. They will reduce their bribes if all firms exercise more restraint from bribing (a).

We then look for the criteria that can maintain long-term stability among all of the firms in the society with regard to their bribery activities. Using techniques offered by Hirsch and Smale (1974), we identify the following conditions:

$$p = a_1 + a_2 > 0; \text{ and} \tag{3}$$

$$q = det\ A = a_1 a_2 - \beta_1 \beta_2 > 0. \tag{4}$$

These equations show that to prevent bribery activities from becoming out of control in the long run, two conditions must be met. First, all firms must exert a positive anti-bribery force ($a_1 + a_2 > 0$); and second, the collective anti-bribery tendency ($a_1 a_2$) must be greater than the collective tendency to bribe ($\beta_1 \beta_2$).

The model that we developed in Li and Ouyang (2007) has three important implications. First, it shows the paramount importance of the overall institutional environment in determining firms' bribery behavior. Equation 1 implies that even if a firm does not bribe at first (namely, setting $B_i = 0$ as an initial condition), it will end up paying bribes as long as the environment (the aggregate level of corruption by all government officials) is corrupt (because $G > 0$, which will lead B_i to be a positive number). In other words, as long as corruption is rampant in the host government, multinational firms cannot refuse to pay bribes for long; otherwise, they will be driven out of the market.

This point can be supported by copious anecdotal evidence. For example, according to a report on corruption in Vietnam, "[c]orruption continues to be pervasive in Vietnam's business environment ... Nearly half of businesses paid a bribe during an administrative inspection in 2016." Moreover, nine out of ten times, the government inspector did not even ask for a bribe; the firm just paid it because the managers did it "out of a belief that it is simply common practice" (GAN Integrity, 2017b).

In the study by Svensson, 81 percent of the firms he sampled in Uganda paid bribes (Svensson, 2003), while we see from Transparency International's survey on bribe payers that bribery in highly corrupt countries is not only prevalent, but shows no signs of decreasing over time (Transparency International, 2011).

The second implication of this model is that, in a corrupt environment, the bribery-resistant force – or "refusal power" (Svenssen, 2003) – must be greater than the bribery tendency within most of the firms in order to keep bribe activities from reaching such a high level that doing business is impossible. Anecdotal evidence seems to support this condition. There is evidence that multinational firms operating in highly corrupt environments refuse to pay bribes, as shown in the study by Pedigo and Marshall (2008). (See the citation of their study earlier in this chapter.)

Third, the collective force of bribery resistance and the collective force of the bribery tendency are contagious (which is implied by the multiplicative terms ($\alpha_1\alpha_2$ and $\beta_1\beta_2$) in Equation 4). The implication is that their collective effect is much bigger than the simple addition of their efforts. If more firms show greater resistance to paying bribes, and if that force is greater than the collective tendency to pay bribes, then the overall level of corruption (G) can be reduced. Intuitively, if a firm that refuses to bribe knows that other firms in the market do the same, the firm will feel more confident in continuing to refuse (Martini, 2013).

In sum, in a highly corrupt environment, it is very difficult for a single firm to resist paying bribes, but the fact that firms hang on in these highly corrupt countries indicate that they are not completely subdued by the force of corruption, and their collective effort in resisting bribery can make a difference.

NOTES

1. BBC. 2018. Argentina notebook scandal: Driver details "decade of bribes." *BBC*, 2): Accessed August 26, 2018, Dube, R. 2018. Argentine ex-president's homes raided in graft probe. *The Wall Street Journal*, August 24: A7.

4 When Public Rules Meet Private Relations: The Importance of Governance Environment[1]

LOS ANGELES INTERNATIONAL AIRPORT (LAX). After a long journey from Qingdao, a seaside city in Eastern China, Mr. Qingbin Pei landed at LAX on May 16, 2018. Upon entering the USA, a US Customs officer discovered that Mr. Pei had a dishonest record and detained him for deportation. While waiting for deportation, Mr. Pei approached a customs officer named Tsai, who was of Chinese origin and was in charge of the detainees, and said to the officer in Chinese, "Please help me, we are all Chinese!" He initially offered $1,000 to Officer Tsai if the officer could expunge his bad record and let him into the USA. Eventually, he arranged for his Chinese friend Mr. Zulei Wang, who lived in the USA, to pay $6,000 cash to Officer Tsai. Mr. Pei also asked for contact details from Officer Tsai for future "business," because, according to Mr. Pei, he had more friends who would need the officer's "services." Officer Tsai reported the bribe to the authorities and Messers Pei and Wang were arrested and charged with "conspiracy to commit bribery."

–*Sing Tao Daily*, July 17, 2018[2]

4.1 WHAT HAPPENED IN EAST ASIA? AN EXPLANATION FROM THE GOVERNANCE AND GOVERNANCE ENVIRONMENT PERSPECTIVE

While the scene in the above case is not uncommon, what is interesting about it is that Mr. Pei did not seem to think that bribing an officer was wrong, especially since Officer Tsai was of Chinese origin. In Mr. Pei's view, a Chinese person must help a Chinese person. It appeared that he was so comfortable in dealing with someone of Chinese origin that he even proposed to Officer Tsai to make this kind of "help" into a regular business. His mistake was that he still used the norm of his home country in the new host country. In other words, he mixed two different types of governance environment, which is vitally important in understanding bribery–corruption behaviors across countries. In this chapter, I will introduce a framework of government environment that my coauthors and I developed, which will help us understand the bribery–corruption relationship.

Our effort to develop the framework of the governance environment was motivated by the difficulty of pinning down the main factors that can differentiate the "East" and the "West" in a systematic and fundamental fashion. Anecdotal observations of different social behaviors between East and West abound. For example, friends in East Asia tend to compete to pay for the entire group when they eat out, while people in the West are more likely to ask for separate checks in the same situation. Strangers in the West tend to exchange greetings when they pass each other, whereas Chinese avoid talking to strangers. More relevant to political and economic significance, we observe that people in the East seem to rely more on private connections and relations to govern socioeconomic exchanges, while Westerners are more reliant on public rules, such as the legal system, to settle differences in socioeconomic interactions.

A major event that further pushed us to seek a plausible explanation of the "Eastern" way was the 1997 Asian Financial Crisis. Before the crisis, the rapid economic development achieved by some East Asian countries, such as Japan, South Korea, Taiwan, Hong Kong, and Singapore had been viewed positively as the "East Asian Miracle" (Page, 1994). One of the major advantages of the East Asian economies, in addition to their high savings and investment rates, was the cordial, close relationship between businesses and governments, which was viewed as a positive factor that contributed to the rapid economic growth (Page, 1994).

And then came 1997, during which a powerful financial hurricane swept Asia. East Asian economies were hit the hardest, and bank runs and currency and debt crises occurred which, in turn, triggered an economic recession in Asia that was later to become known as "the Asian Financial Crisis." This crisis served as a watershed for views of the East Asian development model. Policy makers and scholars began to rethink the East Asian model: the cozy relationship between government and business that had existed in East Asia might not be that benign and admirable after all, because it was a form of corruption, or "crony capitalism" (Hughes, 1999; Krugman, 1998).

What happened to Asia? How could the very same phenomenon, namely, the cozy relationship between government and business, which had been viewed positively when scholars were discussing the Asian Miracle, now be condemned as corrupt after the Asian Financial Crisis? There was a need to develop a more consistent theoretical explanation of the causes of both the Asian Miracle and the Asian Crisis.

One way to help us to understand what is so unique about East Asia is to identify the major institutional factors that distinguish East Asia from the West in terms of how their economic activities are conducted. Attempting to achieve this, my coauthors and I offered an explanation from a *governance* perspective that can more consistently explain both the Asian Miracle and the Asian Crisis, which we call "rule-based versus relation-based governance" (Li, 2009; Li et al., 2004). The basic theme of the framework is that the macro institutional environment determines the micro behavior of individuals and organizations in choosing a particular type of governance mechanism in their socioeconomic exchanges.

At the center of the framework of rule-based versus relation-based governance is *governance*. We define governance as a mechanism that people or organizations use to protect their interests in social, political, or economic exchanges. For example, if, in a society with a fair, open, and effective legal system, a dispute arises, people would rely on the courts of law or on other public arbitrations for a ruling. In contrast, when the laws are biased and the judges are corrupt, then people and organizations tend to avoid the public rules as their means of settling disputes. Instead, they tend to look for a private way to solve the situation, which may include mediation, bribery, or even violence (such as kidnapping). We further argue that the type of governance mechanism people or firms choose in a society

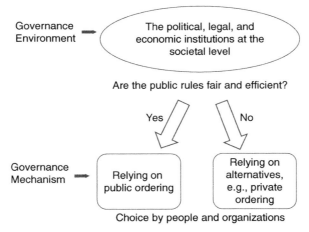

FIGURE 4.1 Governance environment and choice of governance mechanism

is not entirely up to the individual or firm; it is primarily determined by the dominant governance environment of the society in which they live or conduct business. This leads us to the concept of *governance environment*.

Governance environment refers to the set of political, legal, and social institutions that collectively facilitate or constrain the choice of governance mechanism for the individuals or organizations in a society. Social scientists have now come to a consensus that, broadly speaking, all societies can be grouped into two major camps in terms of governance environment: the ones that have good public ordering, or the rule of law, and the ones that do not have good public ordering (Dixit, 2004). This is illustrated in Figure 4.1.

4.2   RULE-BASED GOVERNANCE SYSTEM

Before discussing this particular type of governance system, we need to briefly review two key factors (or dimensions) that are vital in conducting social and economic exchanges: *information* that is needed for making decisions about the exchange, and *enforcement* that is needed to protect one's interest in the exchange.

We distinguish two types of information and enforcement: public and private. A key feature of public information is that it can be verified by a third party other than the two transacting parties, such as an online stock quote, whereas private information can only be shared by the two transacting parties and is difficult or impossible for a third party to verify (such as a mafia boss nodding at a mafia soldier, which can only be understood by the latter). In parallel, public enforcement means relying on judges and police to protect one's rights, whereas private enforcement involves private methods of settling disputes, such as private mediation or private violence.

In most developed societies, we observe that people and organizations primarily rely on public rules – laws and government regulations – to conduct exchanges, including enforcing agreements and rights, and to solve disputes. We call this reliance on public ordering the *rule-based governance system*. The most important reason for people and organizations to prefer public ordering is that they are confident that the law can be fairly applied and enforced. More specifically, a rule-based governance environment must satisfy the following conditions from the information and enforcement perspective: public rules (laws, policies, and regulations) governing social and economic exchanges are fairly made; rule-making, rule-adjudication, and rule-enforcement are separate and keep a check on each other; rule-enforcement is impartial, efficient, and effective; and the public information infrastructure (such as the news media, accounting, auditing, or financial rating) is well established, highly reliable, and trustworthy.

The above features imply that rule-based societies tend to be mature democracies. For instance, for the laws and public rules to be fair, a society must ensure fair participation of all interest groups in lawmaking, which requires a representative democracy. For legal interpretation to be impartial, judges must be free of influences from other government branches such as lawmaking and law enforcement, which implies that checks and balances exist between the three branches of the government. While their names and the number of branches differ, all rule-based societies must have the above functions, and thus they all share these key commonalities. However, non-rule-based societies may take many different forms, ranging from having effective private ordering to having no order at all, such as in civil wars or in anarchy.

We observe that a specific group of non-rule-based societies that rely on private ordering are quite effective and efficient in governing social exchanges and that they have been experiencing rapid economic growth: the East Asian societies. In addition to the absence of fair and transparent public rules, due to the lack of some of the above-mentioned conditions necessary for the rule-based governance system, these societies all have a governance environment based on private information and enforcement that can effectively and efficiently regulate economic exchanges and can solve disputes. We call this particular type of non-rule-based system *relation-based governance*.

4.3 RELATION-BASED GOVERNANCE SYSTEM

A relation-based society has the following characteristics:

1. Public rules (laws, state policies and regulations) are less fair because they are usually biased in favor of certain privileged groups (due to the lack of checks and balances).
2. The executive branch of the government usually overshadows the legislative and judiciary branches and is likely to be controlled by a dictatorial ruling elite; courts and judges are controlled by the ruler(s).
3. Government operations are secretive, and public information and the press are controlled and censored by the government.
4. Industries and markets tend to be controlled by a small number of insiders (e.g., people who have connections with the government) and are closed to outsiders.
5. Officials and business insiders are usually locked in a bribery–corruption relationship.
6. The informal network among the insiders in an industry is so closely knit and powerful that if one of the insiders is said to have broken the

(unwritten) norms of the trade, word of mouth by other insiders will effectively put him or her out of business.

For example, in Thailand, a relation-based society, there exists a class of powerful businessmen called *"chao pho,"* or godfathers, who "cultivate close links with local officialdom . . . to secure the licenses, permits, land deeds . . . to corner the lucrative government contracts." These godfathers also provide "some measure of security [and] justice . . . more speedily and more accessibly than officialdom." Also, "whenever these [ordinary] people have any problems they go to the *chao pho*" (Phongpaichit & Baker, 2000, pp. 37–47). Similar private, informal social networks have also existed in Malaysia. Historically, because the government was unable to provide many public services, residents, especially the Chinese there, began to form a *sherh-hui-tarng*, commonly known as a "secret society," to help each other in political, economic and legal matters (Siaw, 1983). Vietnam particularly, as a seasoned business writer summed up, relied on an "informal system of rule by people, rather than rule by law" (Hiebert, 1996). In Russia, courts are known to be corrupt and to use "fabricated cases," according to Russian lawyers and activists. Most of the business-related cases are brought by plaintiffs who have already bought off the judges. As a result, "Russian courts found 99.8% of defendants guilty, according to court data" and "[b]usiness owners often prefer to cut a deal rather than end up in court" (Marson & Grove, 2018, A8).

4.4   HOW DO PEOPLE GOVERN TRANSACTIONS IN A RELATION-BASED SOCIETY?

Unlike in a rule-based society, where public information is credible and is heavily relied upon by citizens and businesses (making the protection of business transactions by public ordering feasible and efficient), public information in a relation-based society is usually untrustworthy. As a result, people and firms rely on private information to govern their transactions. There are several reasons why public information is not trusted. First, the government controls public information and the media, in order to support its rule and agenda. For instance, it is well known that the governments in China and Vietnam (both relation-based societies) tightly control the media and decide what news can be published (Kalathil & Boas, 2003). They even doctor news stories and time news releases in order to reinforce their rules. For example, news of major scientific discoveries is often saved and released on major political holidays (e.g., the National Day, the Communist Party's birthday). According to a *Wall Street Journal* report, the government of Saudi Arabia pressured independent analysts to alter their estimates of the kingdom's oil output based on what the government told them, rather than on the information that the analysts collected from storage, ship-tracking, and insiders (Said & Faucon, 2018). The practice of manipulating public information at the national level by the government does not help firms to report accurate information. As we will show later in the book, there is strong evidence that firms in relation-based societies such as China manipulate their income reports (Li, Selover, & Stein, 2011).

Another reason why public information is rarely useful as a means for firms to govern their transactions is the nature of these transactions. When the scale of the economy is small, and business people predominantly deal with people they know, they rely on private information restricted to the transacting parties; they do not want to make their information available to a third party because that private business relationship is their most important asset. It is small wonder that, when researchers in Thailand interviewed successful business people about their political activities, few were willing to talk about them (Hewison & Thongyou, 2000). Similar patterns were also found among successful Chinese business people (Wu, 2008).

Such private relationships and information usually are *local* and *implicit*, and the agreement (e.g., a handshake or a pat on the shoulder) is most often *informal* and cannot be verified by a third party (such as a judge in a court). These practices are the opposite of rule-based governance, and as a result, business people must rely on private means to protect their transactions. Specifically, firms in relation-based societies rely on three private monitoring mechanisms to govern their rights in transactions: *ex ante* monitoring capability, *interim* monitoring capability, and *ex post* monitoring capability.

Ex ante means "before the event" and is used in economic analysis to forecast the results of a particular action. Private *ex ante* monitoring capability refers to the effort invested by a transaction party *before* a business deal is made. In the absence of public information and enforcement, a firm must privately investigate its prospective transaction partner in terms of his or her track record and reputation. If the prospect has cheated, do not deal with them. If the prospective partner does not have a stable pool of business partners or clients, it implies that they may have a bad reputation and should be avoided by other insiders. Such a prospect should be ruled out.

Interim monitoring is the ability of one party to obtain ongoing business and operational information about the other party, specifically about whether the other party is on track with a project's schedule or whether the other party is undergoing any financial troubles or disputes. In a relation-based society, such information is not publicly available through credit investigating agencies. This is why news of the financial insolvency of a firm in a relation-based society tends to cause large-scale panic. Due to the lack of reliable public financial data, people do not know whether other firms may also be involved with the insolvent firm and will, thus, be adversely affected. As a result, people stop lending to or withdraw deposits from firms likely to be involved with the insolvent firm (a snowball effect). Therefore, one must invest in the ability to obtain private and reliable information.

The third monitoring mechanism, private *ex post* capability, is the most important of the three. *Ex post*, Latin for "after the fact," is used here to refer to the ability to remedy or deter cheating or other opportunistic behaviors by the other party without resorting to public regulators such as the courts (which tend to be corrupt, unfair, and inefficient in relation-based societies). In a relation-based society, it is not uncommon for a promisee to resort to kidnapping in order to force a promisor to fulfill a promissory obligation (which may be an implicit, oral promise). For relation-based governance to work efficiently, private *ex post* monitoring must be effective and efficient. A *New York Times* report about informal, relation-based lending in China vividly describes such *ex post* monitoring (Bradsher, 2004).

> Borrowers default on nearly half the loans issued by the state-owned banks, but seldom do so here on money that is usually borrowed from relatives, neighbors or people in the same industry. Residents insist that the risk of ostracism for failing to repay a loan is penalty enough to ensure repayment of most loans . . . [As one lender puts it], "If it weren't a good friend, I wouldn't lend the money . . ." Violence is extremely rare, but the threat of it does exist as the ultimate guarantor that people make every effort to repay debts. "Someone can hire a killer who will chase you down, beat you up and maybe even kill you."

In Thailand, the powerful business people – godfathers – "built up networks of associates and gangs of subordinates." Because they took the law into their own hands, the areas in which they dominated "acquired a reputation for hired gunmen, sporadic violence, and regular newspaper reports of murders 'arising out of a business dispute'" (Phongpaichit & Baker, 2000, p. 37).

In Vietnam, experienced business people all know that a formal contract is not very useful. "If the contract is not conducted satisfactorily," a successful Vietnamese entrepreneur commented, "we have the option to sue them, but that would be ridiculous. You know the legal system here" (Nguyen, Weinstein, & Meyer, 2005, p. 224).

4.5 THE COSTS AND BENEFITS OF A RELATION-BASED GOVERNANCE SYSTEM

Since we observe that all advanced countries rely on public rules for governance, we may be tempted to rush to the conclusion that relation-based governance is categorically inefficient, and thus detrimental to economic development. However, such a conclusion is premature. Relation-based governance systems are not all inefficient and, thus, hinder economic growth. Under certain conditions, relation-based governance can be quite effective and efficient, due to its differing cost structure.

A well-functioning rule-based system is not free of cost to build and use. Imagine, for instance, the public ordering in the United States, one of the most advanced rule-based countries, and the infrastructure that it must have in place, in order for public ordering to function effectively and efficiently. In general, public ordering needs the establishment of a three-branch government. First of all, the country must build a legislative body, which in the United States means the establishment of the House and the Senate in Congress; the election system in all 50 states, used to select all the senators and representatives; and the infrastructure that supports the operations of legislation in Congress. Secondly, the country must build a court system, which in the USA ranges from the Supreme Court to local courts that are autonomous and well funded. This infrastructure compels the society to invest in an education system that can train a sufficiently large number of judges who are professional, ethical, impartial, and well paid. The society must also invest in training an army of lawyers and other legal workers with high professional and ethical standards. Last but not least, public ordering requires a credible and powerful law enforcement branch: the executive branch of the government, and a police force that must be well trained and adequately paid and, thus, uncorrupted.

Simply put, *a well-functioning rule-based system requires a large investment in legal infrastructure.* This is costly and can take a long time to build. From a cost accounting perspective, such an investment at the national level can be viewed as a *fixed cost* that does not vary, regardless of how many people use it. Once the legal infrastructure is built and functioning, *the incremental cost of drafting and enforcing one more contract is relatively low.* In other words, whether the legal system enforces one contract or 1,000,000 contracts, the fixed, upfront investment for the legal infrastructure is the same (and *sunk,* in the sense that it cannot be recovered), and the *marginal cost* (the incremental cost of enforcing an additional contract) is minimal.

Meanwhile, *in a relation-based society, business can thrive with minimal social order.* As long as crimes, such as robberies, are not out of control, business can be conducted and governed by well-functioning social-industrial networks maintained by private players (individuals or firms). In Thailand, where the public protection of business is not very effective or efficient, and the formal channel of financing (through banks) is expensive because of stringent rules, the Chinese Thai business community has resorted to informal financing among themselves. As one researcher observed, "Chinese [Thai] merchants ... could inform themselves much more efficiently than branch offices of Bangkok banks about the credit status of other local Chinese ... Their businesses were based on personal relationships ... They arranged [private financing] to cut down fellow businessmen's transaction costs ... Ultimately, they helped to increase the efficiency of Chinese business transactions and to redress a resource allocation distorted by economic regulation" (Ueda, 2000, p. 175).

Another interesting difference in contract fulfillment and enforcement between the two systems is that, unlike public enforcement of contracts, which relies on third-party verifiable information that may be only part (the written part) of the general agreement between two parties, private enforcement is based on private information, which may not need to be verified by a third party. In this sense, private enforcement can be more complete than public enforcement, even including implicit agreements based on mutual understanding, the spirit of cooperation, or past practices.

In general, compared to the cost structure of the rule-based system, the relation-based governance system incurs few fixed costs (since it does not rely on a nationwide legal infrastructure). But *the marginal (incremental) cost of privately enforcing contracts increases as the scale and scope of one's business expands.* For example, if one only does business with one's siblings, the marginal cost of the three types of monitoring (*ex ante*, interim, and *ex post*) is low, because one knows their reputation, their ability to deliver, and where their assets are (in case it becomes necessary to seize them). But when the business grows and the business person runs out of family members, they may have to deal with people they do not know as well, such as neighbors or distant relatives, and the marginal cost of monitoring increases. In general, the marginal (incremental) cost of establishing new relationships rises because cultivating new relationships becomes more and more expensive and time-consuming when one's private network expands from family members to strangers. For this reason, in a relation-based society, people first do business with family members and then with friends and people they know. They try to avoid dealing with strangers because it takes a long time to develop close relationships, and the costs of private monitoring and enforcement are high.

Therefore, *when the scale and scope of the economy are small, relation-based governance may be effective and efficient,* as the society avoids costly investment in developing and maintaining the legal infrastructures. People and firms are constrained to deal with family members, friends, and people in closely knit circles and are content to do so. As illustrated in Figure 4.2, when the market is small, the average governance cost is lower in relation-based societies, giving them a comparative advantage during the take-off stage of their economy.

However, when an economy expands from local to national and international scope, relation-based governance becomes inefficient. The average cost of finding and establishing new relationships rises, and thus the average cost of governance surpasses that of rule-based economies, as illustrated at the turning point in Figure 4.2. At this point, a relation-based society begins to lose its comparative advantage in governance costs over a rule-based society. It faces the pressure to evolve into a rule-based governance environment. A postponement

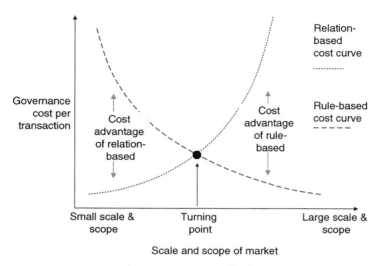

FIGURE 4.2 The governance cost of rule-based and relation-based systems

of the transition caused by resistance from people who are deeply entrenched and invested in the existing relational network will hinder a country's economic development. This point will be further elaborated upon later.

We now have a clearer understanding of the "East Asian economic miracle": these countries have extensive informal social networks that enable them to rely on the relation-based system to govern economic activities. This system has helped them to save the huge fixed cost of building an effective public governance system. In other words, they did not have to wait until they could build a vast, expensive legal infrastructure for their economy to take off. These countries, rather, have relied on private governance mechanisms maintained and enforced by family members, friends, cronies, and related people in high places (possibly through bribery) to protect their business interests and operations. *The "East Asian economic miracle" has been achieved with the help of its relation-based governance system.*

Furthermore, we can now see that the Chinese heavily rely on *guanxi* (Chinese for *connection and relation*) in business activities, not only because of their cultural heritage, but also, and more importantly, because the public rules are not effective and efficient in providing fair protection for their property rights and interests. *Relying on the relation-based way of conducting business activities is not merely a cultural phenomenon, it is fundamentally determined by the stage of the political and economic development in a society.* Relying on private relations to settle business disputes is not unique to East Asian societies. Historically, feudal Europe and the United States were primarily relation-based societies (Li, 1999). Contemporarily, many developing and transition economies such as those of Azerbaijan, Bahrain, and Kazakhstan are, to various degrees, relation-based, even though they do not have the Chinese or East Asian cultural heritage (see discussions later in this chapter). Table 4.1 highlights the main contrasting features of the two systems that we have discussed so far.

4.6   FURTHER CLARIFICATIONS OF THE RULE-BASED AND THE RELATION-BASED SYSTEMS

Now that we have presented the rule-based versus relation-based governance framework, several important clarifications must be made. Like all theories that must use idealized situations to make the key features clear (just as basic dynamics theory must assume away frictions), in our framework, we need to contrast the rule-based versus the relation-based governance systems in an idealized fashion in order to help understand their key (and contrasting) features. However, in reality, the governance environment in a society is not so clear-cut, and we should make clarifications.

First, the distinction between rule-based and relation-based societies is not absolute. It should be noted that all human societies, including relation-based ones, have various degrees of formal rules. When we say that a country is relation-based, it does not mean that this country has no formal laws. Even the most lawless

Table 4.1 *Differences between relation-based and rule-based governance*

Relation-based governance	Rule-based governance
Relies on private and local information	Relies on public information
Complete enforcement possible	Enforces a subset of observable agreements
Implicit and non-verifiable agreements	Explicit and third-party verifiable agreements
Requires minimum social order	Requires well-developed legal infrastructure
Low fixed costs to set up the system	High fixed costs to set up the system
High and increasing marginal costs to maintain	Low and decreasing marginal costs to maintain
Effective in small and emerging economies	Effective in large and advanced economies

Source: Based on Li et al., 2004

country must have a set of published legal codes of some sort. But the state may not follow the laws, and the ruler may simply ignore them. What distinguishes relation-based societies from rule-based ones is not who has the most comprehensive written laws, it is that people in relation-based societies tend to *circumvent* formal rules because the rules and the enforcement tend to be unfair, particularistic (depending on who has better relationships with people in power), and corrupt.

Second, relation-based governance is not the same as doing business using personal relations, such as relational marketing or customer relationship management (CRM). The latter is about using personal connections to enhance services to the customer, such as providing customized products or services based on the individual characteristics and preferences of the customer. This is perfectly legal, and thus can (and does) exist in a rule-based society. The former is different from the legalistic perspective: it is about obtaining public goods and services, such as lucrative government projects, licenses, or government protections, through private means, such as bribery, kinship relations, or even blackmail. This relation-based way of obtaining public goods circumvents the formal, public channel and rules, and, by its definition, is illegal. As a result, relation-based systems are inherently prone to corruption. In this sense, they are not compatible with the rule-based system. Logically, we can argue that both relation-based and rule-based governance systems can be in a stable state (equilibrium), and can have their own competitive advantages in terms of cost structure, as we discussed earlier in this chapter. A mixed system, with both rule-based and relation-based governance practices, is bound to be confusing and unstable. This can happen during the transition from relation-based to rule-based system (Li et al., 2004).

A third type of governance system is to be found in societies that do not have good public ordering or private ordering (such as a relation-based system). To paraphrase Tolstoy's famous saying that "Happy families are all alike; every unhappy family is unhappy in its own way," we can say that, in terms of the governance system, rule-based societies are all alike in the sense that they all have an environment that ensures checks and balances between lawmaking, law interpreting, and law enforcing, a publicly verifiable information infrastructure to support the consistent and impartial enforcement of public rules. In contrast, non-rule-based societies may have various ways to fill the vacuum of fair and effective public rules. Relation-based governance is one of the major systems that provide governance in these societies. Unfortunately, not all non-rule-based societies have the extensive informal social networks that the relation-based societies do. So, expanding the rule-based versus the relation-based framework, we can make a typology of three types of societies: (a) societies that rely on a rule-based governance system (most developed countries); (b) societies that lack fair and efficient public rules and rely on a relation-based governance environment (developing countries with strong relation-based networks); and (c) societies that lack fair and efficient public rules and do not have efficient and effective relation-based networks either.

4.7   A THIRD TYPE: NON-RULE-BASED SOCIETIES THAT LACK EXTENSIVE RELATIONSHIP NETWORKS

As we discussed earlier, a country that is not rule-based may not necessarily be relation-based; it can be governed by anything but public rules. Conceivably, there are countries that have neither strong public rules nor extensive informal social networks (i.e., relation-based governance) to conduct and protect business. More generally, how do we distinguish which countries are more relation-based among the non-rule-based countries?

4.7.1   *The Role of Different Types of Trust in Governance*

Based on the literature, a key indicator that can help us to do this is the level of trust in a country. Broadly speaking, there are two types of trust in terms of *who* people trust: *"generalized trust"* (also called public trust, as considered above) and *"particularized trust"* (Uslaner, 2002). People who have generalized trust believe that most people, including strangers, can be trusted. If a society has a high level of generalized trust, then the cost of testing and verifying the integrity of prospective business partners will be lower, thus increasing economic efficiency for a society. Data show that affluent societies – countries with a high economic development level – have high levels of generalized trust, as shown in Figure 4.3. From the perspective of the political system, a higher level of generalized trust means that people have confidence that others will abide by the rule of law and will cooperate in maintaining it. This confidence makes a pluralistic political system, such as a democracy, work more efficiently.

By contrast, in countries with low economic development and a weak rule of law, the level of generalized trust tends to be low (Figures 4. 3 and 4.4) and there seems to be a mutually reinforcing interaction between trust and economic development: the lack of generalized trust creates more friction in the political and economic

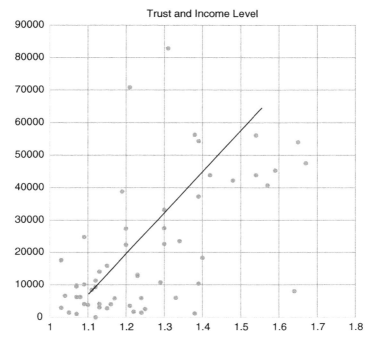

FIGURE 4.3 Trust and income level across countries, 2010–2016
Note: X (1 = do not trust people, 2 = trust people) (WVS Wave 6,
2010–2014). Y = Income per capita in US dollars, three-year average
2014–2016. Each observation (dot) is a country.
Source:(World Bank, 2018; World Values Survey, 2005–2014)

activities in a country, which, in turn, makes economic activities less
efficient.

When a society does not have sufficiently high levels of generalized trust, it must have another kind of trust to make social exchanges
possible. As economics Nobel laureate Kenneth Arrow (1972) stated
succinctly, "Virtually every commercial transaction has within itself
an element of trust." When people have very little confidence or faith
in strangers, they rely on people they know well, such as family
members or close friends. Such trust is called *particularized trust.*
People who adhere to particularized trust do not believe that people, in
general, can be trusted. They only trust the people whom they know

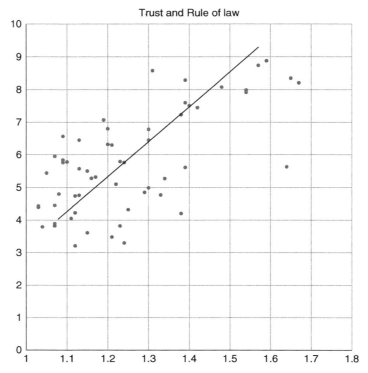

FIGURE 4.4 Trust and rule of law across countries, 2010–2016
Note: X = (1 = do not trust people, 2 = trust people) (WVS Wave 6
(2010–2014); Y = Rule of Law Index (high value = high degree of rule of law)
2016. Each observation (dot) is a country.
Source: (Gwartney & Lawson, 2012; World Values Survey, 2005–2014)

through certain groups (networks) to which they belong, such as
relatives, friends, or the members of one's club. In general, particularized trust is based on the close relationship that one has with the
person to be trusted (so that they can easily be held accountable).
Implicitly, maintaining particularized trust relies on the three monitoring mechanisms discussed earlier in this chapter: *ex ante*, interim,
and *ex post*. For example, A trusts B only because A knows B's history
well (B should not have a bad record in business dealings), because A is
able to follow up on B's ongoing activities, and because A can punish
B if he or she cheats.

Upon further examination, we find that the closeness, or the distance, of one's relationship varies. The closest relationship is among the direct members of the family: spouse, parents, and children. The second closest relationship may be with relatives, such as in-laws, cousins, and other close family. Friends, neighbors, and coworkers usually belong to the next circle. The level of particularized trust that people place on these different relationships varies across societies.

Take the case of Chinese society, for example. The conventional view is that the Chinese give paramount importance to the family and rely almost exclusively on family ties to conduct and safeguard their business. This view is actually quite misleading. Recent studies and surveys on the sources of particularized trust in China have revealed that the Chinese place more trust in neighbors and friends than in family (Li & Wu, 2010; Tang, 2005; World Values Survey, 2005–2014).

Such relationship building was practiced among Chinese Thais in Thailand. As observed by researchers among the Chinese Thais, "They invested in one another's enterprises to share risks and rewards, and they exchanged marriage partners to strengthen links, often with little reference to traditional boundaries on such alliances" (Phongpaichit & Baker, 2000, p. 33).

The Chinese *guanxi* culture is not about trusting family members only; it is about relying on an extended informal social network of friends and friends' friends to conduct business and to protect property rights. In China, for historical reasons, the *guanxi* culture is very strong. Everyone must have his or her circle of close friends. The members of the circle help each other in social interactions and exchanges. The mutual help is effectively and efficiently enforced through the three monitoring mechanisms (*ex ante*, interim, and *ex post*) with minimal cost, since the members know each other well. This familiarity includes a knowledge of one's history in dealings (so as to exclude cheats) and asset information (in case it becomes necessary to seize someone's assets as compensation). In China, almost everyone must belong to a circle in order to survive. (People who do not belong to any

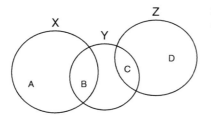

FIGURE 4.5 Circles representing private networks

A, B, C, D: Members of a network
X, Y, Z: Networks
Through mutual assurance between members in the same network (A and B, B and C, and C and D), a particularized trust can be established between A and D.

close circles tend to be those with a shady past or dubious character, such as those who have cheated; thus, they are avoided by others.) Therefore, Chinese society can be viewed as consisting of numerous circles of close friends (see Figure 4.5). Resourceful people are those who belong to multiple circles. They act as liaisons to link different circles by introducing the members of one circle to another. This kind of introduction is very powerful; it is not merely a friend introducing someone to a new friend, it is used to link two or more circles together, with minimal monitoring cost for potential cheating. For example, as depicted in Figure 4.5, A and B are members of Circle X. A, a developer, needs approval from D, a powerful official who controls a lucrative real estate project. But A does not know D directly. Fortunately, B belongs to two circles (X and Y), which enables B to ask C for help. C belongs to the same circle as B (so they can trust each other) and also to circle Z, in which D is a member. Once the chain of circles has been established and the introduction is made, then A and D can have almost instant trust in each other, because the monitoring cost between them is low: if D cheats A, A can punish B easily in Circle X, and B can, in turn, punish C in Circle Y, and C can hold D responsible. If D does fail to perform what he or she was asked and has promised to do, he or she will be kicked out of Circle Z. In a relation-based society, if one were kicked out of his or her circle, it would be devastating, because his or her livelihood heavily relies on such circles. This strong deterrence will ensure that D will not cheat, even though he or she barely knows A.

The case of secret societies in Malaysia provides further evidence on such cross-memberships. It is not uncommon for the members of a family to join different societies so that the family gets "the best of both worlds," in the sense that they can get protection and business opportunities from all of the societies and the members with whom they have linked up (Siaw, 1983, p. 127).

When a researcher in Vietnam interviewed a "highly successful land broker," he attributed his success to an informal network resulting from "shared history through alma maters, military services, neighborhood associations, parties, anniversaries, and memorial services that bring people together" (Kim, 2008, p. 60). Interestingly, he did not mention the word "family." In another study on trust and interfirm relationships in Vietnam, the authors found that an important way to quickly establish trust and a close relationship between two new partners is through a third party. A natural way to start a conversation between two prospective partners is to find a mutual friend and talk about their relationship with the mutual acquaintance. As a Vietnamese business executive commented, "It is easier to talk about common friends. But more importantly, we feel more secure when there are [sic] someone who knows both of us" (Nguyen et al., 2005, p. 228).

Particularized trust that goes beyond family members and extends to neighbors, friends, and friends' friends can be termed "*extended* particularized trust." These thick private networks based on extended particularized trust that overlap and reach every corner of a society make up what we call *relation-based governance*.

4.7.2 *Non-Rule-Based Societies That Lack Extended Particularized Trust*

There are also non-rule-based societies that lack trust of any kind. People there do not have much confidence or faith in anyone. But in order to conduct business, they have to rely on someone. In such a situation, family members come in handy, and the saying that "blood is thicker than water" makes the most sense. In general, when a society has extremely low levels of trust, people mostly rely on family members to conduct business and to protect property rights. Borrowing from the sociological term "nuclear family," we refer to the narrowly particularized trust that is only applied to family members as "*nuclear* particularized trust." Correspondingly, the type of governance environment that is associated with nuclear particularized trust is not relation-based; we will call it "clan-based."

Clan-based governance is more primitive than relation-based governance because the economic cooperation is limited to family members only and may not always be the most efficient choice. For example, within a family business, the key posts are held by family members who may not be best qualified, and in firm-to-firm or government-to-firm relationships, a government official or a firm's head tends to award projects to a firm owned by his family, which may not be the most efficient or highest quality (this will be further discussed in Chapter 5).

Therefore, we can distinguish relation-based countries from non-relation-based countries by examining the dominant type of particularized trust. The countries that have a relatively high level of extended particularized trust are relation-based. In other words, people in relation-based countries tend to have a high level of trust beyond trusting family members only; they also place a high level of trust on nonfamily friends, such as neighbors. Table 4A.2 summarizes our categorization of trusts.

4.8   HOW TO MEASURE GOVERNANCE ENVIRONMENT

The previous sections of this chapter give us an overview of the theory of rule-based and relation-based governance. An immediate question is this: which countries are rule-based and which are relation-based? For instance, if we are considering entering the market of Malaysia, how do we know to what extent it is rule-based? In this section, we will discuss how to evaluate whether a country is relatively more rule-based or relation-based, and we will measure the governance environments of the countries on which we have data. For business readers, understanding the criteria that we use to evaluate the governance system will provide a tool that can be used to assess the business environment of a target country in the future.

4.8.1 Measuring Governance Environment: The Governance Environment Index (GEI)

Based on the literature on governance environment, we created a Governance Environment Index (GEI), which is a sum of five governance-related indicators (Li & Filer, 2007): political rights, the rule of law, free flow of information, the quality of accounting standards, and public trust. These are explained in more detail below.

1. **Political rights.** This indicator measures the political rights available to a country's citizens. The more political rights that citizens have (as opposed to the political power of the rulers), the more democratic the political system is, which provides more checks and balances among the political forces. Thus, sufficient political rights are the foundation for the rule-based governance system.

2. **Rule of law.** This indicator measures the degree to which a country has the rule of law. As we discussed earlier, a fair, effective and efficient legal system is a necessary condition for citizens to rely on public ordering, or rule-based governance, to solve disputes and to protect property rights.

3. **Free flow of information** (as opposed to governmental control over the flow of information) is a necessary condition for a rule-based society, as it depends on high-quality, publicly available economic information. It is assumed that, if information can be freely disseminated in a country, the competition between all of the sources of information will force the information providers to offer more accurate and timely information. On the other hand, if the state controls and censors information, then the quality of publicly available information will be poor, and people will trust it less.

4. **Quality of accounting standards.** This indicator, closely related to the free flow of information, specifically measures the quality of publicly verifiable financial information, such as company financial disclosure and auditing, which are fundamental for rule-based governance to work efficiently.
5. **Public trust (generalized trust).** To put it simply, trust is a confidence that one places in the other person's reliability. Public trust, or generalized trust, is the belief that most people, including strangers, can be trusted. A higher level of public trust reduces the cost of information verification and the cost of sanctioning cheats, making rule-based enforcement efficient. Based on the same rationale, political scientists find that a high level of public trust is conducive to democracy, which, in its mature form, is a highly rule-based governance system.

All the five indicators are positively correlated with a rule-based governance environment. In other words, the higher the degrees of political rights, the rule of law, free flow of information, the quality of accounting standards, and public trust, the higher the degree of rule-based governance in a country. (Please see Table 4. A.1 in the Appendix for detailed information on the data sources of the five indicators.) Based on the five indicators, we created the GEI, which is the sum of the standardized value of the five indicators. Table 4. 2 lists the GEI of all of the countries for which we have available data.

The GEI measures the degree to which a country is rule-based. It is a relative measure. For example, based on Table 4.2, we can say that, compared to Thailand, South Korea is more rule-based. The countries that are ranked at the top, such as Sweden, the Netherlands, and the United States, are the most rule-based countries, whereas the countries at the bottom, namely Bahrain, Azerbaijan, and Libya, are the least rule-based. Since the GEI score is constructed by the sum of the five standardized indicators, the mean of the GEI is zero. The simplest way to categorize the countries in Table 4.2 is to divide them into two groups, one with positive GEIs and the other with negative GEIs. We may say that the countries with a positive GEI are more rule-based and the ones with a negative GEI are less rule-based.

Table 4.2 *Governance Environment Index (GEI) by country, 2018*

Country	GEI 2018	Country	GEI 2018
Sweden	6.03	Romania	–0.46
Finland	5.98	Georgia	–0.64
Netherlands	5.85	Philippines	–0.66
New Zealand	5.43	Ukraine	–0.67
United States	4.82	Nigeria	–0.88
Australia	4.63	Colombia	–1.04
Switzerland	4.38	Trinidad and Tobago	–1.45
Japan	4.35	Peru	–1.59
Estonia	3.67	Kyrgyzstan	–1.65
Germany	3.65	Kuwait	–1.78
Uruguay	3.27	Brazil	–2.05
United Kingdom	2.83	Morocco	–2.11
Singapore	2.79	Armenia	–2.21
Taiwan	1.89	Qatar	–2.34
Tunisia	1.71	Mexico	–2.55
Spain	1.71	Turkey	–2.55
France	1.58	Pakistan	–2.56
Hong Kong	1.55	Egypt	–2.64
Slovenia	1.19	Lebanon	–2.81
Korea S	0.98	Ecuador	–2.89
Chile	0.95	Malaysia	–2.93
Poland	0.7	Zimbabwe	–3.13
South Africa	0.7	Kazakhstan	–3.18
Cyprus	0.37	China	–3.31
India	0.35	Jordan	–3.57
Ghana	0	Russia	–3.95
Argentina	–0.09	Bahrain	–4.02
Thailand	–0.35	Azerbaijan	–4.80
		Libya	–6.50

Source: Compiled by Jun Wu and Shaomin Li, 2018, based on Li (2009). For data sources, see Appendix.

Countries with high GEIs, or rule-based countries, are characterized by strong political rights, the rule of law, free flow of information, high public trust, and high quality in their accounting standards.

An important caveat is that the GEI only measures how much a country is rule-based; it does not measure to what extent a country is relation-based. A negative GEI means that the country is less rule-based, but it does not mean that it must be relation-based. Some less rule-based countries are relation-based and some are not. We need to find a way to distinguish between them.

4.8.2 Measuring Governance of Non-Rule-Based Societies

Based on our discussion above, in Section 4.7.2, "Non-Rule-Based Societies That Lack Extended Particularized Trust" we use measurements of different trusts to distinguish the more relation-based from the less relation-based (or clan-based) among the non-rule-based societies.

The World Values Survey has several questions on trust, ranging from trust in one's own family (which is the most narrow particularized trust), to trust in people of another nationality. These trust variables provide a good way to distinguish relation-based societies versus clan-based societies. Based on our conceptualization, in the clan-based societies, people tend to have high trust in their own family and low trust in other people in the society. People in relation-based societies are able to trust people beyond their family members. In other words, they demonstrate relatively high generalized trust.

Based on the above rationale, we conducted a clustering analysis of the 31 countries that have negative GEIs (the non-rule-based countries), based on two variables. The first is the World Values Survey variable that measures generalized trust. The other is the World Values Survey variable that measures how much one trusts one's own family (see Table 4. A.2 in Appendix). We computed the gap between the generalized trust and the trust in family to distinguish the clan-based and relation-based societies. Table 4.3 shows the result of the clustering analysis.

On average, as compared to those in Cluster 0, countries in Cluster 1 have (a) a higher level of generalized trust and (b) a smaller gap between their level of generalized trust and trust in family. They fit our description of relation-based countries.

Table 4.3 *Clustering of more relation-based versus more clan-based countries*

Country name	Cluster	Country name	Cluster
Argentina	0	Turkey	0
Armenia	0	Ukraine	0
Brazil	0	Zimbabwe	0
Colombia	0	Azerbaijan	1
Ecuador	0	Bahrain	1
Georgia	0	China	1
Jordan	0	Egypt, Arab Rep.	1
Libya	0	Kazakhstan	1
Morocco	0	Kyrgyz Republic	1
Mexico	0	Kuwait	1
Malaysia	0	Lebanon	1
Nigeria	0	Pakistan	1
Peru	0	Qatar	1
Philippines	0	Russian Federation	1
Romania	0	Thailand	1
Trinidad and Tobago	0		

Note: 0 = more clan-based; 1 = more relation-based.

In comparison, countries in Cluster 0 have lower generalized trust and show a bigger negative gap between their generalized trust and their trust in family. These are countries in which most people do not rely on public rules and lack extensive informal social networks.

In the next chapter, we will discuss the implications of governance environment and trust on the effects of corruption on economic development.

APPENDIX 4.A

Table 4.A.1 *Data used to calculate the GEI*

Indicator	Description	Source
Political rights	Adopted from the Freedom House survey of "Freedom in the World." The survey asks ten political rights questions in three categories: (a) electoral process, (b) political pluralism and participation, and (c) functioning of government. The raw points are then used to calculate the score of political rights in a country. It ranges from 1 (highest amount of political rights for citizens) to 7 (lowest).	Freedom House: htt ps://freedomhouse .org/report/freedom- world/freedom-worl d-2018
Rule of law	Derived from the Economic Freedom of the World Annual Report by James Gwartney, Robert Lawson, and Joshua Hall. It measures the degree to which the court system in a country is impartial. It ranges from 1 (least impartial) to 10 (most impartial).	www .fraserinstitute.org/s tudies/economic-fre edom-of-the-world-2 016-annual-report
Free flow of information	Based on the "2017 World Press Freedom Index," which measures the degree of freedom that journalists and media have in more than 160 countries. It is based on annual surveys that ask 50 questions in seven areas: (a) physical attacks, imprisonment and direct threats on journalists and media assistants; (b) indirect threats and access to information; (c) legal situation and unjustified prosecution; (d) censorship, self-	Reporters without Borders: https://rsf .org/en/ ranking_table

Table 4.A.1 (cont.)

Indicator	Description	Source
	censorship; (e) public media; (f) economic and administrative pressure; (g) the Internet and new media. The score ranges from 0 (most free) to over 100 (least free).	
Quality of accounting standards	Based on Deloitte's report on the adoption of the International Financial Report Standard (IFRS) across countries. The indicator is from 1 (not adopting IFRS – low standard) to 4 (compete adoption – high standard), with 2 and 3 indicating partial adoption.	Deloitte, "Use of IFRS by Jurisdiction" (www.iasplus.com/en/resources/ifrs-topics/use-of-ifrs#Note14). Accessed June 14, 2018
Public trust	Adopted from the 2005 World Values Survey conducted by Inglehart et al. The indicator is derived from the replies to the following question (V24): "Generally speaking, would you say that most people can be trusted or that they need to be very careful in dealing with people?" 1 = "most people can be trusted" and 2 = "need to be very careful."	World Values Survey, Wave 6 (2010–2014) (www.worldvaluessurvey.org/)

Table 4.A.2 *Data used to measure relation-based versus clan-based societies*

Type of trust	Measurement (variable) used	Source
Generalized trust	V24: "Generally speaking, would you say that most people can be trusted or that you need to be very careful in dealing with people?" 1 = "most people can be trusted" and 2 = "need to be very careful"	World Values Survey, Wave 6 (2010–2014)
Particularized trust	V102: "Do you trust your family?" 1 = "trust completely" and 2, 3, 4 = "Do not trust at all"	As above

NOTES

1. This chapter is based on Li., S (2009), *Managing International Business in Relation-Based Versus Rule-Based Countries*. New York: Business Expert Press.
2. Sing Tao Daily. 2018. "Please help me, we are all Chinese": Chinese male indicted for attempting to bribe LAX official. *Sing Tao Daily*, July 17. (www .singtaousa.com/la/453-南加新聞/1008810-「幫幫忙％EF％BC％8C都是中國人」+華男涉賄LAX官員被起訴/): Accessed August 7, 2018.

5 Why Some Societies Thrive Despite Corruption: A Relation-Based Explanation[1]

> The ministers of transportation of the world convened in a main capital city in Asia. The host country minister invited his close friend, a minister from Latin America, to his home in a posh high-rise apartment building. The Latin American minister was impressed by the expensive home and joked with his friend: "I know your salary; how could you afford this?" The Asian minister took him to the window to look out. They saw newly built highways. "I built them!" The Asian minister said, and then patted his pocket: "Ten percent!" Next year, the convention was held in Latin America, and the Latin American minister invited the Asian minister to his home, which was much bigger than that of the Asian minister's. "Wow," the Asian minister asked, "how could you afford this?" The Latin American minister took him to the window to look out. The Asian minister saw nothing and was puzzled. The Latin American minister smiled at him and patted his pocket: "100 percent!"
>
> –Told by an international executive in the author's class

The above joke, which I have heard quite a few times in different versions, suggests an important unanswered question in the study of corruption. That is, why does corruption seem to hurt some countries less than others? Or, looking at corruption from an even more positive perspective, why are some countries able to achieve rapid growth under rampant corruption? This, I think, has been the biggest and most persistent puzzle for scholars of corruption.

In this chapter, I will build on Chapter 4, especially on the arguments of relation-based governance, to offer a framework that may help to solve the puzzle and to explain why some countries thrive despite corruption.

5.1 THE PUZZLE

As we have discussed in this book so far, corruption, in general, has a negative relationship with the level of economic affluence

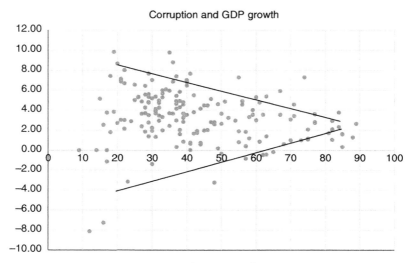

FIGURE 5.1 Corruption and GDP growth rate across countries,
2012–2016
X = Corruption Perception Index 2017, 0 = most corrupt, 100 = most clear
Y = Average GDP growth (2012–2016). Each observation (dot) is a country.
Source: (Transparency International, 2017; World Bank, 2018)

(measured by the level of per capita income) across countries, as
shown in Figure 1. 1 in Chapter 1. However, the way in which corruption affects economic growth, especially the economic growth of the
less developed countries, is far from clear (Svensson, 2003).

For example, if we make a chart of the relationship between the
perceived corruption level and the economic growth rate across countries, we get an interesting and very mixed picture: it seems that
growth rates diverge more sharply for countries with high-level corruption. In other words, while many highly corrupt countries have low
economic growth rates, there are some countries that have achieved
rapid economic growth under rampant governmental corruption
(Figure 5.1). This at least suggests that some countries may achieve
high economic performance despite high corruption.

China provides such a case. Both domestic public opinion polls
in China and surveys by international organizations show that the

level of corruption in China is high, it is deeply rooted, and it is widespread (Transparency International, 2017). However, despite the rampant corruption, the Chinese economy has been growing rapidly, with an average annual growth rate of approximately 10 percent during the past three decades or so. Moreover, China is not alone; there are other countries with relatively high corruption and high economic growth rates. Presumably, one can argue that this is because there are many factors that affect economic growth, and corruption is only one of them. However, we are not satisfied with this argument, because the observation that *all* of the poorest countries are highly corrupt (see Figure 1. 1 in Chapter 1) does suggest that corruption hurts economic growth in the long run.

This poses an important puzzle, not only to scholars of international business, but also to society in general and to policy makers in particular: why does corruption seem to be more harmful to the economic growth of some countries and less harmful to others?

Scholars of corruption first tried to solve this puzzle by constructing various theories of corruption. Broadly speaking, there are two major theoretical streams on the role of corruption on economic growth. One stream argues that corruption is a pure waste and, thus, is bad for economic growth (Choi & Thum, 1998; Murphy, Shleifer, & Vishny, 1993; Svensson, 2003). The other argues that, under a political and economic environment where regulations are extremely rigid and anti-business, corruption (and bribery) may serve as a lubricant to circumvent stifling regulations and, thus, can be conducive to economic growth ("efficiency-enhancing" corruption) (Leff, 1964; Lui, 1985; Wedeman, 1997, 2002). While both theories are internally consistent and make sense, the empirical evidence did not seem to support either.

A weakness in the previous studies is the inability to systematically distinguish the more "efficiency-enhancing" corruption from the more "predatory" corruption by identifying some moderating factor(s) that may alter the circumstances in which the effect of corruption on economic efficiency can be more harmful or less harmful.

Presumably, we could imagine that some countries tend to have more "efficiency-enhancing" corruption, while other countries tend to be plagued by "predatory" corruption (as implied in Wedeman, 1997). If this is the case, without being able to identify the factors that may determine the type of corruption, then the overall effect of corruption on economic growth across countries may be obscured, with the "efficiency-enhancing" and "predatory" effects canceling each other out, thus failing to support either view.

My coauthor and I have been studying this puzzle for ten years, and we have come up with the argument that a major factor that may systematically distinguish countries with predominantly "efficiency-enhancing" corruption from countries with predominantly "predatory" corruption is the level of trust in the society (Li, 2009; Li & Wu, 2007, 2010). More specifically, we argue that, in a society with a high level of trust, corruption tends to be more "efficiency-enhancing" (or less harmful to economic growth), whereas in a society that lacks trust, corruption tends to be more predatory (or more harmful to economic growth).

This argument seems ironic: corruption and bribery are dishonest and immoral behaviors, whereas trust usually has the connotation of honesty and high morality. But in our studies, we used case studies and statistical analyses to show that there is a complementary relationship between corruption and trust regarding the way in which they interact to affect economic efficiency.

In this chapter, drawing on the framework of governance environment laid out in the last chapter, I will further develop our trust argument to show that among the non-rule-based societies, the relation-based ones tend to have "efficiency-enhancing" corruption, whereas the societies that do not have strong relation-based networks (i.e., clan-based) suffer more from predatory corruption.

5.2 PREVIOUS STUDIES ON CORRUPTION AND ECONOMIC GROWTH

The literature on corruption is multidisciplinary, rich, and growing. Scholars from virtually every discipline in the social sciences and the business schools study it (e.g., Jain, 2001; Nwabuzor, 2005; Rodriguez, Siegel, Hillman, & Eden, 2006; Svensson, 2003; Uslaner, 2004). For the topic of this chapter, we will restrict our literature review to the effect of corruption on economic growth across countries.

As briefly mentioned earlier, there are two contrasting views on the effect of corruption on economic growth. One school, which may be termed the "efficiency-enhancing" view, argues that, under certain conditions, corruption may improve the efficiency of a government bureaucracy (Leff, 1964). If a country's political system is characterized by a long and complicated business approval process, and if the laws and regulations are anti-business and rigid, then paying bribes to officials to circumvent the bureaucracy will improve the efficiency of business and, thus, will help the economy to grow. This is the so-called "grease-the-wheels-of-bureaucracy" argument for corruption. Lui (1985) develops a queuing model, demonstrating that if corrupt officials award business licenses or contracts according to the size of bribes, and if more efficient firms can offer larger bribes to get licenses or contracts, then such corruption is efficiency-enhancing: resources can achieve optimal allocation.

Other scholars are skeptical of the "efficiency-enhancing" view. Their main criticism is that the efficiency-enhancing view treats rigid bureaucracy and anti-business regulations as a given. However, in most countries with high corruption, the officials have a strong incentive to make the regulations more rigid so that they can demand more bribes. In this regard, the critics argue that both corruption and rigid regulations are symptoms of other underlying factors (Kaufmann & Wei, 2000; Svensson, 2005). Furthermore, we should point out that Lui's model implicitly assumes that corrupt officials are comfortable accepting bribes from *anyone*, including from people they do not know well. This is not realistic, since the risk of accepting bribes from a stranger is high in a society with little trust. It is more likely that a corrupt official would choose only to accept bribes from related people, in order to reduce the risk of being turned in, which might, then, lead to a sub-optimal allocation of resources.

The argument that corruption negatively affects economic growth is primarily based on resource allocation. Corrupt officials may select and approve projects that make it easy to extort bribery, rather than ones that can create the greatest economic welfare for the society (Murphy et al., 1993). These corrupt officials tend to award contracts to firms that are willing to lower quality and then use the savings to pay a higher bribe to get the business; this method would encourage inefficient firms (Rose-Ackerman, 1978). Responding to a corrupt environment, firms may try to avoid long-term, irreversible investment, and may opt for "fly-by-night" technology to guard against future escalation in bribe demand (Choi & Thum, 1998; Svensson, 2003). Corruption can also drag down economic growth by diverting entrepreneurial talents from productive work (such as starting new businesses) to unproductive work (e.g., seeking government jobs). Despite the theoretical efforts in understanding the impact of corruption on the economy, empirical testing is inconclusive on this issue (Svensson, 2005).

Research on corruption has further distinguished different types of corruption (Shleifer & Vishny, 1993; Sun, 2004; Wedeman, 1997). As we briefly discussed earlier, Wedeman (1997) proposed a classification of three types of corruption: looting, rent-scraping, and dividend-collection. Wedeman argues from case studies that looting corruption hurts a country's economic growth, whereas dividend-collecting corruption may explain the situation in high-corruption, high-growth countries. Sun (2004) distinguishes between transaction-type corruption and non-transaction-type corruption. According to Sun, transaction-type corruption involves "two-way exchanges between officials and citizens" (p. 53), whereas the non-transaction type includes "embezzlement, misappropriation, accounting violation, squandering, and negligence" (p. 87). Sun's non-transaction type is close to Wedeman's looting and rent-scraping, whereas Sun's transaction-type is similar to Wedeman's dividend-collection type.

These studies provided insights into how different types of corruption may affect economic growth differently. But why do some (lucky) countries have dividend-collecting corruption, while others are plagued by looting? What social factor determines, or explains, the type of corruption that a society tends to have? The above studies did not address this. We think that one of the important factors that may help us address this issue is the level of trust in a society, which has been overlooked in previous studies on corruption.

5.3 THE ROLE OF TRUST IN CORRUPTION AND ITS EFFECT ON EFFICIENCY

5.3.1 Why Trust Matters

Corruption is illegal in almost all societies, at least nominally. Thus, an important factor in taking bribes is the risk of being caught. Scholars have studied the probability of being caught in corrupt activities (e.g., Becker, 1968). However, there does not seem to be any study on the systematic variations, or patterns, in the probability of being caught across countries, except for the general notion that in a more corrupt society, bribery and corruption tend to be perceived as less dangerous and more acceptable: "this is the only way to do things here" (Jain, 2001).

In this regard, my coauthor and I have argued that one important factor that has been overlooked is the level of trust (Li & Wu, 2010). Although the way in which trust affects the level of corruption had been well studied (e.g., Gambetta, 1993; Uslaner, 2004), no study had examined how trust moderates the degree to which corruption affects economic efficiency.

From an economic exchange perspective, trust can be defined as a "willingness to rely on an exchange partner in whom one has confidence" (Moorman, Deshpande, & Zaltman, 1993, p. 82). It is a confidence that one has in a prospective partner's reliability (Morgan & Hunt, 1994; Rotter, 1967). Rotter (1967, p. 651) calls trust "a generalized expectancy held by an individual that the word of another ... can be relied on."

While definitions vary, most conceptualizations of trust by economic and business scholars can be summarized in two views. One view focuses on personal traits that characterize trust, such as consistency, responsibility, and fairness (e.g., Dwyer & LaGace, 1986), while the other view emphasizes the perceived outcomes of trust, such as the expectations that a trusted partner will deliver the promised results (e.g., Anderson & Narus, 1990).

Putnam (1993) and Fukuyama (1995) were among the first to argue that trust, or social capital, affects economic performance. Later on, La Porta, Lopez-de-Silanes, Shleifer, and Vishny (1997) argued that trust promotes cooperation, which in turn promotes economic performance, and the authors provide statistical evidence to support their argument.

Scholars of trust (e.g., Bjørnskov, 2006; Uslaner, 2002) further distinguish two types of trust – generalized trust and particularized trust – which are important for our study. As discussed in Chapter 4, generalized trust is the belief that most people can be trusted, including strangers. Its presence or absence can be measured by the following question from the World Values Survey (Inglehart, 1995–2005): "Generally speaking, do you believe that most people can be trusted or that you can't be too careful in dealing with people?" This question is widely used to examine respondents' trust in people whom they meet randomly on the street or in any occasions. Particularized trust, in contrast, is the belief that trust can only be applied to specific individuals or to individuals associated with a certain network or group, such as family members, relatives, friends, or members of one's organization.

The effects of the two types of trust on the level of corruption in a society are quite different, as scholars (e.g., Uslaner, 2002; Uslaner, 2004) have argued. For instance, according to Uslaner, if a society has a high level of generalized trust, it would be difficult for politicians to "rob the public purse" (Uslaner, 2002, p. 221). Empirical studies have also confirmed that the correlation between societal corruption and generalized trust across countries is negative, with the exception of China.[2]

Particularized trust, on the other hand, seems to facilitate corruption (Uslaner, 2004), with the following logic. To form a bribery–corruption relationship (transaction-type corruption), some minimal trust must exist, because of the time lag and the geographic separation between the bribe payment to the corrupt official and the delivery of the public good to the briber. This is especially true in large-scale instances of corruption that involve government contracts or market access worth hundreds of millions of dollars (whereas petty corruption, such as paying a police official to cancel a ticket for a traffic violation, may be accomplished on the spot). Both sides want to make sure that their partners will deliver as they promised (Lambsdorff, 2002). As in any economic transaction, a key issue is: Should the briber pay first, or should the official deliver the goods first? If there exists a high level of trust between the briber and the official, it is less of a concern. Otherwise, the deal cannot be done, since there is very little legal protection for the bribery–corruption relationship. In this sense, Gambetta (1993) argues that high levels of particularized trust are the foundation for the corruption between the Italian Mafia and government officials.

While the argument about particularized trust and the level of corruption had been well made, what had been less studied and, thus, less understood was how trust affects the economic outcome of corruption. This was the focus of the Li–Wu study. In our study, we used the following example to illustrate our rationale:

Suppose that there are two types of societies in terms of the level of trust.[3] Society M has a very high level of trust, whereas Society N has virtually no trust. In Society M, where people tend to trust each other (keep their promises to each other in social exchanges), corrupt officials feel comfortable taking bribes from almost anyone, because the likelihood of being turned in by the bribe-giver is very low.

Furthermore, whether the briber pays first or the official delivers first is not a major issue, since they trust each other. Thus, it can be logically argued that in Society M, there is an extensive and efficient bribe-taking (transaction-type) corruption market; corrupt officials will sell the public goods (contracts or market access) to the highest bidder with the most efficient firm (approximating the "efficiency-enhancing" hypothesis). In essence, bribers pay and officials deliver.

In Society N, people are highly suspicious of each other, and corrupt officials only accept bribes from people they know well, such as their family members or relatives. In these close relationships, the time lag between payment and delivery is not a big problem. But such transactions are only limited to a small number of people. If corruption is rampant in Society N, then it implies that corrupt officials must extract payments from strangers. With people one does not know directly, the time lag and the geographic separation (such as delivering the public goods in one city and paying bribes in another city) becomes a difficult issue. Since there is little trust and, thus, no guarantee that the official will deliver, potential bribers have little incentive to pay up front. Likewise, the official will not deliver without payment first. The likelihood of closing a bribe-taking deal is further reduced because there is a risk of being turned in, coupled with the threat of future extortion, since the people involved do not know each other directly and thus have little trust between them. However, if corruption is rampant in such a society, it implies that officials control most resources and have absolute authority to extract payment from ordinary citizens and private firms. Then corruption becomes predatory, pure extortion that does not deliver value either to the briber or to the society and, hence, it is detrimental to economic growth. This would be close to the non-transaction corruption in Sun (2004) or to the looting or rent-scraping corruptions in Wedeman (1997).

Which countries tend to have a higher level of trust? Literature on trust suggests that public trust can be nurtured and positively reinforced by good political and economic institutions (La Porta et al., 1997). More pertinent to our study, public trust in a society is a culture (commonly observed social norms and values) that is formed during a long history of "horizontal networks of association" (Putnam, 1993) between people in social, economic, and political exchanges. In this regard, a voluntary (or informal) social network can be viewed as a governance mechanism that uses private relations, rather than official laws or regulations, to conduct and protect business and other social interests including property rights (Li & Filer, 2007). Imagine that, in a society in which people tend to make a great effort to cultivate personal relationships and to build private networks (recall Figure 4.5 in Chapter 4), person A tends to place a higher level of trust in person D, whom A does not know well, as long as A's personal network reaches D through the connection of networks (i.e., through B and C, as illustrated in Figure 4.5 of Chapter 4). In other words, if D cheats A, A can always rely on his/her network to reach D's network to punish D. A logical extrapolation is that, in this society, the level of trust tends to be higher as a result of the society's heavy reliance on overlapping personal networks.[4]

Based on the above discussion, we proposed that, in countries with a more expansive, stronger, and thicker social network, as reflected in the higher level of trust, bribery–corruption relations tend to be more extensive (with more people participating) and relatively more efficient (or less harmful to efficiency) in the following sense. First, the briber pays and the corrupt official delivers public goods (such as licenses, permissions, or contracts) to the briber, thus facilitating business activities. Second, more efficient firms can afford to pay higher bribes and the firm that pays the largest bribe (highest bidder), which tends to be the most efficient firm, will get the public goods, thus enhancing economic efficiency, which, in turn, contributes to economic growth. In contrast, in countries with weak social networks, as evidenced in a low level of public trust, bribery–corruption relations tend to be limited to a small number of closely related people (such as family members or long-time friends), who may not necessarily be the most efficient users of the public goods that they receive as a result of their bribe. The bribe payment by strangers will degenerate into pure extortion or looting (as demonstrated by Society N in our example), producing a deadweight loss to the briber and no efficiency gain for the economy.

To summarize the above discussion, we hypothesized that the following three relationships hold. (1) Corruption has a negative effect on economic growth across countries, while controlling for other major factors that may also affect economic growth. (2) Trust exerts a positive effect on economic growth, *ceteris paribus*. (3) If the first two relationships hold, then the negative effect of corruption on economic growth is moderated by trust. In other words, we believed that in countries with a higher level of trust, the negative effect of corruption on economic growth is mitigated by the higher level of trust. Since these arguments were new, we then decided to conduct a case study and then multi-country statistical analyses to verify our arguments. First, we conducted a case analysis of China versus the Philippines.

Case Study

CORRUPTION IN CHINA AND THE PHILIPPINES

The cases of China and the Philippines may illustrate our argument. As shown in Table 5.1, both countries have similar scores in the Corruption Perception Index, but they are widely different in their levels of public trust and economic growth rates, with China being high and the Philippines being low on both measures. While we realize that China and the Philippines share some commonalities in corruption activities, which have been observed in most corrupt countries in the world, such as officials stealing from the state coffers and practicing extortion in the private sector, what we try to illustrate here is that, in a comparative perspective, corruption in China and the Philippines tends to be of different types.

Table 5.1 *Corruption, trust, and economic development in China and the Philippines*

Country	GDP annual growth rate (%) (1990–2000)	GNI per capita (2001)	Corruption Perception Index (10 = best, 1 = worst) (2000)	Trust (1999–2004)
Philippines	3.3	1050	2.8	8.6
China	10.3	890	3.1	54.5

Source: (Transparency International, 2017; World Bank, 2018; World Values Survey, 2005–2014)

CORRUPTION IN CHINA

China is best known for its *guanxi* culture and practice (Li & Park, 2006; Li et al., 2004; Park & Luo, 2001; Xin & Pearce, 1996; Yang, 2002). *Guanxi* refers to the informal social networks based on private relations among people. *Guanxi* functions as a relation-based governance system that provides private means to facilitate and protect economic transactions. In the last chapter, we discussed the way in which a relation-based governance system can perform three monitoring mechanisms to ensure smooth economic transactions when public laws and regulations fail to provide fair and efficient ordering: first, the *ex ante* ability to privately check the prospective party's history of honoring commitments; second, the interim ability to follow the progress and status of the other party after entering into a business deal; and finally, the *ex post* ability of deterring opportunistic behavior by private means (such as bad-mouthing, seizing assets, or even physical harm). From a game-theoretical perspective, in repeated dealings, these private mechanisms can be efficient and effective. As such circles (see Figure 4.5 of Chapter 4) of related people (with particularized trust) increase, they tend to be interconnected and to improve the level of trust in a society, similar to the way in which generalized trust works. Moreover, in a society with a high level of trust, the likelihood of cooperation between two people who have just met for the first time (such as between a potential briber and a prospective bribe-taker) is high (Kreps, Milgrom, Roberts, & Wilson, 1982) and private governance mechanisms can be quite effective and efficient.

The corruption–growth relationship in China closely resembles such conditions. In China, due to the monopolistic control of most of the economic resources by the government, corruption is rampant. The widely accepted view in China is that "power cannot be deposited in a bank, so you had better profit from it while you can" (see, e.g., Taihang Luntan, 2007). Furthermore, the strong and thick social networks make the bribery–corruption relationship extend beyond family members and close friends. A common practice in China is this: if a business person needs a highly restricted permit from a specific government department, he or she would go around asking all of his or her friends who might know someone in that department. It is very likely that one of the friends would say, "I don't know anyone there directly, but my sister-in-law has a co-worker who knows someone who has a student who is the son of a senior official in that department." In a society with low trust, such an indirect relationship is too risky to discuss bribery. But in China, many bribery–corruption relationships can be established in just this way, due to its strong *guanxi* system, as evidenced in a number of known corruption cases, most of which involve people beyond the extended family ties (see, e.g., cases in the section on "corruption" in Chinaaffairs .org, 2007).

This high level of trust can be seen from the following quotation from a multinational executive explaining how his firm gave a large "slush fund" to a consultant to pay bribes in

China: "The terms of the deal was [*sic*] ... a ten million-dollar discretionary fund. Hands off, no questions asked. Don't ask [the consultant] where the money goes ... We knew exactly what he was up to, and exactly how successful he would be ... " (Gutmann, 2004, p. 124).

The following act of bribery is quoted from a reliable source.[5] "I [the briber] invite my client [corrupt official] to a well-known Cantonese restaurant with several branches in Beijing. The meal costs an astronomical 20000 rmb [$2,400] for two. On the way out, the restaurant passes a gift to my client and the client is told he or she can exchange the gift for cash if he or she does not like it. The gift is then exchanged by my client for about 10000 rmb. I have not discussed any such exchanges with my client. But just in case people get the wrong impression, the restaurant has covered my car's license plate in the restaurant's parking lot." This restaurant is known for providing such a service to facilitate bribery and corruption. Needless to say, this kind of bribery–corruption is only possible when there is a very high level of trust.

Even the Chinese government admits that corruption in China has become quite innovative and very sophisticated. According to *Takungpao*, a Chinese government newspaper, bribers and corrupt officials have invented new arrangements in the bribery–corruption relationship (Hu, 2006). One of the new features can be called the "globalization" of bribes. Bribes are paid not in China, but outside of China, in the form of luxury homes, bank accounts, or gambling trips (Chinaaffairs .org, 2007). The reason that these activities and assets are out-side of China is to reduce the risk of being caught. But the geographic and temporal separation of payment and delivery also means that there is a high level of trust between the briber and the official. Perhaps the most interesting new feature of corruption in China is that it has taken the form of futures options. The briber and the official have developed an understanding: the incumbent official will help the briber now, but will not get paid immediately. Years later, when the official is retired or has changed jobs, the briber will pay him in some way. Obviously, this arrangement substantially reduces the risk of being caught. Again, without a high level of trust, the corrupt will not choose this option.

CORRUPTION IN THE PHILIPPINES

The case of the Philippines is very different from that of China. Although it has a similar level of corruption and its income per capita is close to China's, it has a much lower level of public trust and a slower rate of economic growth than China (see Table 5.1).

A major type of corruption in the Philippines, at least historically, was that the head of the state would control entry to an industry or simply monopolize it, and would impose a tax or a surcharge on all of the products of the industry or would extract a fee for entering the industry. The head of the state would appoint one of his or her cronies to be in charge of the industry and steal all the collections from the state coffers. To the private sector payers, these taxes, surcharges or fees would be nothing more than robbery, a deadweight loss in economic efficiency. The collecting officials would simply impose them on the payers, without facilitating or helping any business activities. Furthermore, the victims of the corruption, the payers, would have no evidence with which to turn in the official collector, because the latter was simply executing a state order, as shown in the following examples of major industries in the Philippines.

In the coconut sector in the 1970s (accounting for, roughly, 25 percent of Philippines' export income), former President Ferdinand Marcos imposed a tax on all sales of coconuts and copra. The agency in charge of collecting this tax was headed by his close friend, Manuel Conjuangco. Conjuangco then used the extorted money to buy banks, which in turn funded his acquisition of many coconut oil pressing mills. Then he put all of the tax money into a fund and used the fund to subsidize the mills he and Marcos controlled (Wedeman, 1997).

There is a similar corruption pattern in the cigarette industry. In 1975, Marcos imposed a 100 percent import duty on cigarette filters, but gave a special 90 percent import duty reduction to the Philippine Tobacco Filters Corporation, a company owned by one of his close friends, Herminio Disini. Disini, in turn, supplied the filters at below market prices to Fortune Tobacco, a major cigarette maker owned by another Marcos ally, Lucio Tan. Together, they drove the competition out of the market and monopolized the cigarette industry (Wedeman, 1997).

In the sugar industry in 1974, Marcos ordered that all sugar exports be monopolized by the Philippine Exchange Company, which was controlled by his college friend, Robert Benidicto (Wedeman, 1997). With the blessing of Marcos and with subsidies from state funds, Benidicto manipulated sugar prices and took advantage of the differences between the monopolized domestic price and the international price to profit at the expense of sugar farmers and producers.

In all of these corruption anecdotes in the Philippines, there was little collaboration between the briber (the payer of surcharges, entry fees, and other types of extortions) and the corrupt official. The briber was forced to pay, and the official did not enhance the efficiency of the briber's business. It is estimated that, through these extractions, Marcos and his associates amassed wealth valued between $3 billion and $6 billion (Bhargava & Bolongaita, 2004; Wedeman, 1997).

The above comparative case study of the corruption in China and the Philippines demonstrates that the types of corruption in China (i.e., the futures options type, third party brokering (the restaurant example), and the "no-questions asked" slush funds)

> require a high level of trust between the briber and the bribee, whereas, in the Philippines, a high level of trust between the extorting official (bribee) and the extorted business people (briber) is not required and, in fact, does not seem to exist.

5.3.2 Further Examination Using Statistical Data

In the statistical test, we used a pooled data set from the World Values Survey conducted by Inglehart (1994–2005) of 65 countries in two periods (the number of countries was limited by data on trust). We were able to obtain the two most recent waves of the World Values Survey back then, 1994–1999, and 2000–2005, and we collected other variables based on the same time periods to construct a pooled data set (Woodridge, 2003) for our statistical test.

Essentially, in our statistical test, we wanted to find out whether the three relationships hold: (1) whether corruption has a negative effect on economic growth across countries; (2) whether trust exerts a positive effect on economic growth; and (3) if (1) and (2) hold, whether the negative effect of corruption on economic growth is moderated by trust. In other words, we wanted to learn whether, for countries with a higher level of trust, the negative effect of corruption on economic growth is mitigated by the higher level of trust.

In the test, we controlled for other major factors that may also affect economic growth, including the economic development level measured by GDP per capita, the education level, and the political system. The results of the test support our hypotheses: first, corruption negatively affects economic growth; second, trust has a positive effect on economic growth, and third and most importantly, we find that trust reduces the negative effect of corruption on economic growth (see the Appendix for details of the statistical test).

5.4 COMPARING RELATION-BASED AND CLAN-BASED SOCIETIES IN THE CORRUPTION–EFFICIENCY RELATIONSHIP

After the 2010 Li and Wu study, I continued to think about and work on the relation-based versus rule-based framework and on the corruption–efficiency relationship, and I have developed a new perspective: what we observed in the Li and Wu (2010) study on why some countries thrive despite corruption can be further explained by the difference between relation-based and clan-based societies.

In Chapter 4, we discussed the distinction between relation-based and clan-based societies, and we used a clustering analysis to distinguish them, based on the gap between generalized trust and trust in family. Applying this framework to the case of China versus the Philippines and the statistical test of Li and Wu, I note that the findings of Li and Wu can be explained by the framework of relation-based versus clan-based governance. In the most recent World Values Survey (Wave 6, 2010–2014), 64 percent of people in China thought that people can be trusted, which is the highest among all of the non-rule-based countries. In contrast, only 3 percent of people in the Philippines said that they trust people in general. In terms of trusting one's own family, both countries showed a fairly high level, 3.89 and 3.68 (1 = "do not trust at all," 4 = "trust completely"), for China and the Philippines, respectively. As a result, the gap between generalized trust and particularized trust (trust in family) is much larger for the Philippines, making China more relation-based and the Philippines more clan-based.

Using the relation-based versus clan-based framework, I conducted preliminary statistical analyses on the non-rule-based countries to test whether corruption has a different effect on economic growth between clan-based and relation-based societies.

5.4.1 Preliminary Analyses of Corruption–Efficiency Relationship Between Clan-Based and Relation-Based Countries

I conducted preliminary analyses to seek support for my argument that corruption is relatively more beneficial, or less harmful, to relation-based countries than to clan-based countries, in terms of economic growth.

Unlike the Li and Wu (2010) study, which uses all countries with valid data, I limited my sample to the non-rule-based countries (see Section 4.8.2 in Chapter 4), which includes both relation-based and clan-based countries. Table 5.2 lists the countries in the current analysis.

The classification of clan-based and relation-based countries is done by using SAS clustering analysis (see Section 4.8.2 in Chapter 4). As can be seen in Table 5.3, relation-based societies have a higher level of generalized trust and relatively lower trust in family (as shown by the relatively smaller gap between them), confirming our argument.

Table 5.4 compares economic growth rates between clan-based countries and relation-based countries, using growth rates of different durations. Overall, relation-based countries do better in economic growth than their clan-based counterparts.

I then conducted a multiple regression analysis to see how corruption interacts with the two types of governance: clan-based and relation-based governance. Due to the small sample size, I only included the three variables of interest as the influencers – the independent variables – in the regression analysis: the Corruption Perception Index (2017); a dummy variable differentiating the two types of governance, with 1 being relation-based and 0 being clan-based; and an interaction term between the Corruption Perception Index and the dummy variable. I used three average economic growth rates with different durations as the predicted, or the

Table 5.2 *Countries in the analysis*

Country name	Cluster
Argentina	0
Armenia	0
Brazil	0
Colombia	0
Ecuador	0
Georgia	0
Jordan	0
Libya	0
Morocco	0
Mexico	0
Malaysia	0
Nigeria	0
Peru	0
Philippines	0
Romania	0
Trinidad and Tobago	0
Turkey	0
Ukraine	0
Zimbabwe	0
Azerbaijan	1
Bahrain	1
China	1
Egypt, Arab Rep.	1
Kazakhstan	1
Kyrgyz Republic	1
Kuwait	1
Lebanon	1
Pakistan	1
Qatar	1
Russian Federation	1
Thailand	1

Note: Cluster 0 are clan-based countries, and Cluster 1 are relation-based countries.
Source: Author's calculation (World Values Survey, 2005–2014)

Table 5.3 *Different types of trust in relation-based and clan-based societies*

Means by clusters		
Cluster	Generalized trust (V24)	Gap between generalized trust and trust in family (V24-V102)
1 (Relation-based)	1.30	–1.86
0 (Clan-based)	1.10	–2.49

Source: Author's calculation (World Values Survey, 2005–2014)

Table 5.4 *Economic growth rate by cluster type*

Average annual economic growth rate	Cluster 0 (clan-based)	Cluster 1 (relation-based)
5-year average (2012–2016)	2.88	3.36
10-year average (2007–2016)	3.42	4.91
15-year average (2002–2016)	4.23	6.03

Source: Author's calculation (World Bank, 2018)

dependent, variable. Table 5. 5 summarizes the regression analysis results.

While the regression analysis is simple in design, due to the small sample size, and while some coefficients are not statistically significant, the general pattern of coefficient estimates is consistent, in their directions, with my conjecture. In general, corruption has a positive effect on economic growth for non-rule-based societies. The effect of being a relation-based society on economic growth, without factoring in the effect of corruption, is negative. The most

Table 5.5 *Results of regression analyses for the corruption–efficiency relationship, relation-based versus clan-based (standardized estimate of coefficients)*

Variable	Model 1 (dependent variable = 5-year average economic growth)	Model 2 (dependent variable = 10-year average economic growth)	Model 2 (dependent variable = 15-year average economic growth)
Corruption (Index)	0.107	0.087	0.304*
Cluster (relation-based = 1)	–0.110	–0.886*	–0.319
Corruption X cluster	0.245	1.307**	0.778
N	29	29	29
Adjusted R-square	–0.07	0.27	0.33

** $p < 0.05$ in one tail test;* $p < 0.10$ in one tail test

Source: Author's calculation

interesting and most important finding is the positive sign of the interaction term, (corruption) x (relation-based), which suggests that corruption increases economic growth for relation-based societies.

In sum, my analyses show that first, relation-based countries have a high level of generalized trust and a smaller gap between generalized trust and trust in family; second, relation-based countries have a higher economic growth rate; and third, corruption has a positive effect on economic growth for relation-based countries, but for clan-based societies, corruption has a negative effect on economic growth.

These findings, while preliminary due to the small number of observations, lend support to our main argument on the role of different types of trust, clan-based versus relation-based societies, and how they affect the corruption–efficiency relationship.

5.5 IMPLICATIONS OF THE FINDINGS

The arguments and analyses of this chapter shed light on the mystery of why some countries achieve rapid economic growth with rampant corruption by examining the role of trust in the corruption–efficiency relationship and the effect of corruption in non-rule-based societies between relation-based and clan-based types.

In the 2010 Li and Wu study presented in this chapter, we showed that, in countries with a higher level of trust, corruption tends to be relatively less harmful to economic growth. Our empirical analysis, using both a case study and statistical testing, provides support for our view. I have further developed the 2010 Li and Wu study to argue that among the non-rule-based societies, the relation-based societies tend to have "efficiency-enhancing" corruption, whereas the clan-based societies suffer more predatory corruption.

Our findings have several important implications for the study of corruption, trust, and economic development, as well as for business executives and policy makers.

5.5.1 Different Shades and Evolutions of Trust

The literature on the relationship between trust and political–economic development generally indicates that trust is conducive to economic growth and democratic development (Fukuyama, 1995; Putnam, 1993). Countries with high levels of income and mature democratic systems (with strong rule of law) tend to be associated with high levels of public trust (see Figures 4.3 and 4.4 in Chapter 4). However, China, with its relatively low income level and the lack of democracy conspicuously stands out as a counterexample. The level of generalized trust in China, as measured by the World Values Survey, is very high, which has been a puzzle for scholars of trust (Tang, 2005).

Our argument that relation-based societies such as China have extensive informal social networks, or "circles" (see the discussion on circles of private networks and Figure 4.5 in Chapter 4), may provide clues to solve this puzzle. We show that the common perception of the Chinese *guanxi* that people in China only trust their family is not accurate. Through a series of interconnected circles, within which members can hold each other accountable, the Chinese can extend their form of trust – sanctioned by accountability between members within each circle – to a stranger, which, by definition, is generalized trust. In fact, earlier studies have indirectly supported this view. Tang (2005) found that the most important source of trust in China is not within the family – the core of particularized trust – but beyond the family.

This shift from trusting one's own family the most to trusting broader circles of people may indicate that generalized trust is being nurtured from particularized trust, but in a twisted way: it is secured by *ex ante*, interim, and *ex post* monitoring mechanisms (see Chapter 4, Section 4.4). In relation-based societies, people and firms build their particularized circles and connect their circles with other circles, forming a vast, more generalized social network. This social network may relay trust between people who do not have direct information on each other but are connected through a mutual friend (someone who has memberships in multiple circles). This may supplement Putnam's argument that particularized trust evolves into generalized trust (Putnam, 1993). As shown in our case study, the vast network enables one to trust a total stranger who is connected through (and thus governed by) particularized links.

5.5.2 The Role of Trust in the Economic Outcome of Corruption

Our finding that high levels of trust tend to make the economic effect of corruption less predatory and more "efficiency-enhancing" should be read with caution. We are not claiming that corruption in a society with a high level of trust is a good thing. As stated at the beginning of this book, corruption diverts resources from the investors and the society to corrupt officials' pockets and thus hurts economic efficiency and development. This chapter argues that in a society with a higher level of trust, or in relation-based societies, the market for bribe–corruption exchange tends to be more competitive, and government goods tend to be sold (for corrupt officials' private gains) to the most efficient bidder (briber), making corruption less predatory, or less damaging. As compared to pure looting, which tends to happen in clan-based societies, corruption in relation-based societies tends to be relatively more "efficiency-enhancing." But even in "efficiency-enhancing" corruption, the cost of corruption is still greater than zero; it is still less efficient, when compared to no corruption.

5.5.3   Consequences of "Efficiency-enhancing" Corruption

The so-called "efficiency-enhancing" corruption, under a high level of trust or in relation-based societies, implies that officials steal public goods and provide them below the official price to the briber, enabling the briber to improve efficiency (similar to Shleifer and Vishny's corruption with theft (1993) and to Wedeman's "dividend-collecting corruption" (1997)). The so-called "predatory" corruption is more like the corruption without theft in Shleifer and Vishny's model (or the "looting" or "rent-scraping corruption" in Wedeman, 1997), in which the bribe is an extra, on top of the official price of the public good in question.

Efficiency-enhancing corruption may have the following aspects. First, it lines corrupt officials' pockets. Second, it improves the bottom line of the private firms who bribe (and the number of firms who bribe is extensive, due to the high level of trust). Third, in the case of "victimless corruption" (see Chapter 2, Section 2.1), corrupt officials, colluding with a bribing firm, may create a new project that fills a need in the society, increasing social welfare. Fourth, the corrupt officials have strong incentives to maintain and increase the state's political and regulatory power so that they can continue to sell licenses and permits for their private gains. Thus, we may conjecture that, under efficiency-enhancing corruption, the society will have a government with a strong and monopolistic political power and an efficient and wealthy business class, and many new, huge projects, some of which may actually benefit the society, such as high-speed rails or other infrastructure projects – providing they can be efficiently completed, of course.

5.5.4   Policy Implications for Cleaning up Corruption

The high level of trust (or personal reliance sanctioned by a vast informal social network) in the relation-based societies with predominantly "efficiency-enhancing" corruption implies that cleaning up corruption is very difficult for the following reasons.

First, as Shleifer and Vishny point out, "corruption with theft" may lower the total cost of business for the briber, and thus the briber will have little incentive to turn in the corrupt official, making corruption with theft difficult to detect.

Second, in societies that have extensive and expansive particularized circles that form a strong and thick general social network, it is very difficult to "blow the whistle." I once had a rare opportunity to chat with a jailed official charged with corruption about whether private contractors who bribe to get projects would confess if they were caught. He said that the unwritten rules are as follows. If the anticipated sentence is relatively short, the contractor would not implicate the bribed officials, so that the contractor could build a reputation that he or she can be trusted by corrupt officials for future deals after he or she is released. If the anticipated sentence is death or life in prison, then the contractor would confess, in order to save his or her life. Thus, in general, my interviewee concluded, most bribing business people tend to be tough and not confess – if it is a repeated game, of course. (In game theory, a *repeated game* refers to a game that is played by the same players repetitively, as opposed to a *single-shot game*. In repeated games rational players take into consideration how their current actions will affect the future actions of other players.)

If this logical conjecture is true, then the prospect of eradicating corruption in highly relation-based countries is less likely. On the other hand, corruption in societies with a low level of trust (resulting in thin and sparse particularized circles), may, ironically, be easier to clean up, since it absolutely dissipates values from the business and citizens.

Third, the difficulty of cleaning up "efficiency-enhancing" corruption may be further exacerbated by the "futures option" type of corruption. The time difference in bribe payment and public goods delivery implies that both parties – the briber and the corrupt official – have strong incentives to preserve the current political order in order to protect their futures options. We may call it a "lock-in effect" of the bribery–corruption relationship.

Our analysis and findings bring a new challenge to the "good governance" policies formulated by international organizations such as the World Bank. These policy makers need to realize that the "one-size-fits-all" policy of anticorruption that treats all countries indiscriminately may not work effectively and efficiently. They should also consider the level of, and the relationship between, particularized and generalized trust in a country, or the Governance Environment Indexes, in order to distinguish relation-based and clan-based countries, as they affect the economic outcome of corruption.

APPENDIX 5.A STATISTICAL ANALYSIS OF LI AND WU (2010)

In Li and Wu (2010), we performed a statistical test to verify three hypotheses:

Hypothesis 1: Corruption has a negative effect on economic growth, *ceteris paribus*.

Hypothesis 2: Trust has a positive effect on economic growth, *ceteris paribus*.

Hypothesis 3: The effect of corruption on economic growth is moderated by trust. There is an interaction effect between corruption and trust on economic growth. In countries with a higher level of trust, the negative effect of corruption will be mitigated.

We use a pooled data set consisting of 76 observations with 53 countries in two time periods (see Table 5.A.1). A major limitation in building a testing data set with a large number of countries with multiple time periods is the lack of data on trust. The only publicly available data on trust across countries is the data from the World Values Survey conducted by Inglehart (1995–2005). We were able to obtain the two most recent waves of the World Values Survey, 1994–1999, and 2000–2005, and to collect other variables based on the same time periods to construct a pooled data set (Woodridge, 2003) for our statistical test.

Table 5.A.1 *Countries included in the statistical test*

Period 1: 1994–1999		Period 2: 1999–2004			
1	Australia	1	Argentina	24	Jordan
2	Brazil	2	Austria	25	Korea, Rep.
3	Chile	3	Bangladesh	26	Mexico
4	China	4	Belgium	27	Netherlands
5	Colombia	5	Bulgaria	28	Pakistan
6	Czech Republic	6	Canada	29	Peru
7	Finland	7	Chile	30	Philippines
8	Germany	8	China	31	Poland
9	Hungary	9	Czech Republic	32	Portugal
10	India	10	Denmark	33	Romania
11	Japan	11	Egypt, Arab Rep	34	Russian Federate
12	Korea, Rep.	12	Finland	35	Singapore
13	Mexico	13	France	36	Slovak Republic
14	Netherlands	14	Germany	37	South Africa
15	Norway	15	Greece	38	Spain
16	Pakistan	16	Hungary	39	Sweden
17	Philippines	17	Iceland	40	Tanzania
18	Poland	18	India	41	Turkey

Table 5.A.1 *(cont.)*

Period 1: 1994–1999		Period 2: 1999–2004			
19	Romania	19	Indonesia	42	Uganda
20	Russian Federate	20	Ireland	43	United Kingdom
21	South Africa	21	Israel	44	United States
22	Spain	22	Italy	45	Venezuela, RB
23	Sweden	23	Japan	46	Zimbabwe
24	Switzerland				
25	Turkey				
26	United Kingdom				
27	United States				
28	Uruguay				
29	Venezuela, RB				
30	Vietnam				

DATA

Economic growth. This was our *dependent variable.* We used the average annual growth rate of GDP per capita, adjusted by purchasing power parity (PPP), to measure economic growth (World Bank, 2018). Corresponding to the two periods for which we have the data on trust, we used the following two time periods: 1994–1999, and 2000–2005. Although there were no obvious outliers in the distribution of growth rates, after some trial runs, we found that taking the natural logarithm of the growth rate substantially enhanced the goodness of fit in our regression. We thus took the natural logarithm of average annual growth rate of GDP per capita [log (GDPpgr)] to improve linearity. Since there were negative growth rates in our data, we first added a constant to the growth rate and then took the natural logarithm.

Our *independent variables* included the following.

Corruption. Our measure of corruption (CORRUPT) was adopted from the Corruption Perception Index (CPI) developed by Transparency International (1996, 2002). The original CPI ranges from 0 (most corrupt) to 10 (most clean). We reversed the order by multiplying (–1), so that a higher score means more corrupt, which made it easier to interpret the test result. Corresponding to the two time periods, we used the CPIs in 1996 and 2002.

Trust. Our measure of trust came from the World Values Survey (Inglehart, 1995–2005), based on a question in the survey which asks: "Generally speaking, would you say that most people can be trusted or that you cannot be too careful in dealing with people?" The answer is "yes" or "no." We used the percentage of people answering "yes" over the total sample as our measure of trust (TRUST) in a country. We used data from the two most recent survey waves, 1994–1999 and 1999–2004.

Our *control variables* included the following.

GNI per capita. According to the literature, a major factor affecting economic growth is the existing level of economic development (Solow, 1956). We used the average gross national income per capita based on purchasing power parity (PPP) (GNIp) as the measure for economic development and included it in our model as a controlled variable. The periods of the income data were 1994–1999 and 2000–2005 (World Bank, 2018).

Schooling. Studies have shown that human capital stock affects economic growth (Barro, 1997). Furthermore, corrupt countries have significantly lower levels of human capital stock (Svensson, 2005). We thus controlled it in our model and used years of schooling of the total population aged over 15 (SCHOOL) developed by Barro and Lee (2000) to approximate it. Barro and Lee (2000) calculate the data every five years. We used the data in 1995 and 2000 corresponding to the two time periods.

Political system. Scholars of political economy have argued that regime type, such as democracy or dictatorship, affects economic development, although the overall relationship between growth and regime type is not very empirically clear. Przeworski, Alvarez, Cheibub, and Limongi (2000) find that regime type does not have a significant effect on development, whereas Barro (1997) finds a nonlinear relationship between the two. In our model, we control the political system (STATUS), adopted from Freedom House (1972–2018), which classifies the political system of a country into "Not Free," "Partially Free," and "Free." In our preliminary test, we found that there was no significantly different influence on economic growth between partially free and free countries. Thus we coded STATUS as 1 if "Not Free," and as zero otherwise. Corresponding to the two time periods, we used status data from 1996 to 2002.

Time period. As mentioned before, our pooled data were from two time periods: 1994–1999 and 2000–2005. To reflect the fact that the population may have different distributions in the two different time periods, we allowed the intercept to differ across the two time periods by including a time period dummy (TIME). We chose the first time period (1994–1999) as the baseline; that is, TIME = 0, if an observation was in 1994–1999, and TIME = 1, if an observation was in 2000–2005.

TESTING RESULTS

We first estimated the correlation coefficients for all of the variables (see Table 5.A.2). As expected, corruption was negatively correlated with the growth rate of GDP per capita and trust was positively correlated with the growth rate of GDP per capita. The correlation efficient between the GNI per capita and the level of corruption was quite high (–0.872), causing us concern about potential multicollinearity problems in our subsequent regression estimates. We thus

Table 5.A.2 *Correlation coefficient estimates among all the variables*

	Mean	S.D.	GDPpgr	CORRUPT	TRUST	GNIp	SCHOOL	STATUS
GDPpgr	2.94	2.56						
CORRUPT	4.70[a]	2.53	-.220					
			(.056)					
TRUST	28.86	15.53	.290*	-.588**				
			(.011)	(.000)				
GNIp	12.91	12.65	.132	-.872**	.599**			
			(.257)	(.000)	(.000)			
SCHOOL	8.04	2.29	.179	-.625**	.417**	.627**		
			(.123)	(.000)	(.000)	(.000)		
Status	.07	.25	-.016	.241*	.146	-.254*	-.304*	
			(.893)	(.036)	(.208)	(.027)	(.008)	
TIME	.61	.49	.219	.010	-.004	.042	-.067	.016
			(.057)	(.928)	(.976)	(.722)	(.568)	(.363)

P-values are in parentheses. * Correlation is significant at the .05 level, ** Correlation is significant at the .01 level.

[a]0 = most corrupt, –10 = most clear.

decided to run two sets of regressions, one with and one without GNI per capita.[6]

The general model tested is:

Economic growth = f (corruption, trust, corruption*trust, control variables (GNI per capita, human capital stock, political status, time period), error term).

We used three specifications to test our hypotheses. Model (1a) examined the traditional model of the impact of corruption on economic growth, controlling for human capital stock, political status and time period. Model (2a) added "trust" to Model (1a) as an additional independent variable to examine the influence of trust on economic growth. Model (3a) added an interaction term between corruption and trust to Model (2a). We then repeated the above models with one more control variable: GNI per capita (Models (1b), (2b), and (3b)).

The results are summarized in Table 5.A.3. All the six specifications, Model (1a) to Model (3b), are very consistent: corruption has a negative effect on economic growth, trust shows a positive sign in terms of affecting economic growth, and the interaction term is positive. Comparing Models 1a–3a (without GNI per capita) and Models 1b–3b (with GNI per capita), we find that they are similar in terms of the effects of the independent variables and their explanation power, indicating that the relationships between economic growth, corruption, and trust are stable and that our specifications are robust. This robustness can be seen quite clearly from Model 3a and Model 3b: the magnitude of coefficient estimates, the significant levels, and the R-squares are very close. We will thus focus on Model 3b, the model with all of the independent variables, to discuss the testing results.

In Model (3b), the coefficient of CORRUPT is negative (−.059) and highly significant (p<0.000), suggesting that corruption retards economic growth. Hypothesis 1 is supported. Trust has a highly significant positive effect (.011 with p<0.000) on economic growth, supporting Fukuyama's view (1995) as well as our second hypothesis that a high level of trust among citizens accounts for the superior

Table 5.A.3 *Unstandardized coefficient estimates of regression result*

Independent variables	Dependent variable: log(GDPpgr)					
	Model 1a	Model 2a	Model 3a	Model 1b	Model 2b	Model 3b
CORRUPT	−.010	−.001	−.043***	−.025*	−.020	−.059***
	(.008)	(.009)	(.014)	(.013)	(.012)	(.016)
TRUST		.003**	.010***		.003**	.011***
		(.001)	(.002)		(.001)	(.002)
CORRUPT*TRUST			.001***			.001***
			(.000)			(.000)
GNIp				−.004	−.005**	−.005**
				(.003)	(.003)	(.002)
SCHOOL	.004	.001	.002	.007	.004	.004
	(.009)	(.009)	(.008)	(.009)	(.009)	(.008)
STATUS	−.025	−.080	−.130**	−.031	−.103	−.150**
	(.065)	(.069)	(.065)	(.065)	(.068)	(.064)
TIME	.057*	.059*	.055*	.063*	.068**	.063**
	(.031)	(.031)	(.028)	(.031)	(.030)	(.028)
Intercept	2.865***	2.863***	2.650***	2.811***	2.786***	2.582***
	(.064)	(.062)	(.081)	(.073)	(.071)	(.085)
N	76	76	76	76	76	76
R-square	.103	.153	.293	.129	.203	.337
F-statistics	2.040*	2.533**	4.776***	2.071*	2.936**	4.936***

Standard errors are in parentheses.

* Significant at the .10 level, ** Significant at the .05 level, *** Significant at the .01 level.

performance in the economy (measured by economic growth). The interaction term between corruption and trust is positive (.001) and highly significant (p<0.000), showing that the negative effect of corruption on economic growth is reduced by a higher level of trust. The effect of the interaction term can be clearly seen if we rearrange Model (3b) as follows:

$$\text{Log (GDPpgr)} = 2.582 + (-.059 + .001\text{TRUST}) * \text{CORRUPT}$$
$$+.011 * \text{TRUST} - .005 * \text{GNIp} + .004 * \text{SCHOOL}$$
$$-.150 * \text{STATUS} + .063 * \text{TIME} + \text{error},$$

The new coefficient of corruption, $(-.059+.001\text{TRUST})$, means that when the level of trust is extremely low in a society, corruption would impose a strong negative effect on economic growth. For example, if trust equals zero, then the effect of corruption on economic growth would be -0.17% on average; however, as the level of trust increases, it will mitigate the negative effect of corruption on economic growth. On average, every 10 percent increase in trust would reduce the negative effect of corruption by 0.0294%. These results show that trust moderates the effect of corruption on economic efficiency. Hypothesis 3 is supported.

NOTES

1. This chapter is based on Li, S. 2009. *Managing International Business in Relation-based Versus Rule-based Countries.* New York: Business Expert Press; Li, S., & Wu, J. 2010. Why some countries thrive despite corruption: The role of trust in the corruption–efficiency relationship. *Review of International Political Economy,* 17(1): 129–154.

2. Uslaner (2002) found the correlation between societal corruption and interpersonal trust across 52 countries is –0.613. But he eliminated China since he thought that the trust data was suspiciously high. However, Tang, W. 2005. *Public Opinion and Political Change in China.* CA: Stanford University Press. (2005) found that the same trust data were confirmed by several other surveys independently conducted in China (see Tang, 2005, pp. 102–103).

3. To make our argument more general, we do not distinguish generalized and particularized trust here, since both types apply in our example.

4. In our study, we treat the reliance on personal network and its measurement (trust) as exogenous. Discussing the determinants of the development of personal networks or trust is beyond the scope of our study. Interested readers may refer to Putnam (1993), Fukuyama (1995), La Porta et al. (1997) and Child (2001) for further discussion on trust and social networks.

5. This is quoted from a source who wishes to remain anonymous. The quotation and the restaurant name can be verified upon request.

6. This analytical strategy is based on Kennedy (1992), who suggested that "a popular means of avoiding the multicollinearity problem is by simply omitting one of the collinear variables" (p. 182).

6 Corruption and Anticorruption: Two Legs Supporting Dictatorships

Soviet Leader Leonid Brezhnev invited American President Ronald Reagan to visit Moscow. Looking down from his hotel room, Reagan saw several stretch limousines passing by on street.

"Who are the people riding in those limousines?" Reagan asked Brezhnev.

"They are the servants of the people!" Brezhnev answered proudly. Seeing that Reagan was puzzled, Brezhnev continued: "You see, in our country, people are the masters, and government officials are their servants."

"I see!" Reagan replied. "Then, who are the ones driving the limousines?"

"Oh, they are the masters!" Brezhnev replied.

–A Soviet Joke

In earlier chapters, we have laid the theoretical foundation of this book: it is the macro institutional environment that, to a great extent, determines the patterns of bribery and the corruption behaviors of individuals or organizations at the micro level. We have also scrutinized the bribery and corruption behaviors in the non-rule-based societies, with special attention paid to the contrasting effects of corruption on the economic outcomes between relation-based and clan-based societies. All of our discussions have, explicitly or implicitly, pointed to the importance of the political system of a society and the way in which it relates to, and deals with, corruption. In this chapter, we will examine how one of the most important political systems in the non-rule-based societies interacts with and moderates the effect of corruption.

In terms of the political system among the non-rule-based societies, perhaps the most important political system is the one characterized by highly centralized political power and severely restricted political rights for the population. Some examples include the political systems of China, Vietnam, and Saudi Arabia, which are commonly known as dictatorships (described in detail later in this chapter). In this chapter, I will first review regime types and will spotlight the way in which political regimes interact with corruption to affect economic development. I will then focus on the special and important roles that corruption and anticorruption campaigns play for the highly centralized political systems, and will show how, together, they form what I call "the necessary two legs" that support a dictatorial regime's rule and maintain a brittle stability in the society. Finally, I will discuss the cost of the "two legs" on the social and economic development of the society.

6.1 REGIME TYPES AND CORRUPTION

6.1.1 Regime Type

Democracy

Political scientists have a general agreement on what democracy, or at least mature and advanced democracy, looks like. The Merriam-Webster Dictionary defines *democracy* as "a government in which the supreme power is vested in the people and exercised by them directly or indirectly through a system of representation usually involving periodically held free elections" (Merriam-Webster, 2018b).

Democracy is a political system in which the ultimate political power rests in the hands of the people, the constituency, who choose the government heads by election and delegate their authority to those elected. Mature, advanced, and therefore stable democracies all share the following common features: they balance popular democracy (one in which "the majority rules") and a republic system (one in which the minority's rights are preserved); they all have the mechanism of checks and balances between the three branches of government (the legislative, the judiciary, and the executive branches), and their legal system is based on the rule of law that is impartial, transparent, effective, and efficient; the terms of the elected officials are limited; suffrage is universal; and armed forces and civil services are non-political (Li, 2016; Wikipedia, 2018d).

However, while all mature democracies share these common key features, the types of non-mature democracies vary greatly, from the ones in which political power is highly controlled by one person, such as dictatorships, to the ones in which no one controls any effective power, such as anarchies. Furthermore, there is little consensus among political scientists as to how to label various political systems, especially the various types of dictatorship, which is our main interest in this chapter.

Dictatorship

To facilitate our discussion without being dragged into a nomenclature debate, we will explain the two types of dictatorship that are both important and relevant to our study: totalitarianism and authoritarianism.

Totalitarianism   Among the highly centralized political systems (dictatorships), totalitarianism is the most extreme type, as the word indicates, because it is a total control over a society by the ruler. According to the Merriam-Webster Dictionary, *totalitarianism* is a "political concept that the citizen should be totally subject to an absolute state authority" (Merriam-Webster, 2018c). In a totalitarian society, the state's power is absolute and unlimited, and it controls or attempts to control every aspect of the society, including all individuals' lives, including their behaviors and attitudes in both private and public spheres; all organizations, such as business firms, associations; and any groups, regardless of whether they are private or public, political, or non-political. A common feature of the state structure in societies under totalitarian rule is that the legislative and judiciary branches are either nonexistent, dysfunctional, or extremely weak, as compared to the executive branch. The executive branch is totally controlled by the dictator, which may be a single person, a group, or a political party.

Totalitarian regimes maintain their rules in the following ways: culturally, the regime promulgates an official culture (which can be based on an official religion), espouses a political ideology (such as communism or fascism), and bans any views that dissent from the official culture. While the contents vary, they all portray the dictator as the only person or entity to hold the absolute truth and the correct vision about how the society should be ruled and developed. As a result, the society and the people, for their own good, must obey and follow the dictator's rule. The regime promotes its official view in every dimension and channel across the society (even internationally), through the families, schools, organizations, and mass media, as well as through individual sessions. Politically, the regime is highly centralized and hierarchical. The top ruler has ultimate, nearly absolute power without any effective checks and balances. Economically, the regime controls all of the economic resources in the society to the maximum extent possible and feasible. Such control can be realized directly by owning vast economic resources, or indirectly by decrees and regulations that give the state the power to direct, order, and seize any economic resources, including all non-state-owned properties, such as private businesses. In such a society, people have few, if any, rights that usually belong to citizens in a democracy. Thus, in the strict sense, the people in a totalitarian society are not citizens, since they do not have the rights vested in the citizenship of most free societies (see Wikipedia (2018i) for a summary of totalitarianism).

Logically, the stifling political and economic suppression may cause discontent and social unrest in the subjects. So, in order to keep the people and organizations obedient to the totalitarian rule and to ensure that they will not revolt, the regime relies on three pillars – "the iron triangle" (MacFarquhar, 2016). The first is its bureaucracy, or its vast apparatus of officials at different levels of government with different functional departments, whose tentacles reach into every corner of the society, including people's bedrooms. The bureaucracy regulates and manages the people and the organizations in peacetime. The second pillar is ideological propaganda. As mentioned earlier, totalitarian regimes erect an official ideology to justify why they must rule. Since totalitarian regimes do not allow people to choose their leaders as democracies do, they must rely on a legend, or a myth, of their greatness in order to legitimize their ruling. The third pillar is an armed force, consisting of the military and the police (including secret agents). If the ideology is losing ground, which inevitably happens as time goes by, and the bureaucracy can no longer manage the people peacefully, the armed forces are called in. In fact, the presence of such a mighty force and what it may do (and what has been done in the past) to dissenters is a very creditable threat to people who might think of challenging the ruler. Thus, should there be any slight signs of social unrest or even criticisms of the regime, the police and the army will crush the challenges quickly and decisively.

In modern history, the political form that has existed that can incontrovertibly be called totalitarianism is communism, as seen under the leadership of Joseph Stalin in Russia and Mao Zedong in China. Today, North Korea can be classified as existing under totalitarianism. China after Mao's death in 1976 began to shift away from totalitarianism, but the recent changes, such as the elimination of a term limit for the president; a strengthening of censorship and thought control; and the seizing of properties from private companies, have made the Chinese regime closer to totalitarianism (Wikipedia, 2018i).

Authoritarianism Authoritarianism is the next most restricted form of political system in the spectrum of highly centralized political power systems. The Merriam-Webster Dictionary defines *authoritarian* as "of, relating to, or favoring a concentration of power in a leader or an elite not constitutionally responsible to the people" (Merriam-Webster, 2018a).

Unlike totalitarianism, which wants to impose a total control over every aspect of the society, authoritarian rulers' main objective is to maintain their political power and control (Wikipedia, 2018b). They do not allow any challenges to their political power through any forms of political participation by the people, such as genuine, free elections. Authoritarian regimes also have little respect for the rule of law or for constitutions. They do not want to be answerable to the constitution or the people. Laws are the tools they can use to rule and can conveniently change to punish anyone who challenges them. Outside the political sphere, as long as their political power is not challenged or in danger, authoritarian rulers may allow various degrees of freedom in the cultural, social, and economic spheres of the society.

In general, authoritarian regimes exert less control over the society than totalitarian regimes. A key difference is in cultural control and brainwashing. Totalitarianism has as its mission to lead and to rule the people according to its ideology, such as realizing communism. To achieve this, it propagates its ideology widely and deeply in the society, and forces people to believe in it. In contrast, authoritarianism is more practical and may tolerate different views, as long as these views do not pose material challenges to the rulers. It "does not attempt to change the world and human nature" (Radu Cinpoes, 2010, p. 70, cited from Wikipedia, 2018b).

As mentioned earlier, the Chinese regime after Mao had shifted from totalitarianism to authoritarianism, until recently. Tunisia, before the 2011 revolution, can be seen as under the authoritarian rule of Ben Ali. In general, the difference between totalitarianism and authoritarianism is the degree of control and, thus, I believe that the line between them is fuzzy.

For our purpose, the distinction between totalitarianism and authoritarianism is not important. To simplify our discussion without dulling our arguments, in this book we will use the term "dictatorship" to include both totalitarianism and authoritarianism.

6.1.2   Democracy and Corruption

Mature Democracy and Corruption

Both theoretical development and empirical evidence show that corruption is not a major problem in mature democracies (Alon et al., 2016). Politically, high levels of political participation and fair elections enable mature democracies to select public officials who tend to be competent and uncorrupt, and both the free flow of information and the market competition in the mass media place a rigorous check on the behavior of public officials. Economically, the institutional arrangement that keeps the government from operating businesses and limits the power of interference by government reduces opportunities for officials to extort bribes from firms. The high standard of living and the high salary level of public servants make taking bribes unnecessary and bear higher opportunity costs (due to the risk of being caught). Another important reason why corruption is low in mature democracies is that culturally, there is a strong consensus in the society – including both the citizens and officials – to maintain honesty and trust, and to have no tolerance for cheating and a strong will to punish those who cheat (Platteau, 1994). While all of these will substantially reduce corruption, they will not guarantee its complete eradication. As we know, corruption does occur, even in mature democracies. Perhaps the most distinguishing factor that separates democracies from dictatorships is that the former have a well-established legal system that can systematically deal with corruption impartially.

The contrast between the corruption scandals of Tunisia and Virginia, in the USA, mentioned at the beginning of this book (see the opening cases in Chapter 1) can serve as a case in point. In Tunisia, the dictator Ben Ali and his family were beyond the law and stole billions of dollars, whereas the then-governor of the State of Virginia, Robert McDonnell, was charged by the state police (who were under his leadership) with accepting about $170,000 from a businessman for whom he failed to provide a favor.

Empirical evidence shows that mature democracies do indeed have the lowest level of corruption in the world. Table 6.1 is from a study by Alon, Li, and Wu (2016) that calculates the average corruption level by regime type.

Infant Democracy and Corruption
Infant democracies are the countries in which the democratic political system has not fully developed. Many of them are undergoing the democratic transition from a non-democracy to a democracy. During the process, the old power structure is being destroyed, and the new democratic institutions are in the process of being built, and are still weak. The power vacuum left by the old dictator attracts many new politicians who are competing for power, creating "many small mafias," who may demand bribes independently (see Chapter 2 and Alon et al., 2016).

These regimes, while rapidly evolving and unstable, are democratically elected, which gives them more legitimacy than dictatorships. This newly acquired legitimacy affords the government more of a mandate to rule and to impose necessary but unpopular policies, such as levying higher taxes (Yang, 2016). By the same logic, democracies – including infant democracies – are less threatened by corruption than dictatorships are, an argument that I will elaborate in more detail. As can be seen in Table 6.1, corruption is highest in anocracies (including infant democracies).

Worldwide, there is no shortage of corruption scandals in countries in which democracy is the form of government, but whose democratic governments are not yet fully developed and mature. The political system is either unstable, with two steps of progress followed by a one-step backlash, or it is controlled by a popular strongman who has been elected for several consecutive terms. And it is not uncommon that elections are interfered with by the incumbent party. The recent corruption scandals of Malaysia and Brazil are cases in point. In Malaysia's 1MDB corruption case, billions of dollars are missing from 1MDB, the state development fund. The former prime

Table 6.1 *Levels of corruption by regime type*

	Autocracy (N = 20)	Anocracy (N = 44)	Democracy (N = 94)
Average CPI (2008–2012) (1 = least corrupt, 10 = most corrupt)	7.61	8.23	6.27
CPI 2011 (1 = least corrupt, 10 = most corrupt)	7.58	8.22	6.36
CPI 2010 (1 = least corrupt, 10 = most corrupt)	7.48	8.30	6.34
Corruption indicator 2012 by International Country Risk Guide (0 = least corrupt, 6 = most corrupt)	3.83	4.10	3.01
Control of corruption 2011 (Worldwide Governance Indicators by World Bank) (-2.5 least corrupt, 2.5 = most corrupt)	0.48	0.67	-0.23
Control of corruption 2010 (Worldwide Governance Indicators by World Bank) (-2.5 least corrupt, 2.5 = most corrupt)	0.41	0.66	-0.21

Source: (Alon et al., 2016)

minister, Najib Razak, has been accused of pocketing $700 million from the fund (BBC, 2018b). In Brazil's corruption scandal, a state-owned oil company, Petrobras, was found to have been receiving large amounts of bribes for many years. The scandal has implicated many top politicians, including incumbent and past presidents (BBC, 2018a).

Despite all of the problems that face infant democracies, institutionally, they can deal with corruption systematically according to the "rules of the game" (North, 1990) that are built into the modern democratic political system. These rules include the mechanism of changing top government officials (such as election rules), the mechanism of exposing corrupt behavior (such as the free flow of information and competition in the media), and the mechanism of holding corrupt officials accountable (such as the legal system). For example, in Malaysia's 1MDB corruption case involving the former prime minister, Najib Razak, when the top officials of the government were generally recognised to be grossly corrupt, the people chose a new leader who promised to stop the corruption and to hold the corrupt officials accountable (Otto & Ngui, 2018). The corruption case in Brazil was also dealt with according to the law, which led to the removal of the president (BBC, 2018a).

6.2   DICTATORSHIP AND CORRUPTION

The relationship between dictatorship and corruption is a complex one, full of contradictory facts (Yadav & Mukherjee, 2016). It is a love and hate story: there are dictators who are deeply addicted to taking bribes and stealing from the state coffers, such as Suharto of Indonesia and Marcos of the Philippines, and there are dictators who are ruthless in punishing corrupt officials. For example, in Chinese history, many emperors were well known for their zero tolerance for corruption. Some of them used very cruel methods of torture to punish corrupt officials. Ming Taizu (ruled 1368–1398), the founding emperor of the Ming Dynasty (1368–1644), codified "death by a thousand cuts" and "death by flaying" to punish corrupt officials (Fang, 2017). More recently, the dictatorial presidents of Taiwan and South Korea, Chiang Kai-shek[1] (who ruled 1950–1975) and Park Chung Hee (who ruled 1963–1979), have the reputation of being relatively uncorrupt themselves (as compared to more corrupt dictators) and being harsh on corrupt officials (Huang & O'Neil-Massaro, 2001; Taylor, 2011). Hence, a paradox arises: compared to his or her counterparts in democracies, the head of state in a dictatorial political system is categorically more powerful. A dictator can issue a degree without many meaningful checks and balances. So logically, if a dictator hates corruption, why can't he or she use his or her power to eradicate it by mercilessly punishing the corrupt officials? The answer lies in the political economy of dictatorship and the roles of corruption and anticorruption campaigns in authoritarian and totalitarian regimes.

6.2.1   The Need to Allow Corruption under Dictatorship

From a theoretical perspective, scholars of corruption have established convincing theoretical frameworks that link dictatorship with corruption (Bueno de Mesquita, Smith, Siverson, & Morrow, 2003; Clague, Keefer, Knack, & Olson, 1996; McGuire & Olson, 1996; Yadav & Mukherjee, 2016). These studies show that, as the old wisdom says, "Power corrupts; absolute power corrupts absolutely."

The Low Pay of Public Employees under Dictatorship
As we discussed earlier, the legitimacy of a dictatorship is usually built on an ideology, which tends to have lofty ideals, such as developing a communist society in which material wealth is abundant and money is abolished: "from each according to his ability, to each according to his needs" (Marx, 1875). Alternatively, the ideology may be theological, as expressed in the proclamation by Iranian president Rouhani that high pay for government employees is "unacceptable based on the ethical and fair values of this government" (Dehghan, 2016). A common feature of the ideologies used by dictators to justify their absolute rule is that they are altruistic and work for a cause. Such a moral high ground assumed by the dictator logically requires public employees to work selflessly with low salaries. The officials in governments based on a lofty ideology are supposed to be role models for the masses and cannot appear to be greedy, at least publicly. In general, the formal salaries of public employees in totalitarian regimes are set to be more or less in line with those of the general public, and in some cases (such as in Vietnam), they are even lower than the salaries of those in the private sector. Below are some examples.

In Saudi Arabia, which was designated as "Not Free" with an "Electoral Process" score of 0 (0 = most dictatorial, 12 = most democratic) by Freedom House in 2018 (Freedom House, 2018), the average salary in the capital city, Riyadh, is SAR 123,514 (about $32,937) per year (PayScale, 2018), and the average salary of Saudi government employees is only slightly higher, at SAR 130,728 per year (*Saudi Gazette*, 2018).

In Iran, which was designated as "Not Free" with an "Electoral Process" score of 3 by Freedom House in 2018 (Freedom House, 2018), according to the statistics of the Statistical Center of Iran, the average salary of Iranian families is 17,030,000 rials ($470) per month in 2014 (Quora, 2018). The salaries of government employees are not high, with the lowest salary of government employees being about 9 million rials ($249) per month. By Iranian law, the highest salary for government employees cannot be more than 10 times the lowest (Dehghan, 2016). Not surprisingly, in early 2016, when someone put a series of pay records online showing that some high-level officials were paid 50 times higher than the minimum government pay, many Iranians were outraged. In one case, an official received a monthly compensation totaling about 870 million rials ($24,033). What is more interesting and relevant to our discussion here is that the bulk of the 870 million rials in payment was not part of the formal basic salary, but rather "some unconventional payments, bonuses or loans" (Dehghan, 2016).

In Vietnam, which was designated as "Not Free" with an "Electoral Process" score of 0 by Freedom House in 2018, according to Vietnam Online, "[t]he average wage per person in Vietnam is around 3.2 million VND ($150) a month ... Most state officers and employees have very low pay jobs, usually equal to 1/3 or 1/5, or even 1/10 the wage of the private officers in the same post, especially in some core professions such as education and medical care. The salary of the state officers in other industries like banking, petroleum or energy could be higher, but still not matched with the private sector employees"(*Vietnam Online*, 2018).

Table 6.2 *Average monthly salary in the Soviet Union, 1940–1980*

Average monthly salary by year	1940	1965	1970	1975	1976	1977	1978	1979	1980
Overall	33.1	96.5	122	145.8	151.4	155.2	159.9	163.3	168.9
Government	39	105.9	123.2	131.8	133.6	136.7	144.6	147.8	156.4

Note: In 1980, the official exchange rate is about 1 ruble to $1. However, goods were in severe shortage, rationed, and expensive in the Soviet Union.
Sources: (Fxtop, 2018; Reddit, 2018)

In the former Soviet Union, which was designated as "Not Free" with a "Political Rights" score of 6 (1 = most and 6 = least) by Freedom House in 1980 (Freedom House, 1980)), the average salary of government employees was slightly higher than the overall average salary from 1940 to 1970, and then lagged behind from 1970 to 1980 (Reddit) (see Table 6.2).

A member of a history forum on the chat website Reddit comments: "Found some info on lawyers but the numbers don't add up. Apparently in 1955 they were paid 50 to 200 roubles [sic] but that doesn't seem right because they were rather well off" (Reddit, 2018). This implies that lawyers must have had outside incomes, probably from bribery. Another commentator on Reddit made the following observation:

> While they [blue versus white collar workers] were paid similar wages, factory workers ... and Doctors lived very different lives. Doctors received special treatment such as better living conditions. But because they WERE being paid similarly the procedures you could get on "normal wages" were often inferior to those you could pay for on the black market.
> An Appendectomy might cost something like 200 Rubles for face value, but the facilities would likely be sub-par and the doctors less careful. Whereas 1000 Rubles would get you a "Black

Market" Appendectomy most likely at the Doctor's House, but everything would be clean and sterile.

In China, which was designated as "Not Free" with a "Electoral Process" score of 3 by Freedom House (2018), government employees' formal salaries are not higher than those in the private sectors and, in many cases, they are substantially lower. In fact, their salaries were so low that, in 2015, the Chinese government gave a big boost to the salaries of all government employees from the entry-level clerk to the president of the country (Luo, 2015). President Xi's salary was raised from 7,020 yuan ($1,080) to 11,385 yuan ($1,752) per month, a hefty 61.6% increase, whereas the lowest-level public employees' salaries were raised from 620 yuan ($95) to 1,320 yuan ($203) per month, a more than 100% increase! However, even after the huge raises, the salaries of government employees and officials are still low. Perhaps even the reporter who wrote about the big raises realized this and that is why she added in the same news story that "of course, Chinese civil servants have subsidies in addition to their basic salaries" (Luo, 2015). Despite the low salary level, people, especially the young and bright, flock to government jobs in China. The competition is keen: the average success rate for getting a job offer is 1.7% (Chinese Education Online, 2014), much lower than the rate of admission to the elite Ivy League Universities in the USA. They are not attracted by the salary, but by the various in-kind benefits and "gray incomes" (Sohu Finance, 2014).

Inevitably, the low salary level of government employees would reduce the incentive for them to work hard and would hinder government efficiency and effectiveness. As a popular Soviet joke told by government employees goes, "we pretend to work, and they pretend to pay us."

In order to incentivize its workforce to be productive, a dictatorship must, either actively or passively, allow its employees to take bribes.

Table 6.3 *Corruption Perception Index, dictatorship versus democracy*

Regime type	Number of countries	Average CPI 2017 (0 = most corrupt, 100 = least corrupt)
Freedom 2018 = "Not Free" (dictatorship)	49	29.6
Freedom 2018 = "Free" (democracy)	72	58.1
Electoral Process Score = 0 (most dictatorial regime)	23	28.6
Electoral Process Score = 12 (most democratic regime)	44	65.4

Sources: (Freedom House, 1972–2018; Transparency International, 2017)

Corruption of Public Employees under Dictatorship

When we presented the evidence of the low pay of government workers in the last subsection, the signs of corruption began to emerge: how could lawyers and doctors in the former Soviet Union live a much better life when they were paid as poorly as blue-collar workers? Why do the young and bright compete so fiercely for low-paying government jobs in China? The answer lies in the formal and informal benefits and privileges that come with the job, and with the power vested in the job that allows them to extract rents. In sum, it is the opportunity for corruption. Evidences of corruption under a dictatorship abound. In Table 6.3, we show the average Corruption Perception Index for dictatorships and democracies.

In Table 6.3, we use two different measures for dictatorships and democracies. The results using both measures each show that the perceived corruption level is much higher in dictatorships than in democracies. Anecdotal evidence and cases that have come to light all suggest that corruption under or by dictators is severe and, in some cases, is extreme. For example, Haiti's dictator, Jean-Claude "Baby Doc" Duvalier, reigned in Haiti for 15 years (1971–1986) and is believed to have embezzled $300 million to $800 million from a country already impoverished by his rule. Mobutu Sese Seko, who ruled Zaire (now the Democratic Republic of the Congo or DRC) for 32 years (1965–1997), built a vast patronage apparatus that systematically looted the country and enriched himself and his cronies. Various estimates put his take at $4 billion to $5 billion (Sandbrook, 2016).

Permission from the Top to Be Corrupt

In addition to the theoretical argument (Bueno de Mesquita et al., 2003; Clague et al., 1996; McGuire & Olson, 1996; Yadav & Mukherjee, 2016), empirical evidence strongly supports the argument that the rampant and persistent corruption in countries under dictatorship is, to a great extent, permitted by the dictator. In order to incentivize bureaucrats to work efficiently and to carry out the policies of the regime, the dictator must allow subordinates to benefit from working for him or her. In a corruption-ridden government hierarchy, the head of each level must allow subordinates to seek rents.

Only the Corrupt Get Promoted: The Adverse Selection

In such a political system, most officials are corrupt for two reasons. First, in order to get promoted in the hierarchy, one must cultivate a good relationship with the higher-ups, by giving expensive gifts or by providing luxury vacations. All these are costly. So, if promoted, the briber needs to recoup his or her investment by being corrupt and by taking bribes from below. Second, if an official keeps clean and refuses to be corrupt, boss, peers, and subordinates will all be uncomfortable around him or her and will not be able to seek rents on their jobs, fearing that he or she will turn them in. In such a situation, they will all try to nudge the clean official out. In my interviews with officials in China, I got the impression from several interviewees that a "good boss" is someone who subtly hints to subordinates that he or she should also take a "fair share" of extra incomes, assuring his or her boss and subordinates that he or she will play along and will not rock the boat. In the 2014 group corruption case of Shenzhen Customs Office in China, the whole customs control office colluded with smugglers and designed a scientific logistic chain with an efficient division of labor to collect and share the bribes. They set the bribe prices based on the type of the vehicle (in terms of load capacity) and shared the bribes among all of the office staff, based on rank and the risks entailed (the one who actually processed the bribe was considered to have taken higher risks and, therefore, to be entitled to a bigger share). They also set aside a fund from the bribes to cover part of the office expenses (so that their higher-ups – and even the government – would be happy too). To make the opportunity of taking bribes fair, they split the bribes between the staff on duty and those off duty. They even set a policy specifying the payment term for the bribers (e.g. lump sum vs. installments) (Baike, 2016).

More Anecdotal Evidence
Anecdotal evidence also supports this view. Below, we provide evidence that the top rulers of countries under dictatorship allowed corruption.

Indonesia, which was designated "Not Free" in the 1995 Transparency International survey, suffered rampant corruption under the dictator Muhammad Suharto (ruled 1968–1998), with a CPI of 1.97 (1 = most corrupt, 10 = least corrupt). This was the lowest of all the countries surveyed in 1995 (Transparency International, 1995). It is well known that Suharto relied on the armed forces to maintain his absolute rule over the country (Wikipedia, 2018g) and allowed his generals to take bribes and other forms of rents. According to Jeffrey Hays, "Suharto's control of the military was key to his control of Indonesia. He adeptly set off various factions against one another and kept them under a leash by dividing up political power and allowing top military officers to enrich themselves through various enterprises, often in conjunction with Chinese businessmen" (Hays, 2015).

In the Philippines, former president Ferdinand Marcos ruled with an iron fist for almost 20 years (1968–1986). Under his rule, corruption was rampant (CPI score did not exist back then). Marcos not only took from the state coffers and demanded payments himself, but also allowed his lieutenants to collect rents and bribes (Li & Wu, 2010; Wedeman, 1997). For example, Marcos appointed several of his close friends, such as Manuel Conjuangco, Herminio Disini, and Robert Benidicto, to be in charge of various state agencies or related businesses to collect taxes, fees, and other charges. The funds then were shared between them and Marcos (Wedeman, 1997).

The case of East Germany under communist rule provides an example of corruption permitted by those at the top. After World War II, the Communist Party ruled East Germany on the basis that "corruption did not exist under the socialism the party created" (Steiner, 2018). However, very soon after the communists took power, living standards were lagging behind their Western counterparts and the growing gap in living conditions between ordinary people and party officials made people suspect that the party officials were corrupt. Due to the information control by the party, people had little knowledge about the extent of the corruption. The party occasionally released a case of corruption at the lower regional level of government. Whenever such a case was exposed, the party leadership would blame its subordinates. This is a general propaganda position used by all communist parties: the top leader is always correct and is never corrupt. All of the mistakes – including corruption – are due to the misinterpretation and greed of lower-level officials. The fall of the Berlin Wall in 1989 and the subsequent collapse of the East German communist regime exposed the secret corruption under the Communist Party's rule. All this secrecy points to the fact that the corruption originates at the top. The ruling body of East Germany, the Politburo, had been systematically enriching itself during communist rule. For example, the Politburo built housing compound of Wandlitz, which has 23 houses for the members of the party leadership. More than 650 employees worked on the estate, serving the few leaders (Steiner, 2018).

In her study on corruption in the former communist countries, including the USSR, the former communist states in Eastern Europe, China, Vietnam, Cuba, and others, Leslie Holmes lists various methods of corruption by officials. The first way is what she calls "turning a blind eye" (Holmes, 1993, p. 91). This essentially refers to a pattern in which subordinates or patrons extort payments and take advantage of people and of society, and the person in authority does not stop it, implying that the person in authority actually permits (or even protects) such corrupt behavior.

Studies and evidence on corruption in China suggest that the top leaders of the Chinese Communist Party are corrupt and that they allow corruption in the party and in the government (Li, 2017). Like its counterpart in East Germany, the Chinese Communist Party has developed a system of different levels of privileges for its vast army of cadres. Here, we can take a glimpse at the perks of retired officials (see Table 6.4).

In Saudi Arabia, the king and his extended family are, to a great extent, the *de facto* owners of the kingdom. The king, as the head of the state, distributes the privilege of doing business in all sectors dependent upon or controlled by the government to his children and relatives. The current crown prince, Mohammed bin Salman, became a multibillionaire through this patronage system. When he was teenager in the 2000s, Prince Mohammed "scraped together about $100,000 to invest in Saudi stocks," he recalled. Some ten years later, in the 2010s, Prince Mohammed "made billions of Saudi riyals – hundreds of millions of dollars – on the Saudi stock market," he told people. Now, Prince Mohammed is "fantastically wealthy": he has bought "one of the world's largest yachts, a French palace and a $450 million Leonardo da Vinci painting," according to a *Wall Street Journal* report (Scheck & Hope, 2018). Despite the fact that his wealth was indisputably obtained through his royal lineage, he launched an anticorruption campaign in November 2017, accusing other princes of

Table 6.4 *Retirement benefits by rank*

Rank at retirement	Benefits	Estimated number of retirees
National and vice national head level (president, vice presidents, chairman, vice chairmen, premier, vice premiers, general secretary, vice general secretary, senior generals, standing and regular Politburo members, others with equivalent ranks, etc.)	Free housing (size unspecified). Government paid driver/body guard, medical personnel if needed. 4 fully paid vacations, 3 weeks/vacation, all family members. Fly first/business class (up to 4); first class/soft sleeper train travel; 3 cars/2 vans; airports should adjust departure time for need of the retired official and family. Luxury hotel suites and meals, no limit. Special VIP medical service.	100–200
Provincial governor / minister level (governors, ministers, junior generals, commanders, party secretaries, major bureau heads, and other equivalently ranked, etc.)	Free housing of 220 square meters (2200 square feet). Government paid driver/body guard, other assistant(s), medical assistants if needed. 4 fully paid vacations, 3 weeks/vacation, all family members. Fly first/business class (up to 4); first class/soft sleeper train travel; 3 cars/2 vans; airports should adjust departure time for need of the retired official and family. Luxury hotel suites and meals, no limit.	3,742 (estimated in 2015)

Table 6.4 (*cont.*)

Rank at retirement	Benefits	Estimated number of retirees
Vice provincial governor/ vice minister level (vice governors, vice ministers, vice army commanders, major university heads, some bureau heads, mayors of major cities, etc.)	Free housing for 190 square meters (1900 square feet) Shared or dedicated government car for personal use. Shared secretary/assistants, medical assistants if needed. 4 fully paid vacations, 2 weeks/ vacation, up to 5 family members. Fly first/business class (up to 2), first class/soft sleeper train travel (up to 2); 1 car/van. 1 luxury hotel suite and 300 yuan/person food allowance, 200 yuan/assistant.	27,435 (estimated in 2015)

Note: The above information is collected from various public sources, as listed below. They may not be accurate since they are not published by the Chinese government. However, the Chinese government never disputes or clarifies this information.
Sources: (Duowei, 2013; Tang, 2015)

corruption. The message that he sends through the campaign is unmistakable: corruption is a privilege that can only be given and taken away by the king (or by his successor, in this case).

In a *Wall Street Journal* report about police taking and seizing private businesses, the authors write that "Russian companies routinely face harassment from law-enforcement officials seeking to extort money or expropriate businesses," because "Mr. Putin's authoritarian rule relies on security officials and political heavyweights who use their authority not only to squash political opponents but also to squeeze companies for payoffs" (Marson & Grove, 2018, A8).

All of the above examples provide evidence to support my main argument in this section, that corruption under a dictatorship is necessary for the dictator to rule the country, since it provides the needed economic incentives for government employees to keep the government functioning. With the permission of the dictatorship, corruption is widespread in almost all functional departments and regional branches of the government. Only a very small number of functional departments of a dictatorial regime may have difficulty extorting bribes. In former communist countries, a joke mocking the fact that officials of all government departments steal the goods or services they are in charge of says that "only two governmental departments' bureaucrats don't steal what they produce: the toilet-waste collecting department and the ideology propaganda department." Traditionally, the propaganda departments, in charge of promoting communist ideology at various levels of the government in China, were viewed as having little opportunity to demand bribes, since no people or firms desired to get more propaganda products or services. However, now that communist China has embraced markets, propaganda departments are riddled with corruption and are taking bribes. The officials there sell quotas to publish newspapers, magazines, and books. People bribe them to approve the movies they produce. Even printing firms bribe them to direct large projects of printing propaganda materials to the briber's shop. A well-known critic of the Chinese Communist Party, Yu Jie, writes that

> People thought, mistakenly, that the propaganda department was a non-profit, clean agency with little opportunity to corrupt. In fact, the recently exposed high-profile corruption cases of senior officials in charge of propaganda indicate that corruption in the propaganda department is no less severe than those of the "high corruption sectors" such as banking, stock markets, transportation, construction, and public health.
> (Yu, 2006)

In sum, under a dictator, corruption is permitted, grows systematically, and thrives, even in the least profitable and least lucrative segments of the government.

6.2.2 The Need to Curb Corruption under Dictatorship

Interestingly (and also ironically), while all dictators are corrupt and allow their officials to be corrupt, they all rule their countries with a high-profile stance of holding high moral standards and claiming zero tolerance for any corrupt acts committed by government officials and employees. In this section, we will build our argument as to why dictators must informally allow their employees to be corrupt and formally claim that they rigorously fight against corruption.

Dictatorships Are Most Vulnerable to Corruption

Because most dictatorships are built on lofty ideologies that promise a corruption-free society, corruption threatens the very legitimacy of dictatorships. For example, in the former East Germany, the communists ruled with the promise of building and maintaining a corruption-free society, so any information about officials' abuse of power or corruption "became particularly explosive within a society supposedly characterized by egalitarian aims, as well as real shortages of various goods and services" (Steiner, 2018, p. 296). In general, if the dictator allows corruption to run unchecked, discontent may reach boiling point and erupt, which may lead to a revolution, as the cases that we present later will show. Thus, to protect its legitimacy, a dictatorship must keep corruption under control by periodically cracking down on official corruption.

In her study on the communist states, Holmes found that when they faced a legitimation crisis, almost all of them launched campaigns to fight against corruption:

> During the Andropov era of Soviet politics (1982–4), I was struck by
> the energy with which the new leader was attacking all sorts of

social problems—including corruption, which was suddenly
being officially described as one of the most serious problem-
areas in society ... I was reading a collection of Castro's
speeches, and found that he had been highly critical of
corruption in Cuba in the same year as Andropov had started
his campaign ... I looked to China—only to discover that the
Chinese Communist Party had launched a major campaign
against corruption in 1982! Was this coincidence? ... Eventually
I discovered that some of the East European regimes, notably
Bulgaria, Czechoslovakia, Hungary and Poland, had also
launched anticorruption campaigns in the early to mid-1980s,
while Vietnam had been intensifying its fight against
corruption. But *why* had so many leaderships apparently been
'washing their dirty linen in public' or, worse still, 'shooting
themselves in the foot'? (Holmes, 1993, p. xii)

Holmes argued that these communist regimes all had rampant corruption, which seriously undermined the legitimacy of the regimes, and
that is why all of them were waging anticorruption campaigns
(Holmes, 1993).

More recently, several dictatorships have launched anticorruption campaigns. In November 2017, the Saudi government, led by
Crown Prince Mohammed bin Salman, launched a large-scale anticorruption campaign in which "scores" of princes and prominent businessmen were detained in the luxury Ritz-Carlton hotel in Riyadh.
There were no publicly known indictments and there was no verifiable list of detainees. By January 2018, it was reported that the first
phase of the campaign was about to end, with the majority of the
detainees having reached a settlement and having agreed to pay
a total of about $100 billion to the government. The ones who did
not settle would face the prospect of trial. However, by July 2018,
there was no sign of the end of the campaign, with more people having
been arrested and held at a maximum-security prison outside Riyadh.
Some of the detainees were "beaten and deprived of sleep while being

questioned," according to a *Wall Street Journal* report (Stancati & Said, 2018b). In parallel, the government arrested dozens of high-profile Saudis, most of them rights activists and dissidents, who pushed for more opening-up and for women's rights: demands which, ironically, are in the same direction as the reforms carried out by the crown prince. Commentators believe that the purge sends a clear message that only the crown prince, not the people, is entitled to initiate and to make political and social changes (Stancati & Said, 2018a).

The Chinese Communist Party periodically launches anticorruption campaigns, which usually go in cycles, depending on the severity of corruption and the political agenda of the top leader at the time. Beginning in about 2012, the party launched a large-scale anticorruption campaign that has purged hundreds of high-level officials and millions of low-ranking officials. According to the statistics of the Chinese government, during the first five years of the tenure of President Xi Jinping (2012–2017), over two million cadres had been investigated and disciplined for corruption (*Epoch Times*, 2017; Li, 2017).

In 2017, the ruling Communist Party of Vietnam launched a large-scale anticorruption campaign. The General Secretary of the Communist Party, Nguyen Phu Trong, vowed that "Vietnam's fight against corruption must continue to move forward at all costs" (*Vn Express International*, 2017). Since then, many high-ranking party officials have been arrested and prosecuted for corruption (Voice of America, 2018). In 2018, the anticorruption campaign intensified. According to an article on the state-run website, *Vn Express International*, "General Secretary Nguyen Phu Trong, 74, who also chairs the Central Steering Committee on Anti-Corruption, said Vietnam's fight against corruption was at an all-time high. He called for authorities to make great efforts at all costs to take the campaign further" (*Vn Express International*, 2018). According to a party official quoted by *Vn Express International*, as of June 2018, as many as "50 top officials including current high-level officials, former political stars and retired leaders have been subjected to disciplinary action for violations related to corruption and wastefulness" (*Vn Express International*, 2018).

Can Dictators Successfully Eradicate Corruption?

Based on what we have seen above, it seems to be a foregone conclusion that dictators cannot eliminate corruption. However, a comparative discussion of the ways in which dictatorships and democracies deal with corruption will help us to understand why anticorruption campaigns by dictatorships are bound to fail.

Patterns of Fighting against Corruption: Democracy versus Dictatorship

As we briefly discussed earlier, corruption exists in democracies too, especially in infant democracies. In Table 6.1., we see that the corruption level of anocracy, which includes most infant democracies, is consistently higher than that of autocracy (dictatorship). In terms of corruption, what distinguishes democracy from dictatorship is not that the former does not have corruption; the key difference between the two types of regimes is that democracies, especially mature democracies (which have substantially lower – actually the lowest – level of corruption) rely on the rule-based way of fighting against corruption. More specifically, democracies have a set of built-in institutional arrangements that is systematically equipped to deal, and capable of dealing, with corruption.

These institutional arrangements include the following elements. The first is a democratic election system which allows opposition parties to compete. This functions as a political market to reflect the voters' sentiments and preferences; if the incumbent government head is perceived as being grossly corrupt, the voters will vote him or her out. This has happened in many democratic countries such as Brazil, Malaysia, and Mexico. Note that these countries are not mature democracies but can still effectively deal with people's concern about corruption in a systematic manner.

The second factor is a rule of law that is independent of the ruling party, which may systematically and impartially (to varying degrees, depending on the level of development toward the rule-based way) capture and prosecute corrupt officials, including the head of the state, if he or she is corrupt. The third element is a competitive mass media, protected by the law, and free to investigate, expose, and disseminate information on wrongdoing by government officials. We could list the development of a civil society and a culture of low tolerance of corruption, but I believe that the three features above are the most important in setting democracies apart from dictatorships institutionally, regarding the way in which they deal with the issue of corruption. In sum, democracies, while they cannot completely eradicate corruption, can systematically and effectively reduce it to a low enough level for it no longer to be a major concern in the society, as the case of mature democracies (such as Scandinavian countries) shows.

Unlike democracies, dictatorships are inherently unable to deal successfully with corruption. First, as we discussed earlier, fundamentally, the most important principle used by dictatorships to justify their rule is the ideology that the dictator is the only one who possesses the vision for the society and the capability to lead the people to realize that vision. Such a vision requires that government officials be "people's servants" who are full of virtue and who should not be paid lavishly. In order for the "people's servants" to work hard for the dictator, they must be allowed to seek rents on their jobs. This determines that the dictator cannot eradicate corruption, for it will debase his or her rule. Second, institutionally, dictatorships are not rule-based, and they are notorious for not following the laws they make. Public information is controlled by the state and is severely restricted and censored, making the exposure of corruption cases difficult and dangerous. Most importantly, as we discussed earlier, in non-rule-based societies, especially in the ones ruled by a dictator, there are no checks and balances between the legislative, judiciary, and executive branches.

The executive branch, controlled by the dictator, usually overshadows the other two, if they exist at all. All of these, particularly
the lack of the rule of law, make dealing with corruption entirely
dependent upon the will of the dictator. Any anticorruption efforts
are therefore inherently top-down – from the very top: the dictator.
No government agencies can launch any effort against corruption
without his or her approval. And, of course, no one can investigate
the top leader. In sum, the anticorruption efforts are arbitrary and
self-policing.

Furthermore, even if the dictator is not corrupt and is determined to rid the bureaucracy of corruption, he or she will soon find
out that it cannot be done. Without the opportunity to seek rents on
their jobs, the bureaucrats will go on silent strike which will drag the
government to a standstill.

Another issue the dictator faces is that, in a pervasively
corrupt government, virtually every official is guilty of corruption,
to some degree. So who should be arrested? Since it is impractical
and impossible to arrest everyone, some must be selectively
arrested. First, as some researchers conjecture, the dictator would
spare his or her close friends and political allies; second, the campaign would be an opportunity for the dictator to purge his or her
political enemies (Li, 2017; Wedeman, 2017); third, he or she would
arrest some officials known to be more greedy than their peers
(e.g., always exceed their appropriate shares when demanding
bribes). In general, anticorruption campaigns waged by dictators
tend to be political purges in disguise. Even for those begun as
genuine anticorruption campaigns, the inherent handicaps just
discussed will cause them, inevitably, to degenerate into political
purges.

Holmes and Law's Hypothesis Revisited: Can Anticorruption Campaigns Be "Sustained and Decisive?"

In her study on corruption in communist states, Holmes posits
essentially the same question that I ask here, in different wording.

She formulates the following hypothesis, based on David Law's study: "Campaigns against corruption are never sustained and decisive" (Law, 1974 quoted in Holmes, 1993, p. 46 and pp. 267–268).

Holmes points out that while, by their nature, campaigns are supposed to be "relatively short and sharp," they may last for years. As for "decisive," if it means "completely successful," then Law was right: the campaigns are never decisive, Holmes argues. Furthermore, she takes a more tentative view: "wait and see" (Holmes, 1993, p. 268).

By now, with the benefit of hindsight, we can more definitely conclude that, from both the theoretical and the empirical perspectives, anticorruption campaigns waged by dictatorships, such as communist parties, cannot be successful. The failure of anticorruption campaigns is not restricted to communist regimes; it applies to all dictatorships in various forms, as the case below shows.

In Bangladesh, from 2007 to 2008, when the country was ruled by a caretaker government backed by the military, a *de facto* dictatorial rule, the government waged a sweeping anticorruption campaign. At first, the campaign was welcomed by the people, since corruption had been widespread in the country. However, when, due to the extralegal nature of the campaign and the arrests of allegedly corrupt officials by the military, the initial enthusiasm faded; people began to suspect there was a political or partisan motive behind the campaign and to question its fairness and effectiveness. In the end, while the campaign did shake up some corruption-ridden areas of the government bureaucracy, overall, "much of the high profile anti-corruption fanfare of 2007 and 2008 has had little lasting impact" (Hough, 2013, p. 59).

In sum, as we laid out in the introductory chapter of this book, in order to effectively fight against corruption and to keep the society (relatively) clean, six institutional requirements must be met. There must be: (1) a political system that ensures fair and effective political competition; (2) a limited government; (3) the

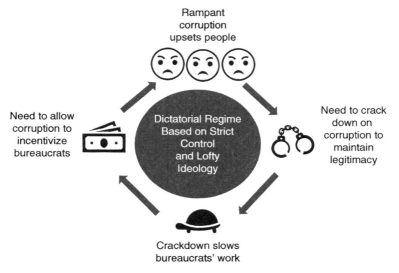

FIGURE 6.1 Cycle of corruption and anticorruption in dictatorships

rule of law; (4) free and competitive media; (5) the development of civil society; and (6) an adequately paid workforce in the government. Obviously, these requirements are not met under dictatorships.

6.2.3 Corruption and Anticorruption Campaigns: Two Legs Supporting Dictatorships

Under a dictatorship, corruption is not only possible, but necessary. At the same time, corruption cannot run unchecked, as it may threaten the legitimacy of the regime, and it can bring down the regime. So, anticorruption measures are also necessary to periodically reduce the level of corruption, in order to pacify the anger of the ordinary people toward the regime. However, the campaigns tend to demoralize the government workforce and to slow down the bureaucratic machine. Therefore, the dictator cannot execute the crackdown on corruption indiscriminately or too severely. The necessity of having both types of campaign, and their cyclical movement (see Figure 6.1), have made corruption and anticorruption campaigns the two legs that sustain dictatorial rule.

Hypocrisy: Cultural Product of the Cycle

The symbiotic relationship between corruption and anticorruption in a dictatorial regime has several effects on the society and the economy. First, it encourages hypocrisy in the government and eventually in the society. Publicly, officials compete to denounce corruption and vow to crack down on it, while privately, they are busy taking bribes in all forms: cash, houses, sex services, or trips. During President Xi's anticorruption campaign, there were several high-profile cases in which a corrupt official was arrested when giving an anticorruption speech at a government meeting.

Ordinary people know that corruption is rampant and that the anticorruption campaigns are not for real, so they have to live with the official hypocrisy. Publicly, virtually every person in the society condemns corruption; privately, they adopt the attitude: "If you can't beat them, join them." Many people cultivate connections with government officials so that they can get preferential treatment in their lives, careers, or businesses. Along with this corruption–anticorruption cycle, cynicism and hypocrisy take root, and permeate, the society.

Some argue that hypocrisy helps fortify a dictator's rule (e.g., Smith, 1984). Dictators do not really mind if people, or even their officials, do not believe government ideology. Even though the people and some officials are disillusioned about the ideology, as long as they publicly support it, the dictator will not persecute them. Instead, the dictator may even promote hypocrites to high positions in the government. People who have become hypocrites are demoralized and feel themselves unworthy. To justify their hypocrisy, they begin to discriminate against people who refuse to be hypocritical. Eventually, the people who behave hypocritically find that supporting the regime makes them feel more consistent and better able to achieve inner peace. Furthermore, materially, supporting the regime, regardless of whether the support is genuine or fake, becomes more rewarding for the hypocrites.

Boom and Bust: Economic Product of the Cycle
Economically, the cycle of corruption and anticorruption under dictatorships helps to create a synchronized boom and bust cycle in the economy. When more corruption is permitted, government officials are more motivated to develop new projects and to make more deals with private businesses, fueling an economic boom. When the dictator clamps down on corruption, government officials lie low and slow down progress on new projects and deals, which may precipitate a recession. In theory, the dictator needs, optimally, to balance corruption and anticorruption campaigns, in order to minimize the cyclical effect and to keep the corruption level high enough to stimulate the economy. In practice, this is hard to do. This is why we see conflicting signals from the dictator about his or her intentions for the anticorruption campaigns. For example, the Saudi government's crackdown on corruption by the princelings and the leading business people is supposed to signal its willingness to reform. However, when people, riding the anticorruption wave, push for more reforms, they are arrested. The Chinese government vowed to make its recent sweeping anticorruption campaign permanent, or a "new normal," but then, realizing that it substantially hurt the morale of public workers, the government toned down the campaign and warned the bureaucrats that "not doing anything" (in Chinese called "bu zuo wei") would not be tolerated either (Wang, 2016). If anticorruption campaigns are overly successful in deterring the corrupt behavior of public employees, without substantial

development in the six institutions necessary for a clean society, the economy will risk being trapped in stagnation (Li, 2015).

NOTES

1. Chiang's early rule in China was ridden with corruption. After he fled to Taiwan in 1948 after his defeat by Mao's Communist Party, he successfully contained corruption. See Taylor, J. 2011. *The Generalissimo: Chiang Kai-shek and the Struggle for Modern China*: Harvard University Press.

7 Paths to Transition Away from Corruption

It's tough to make predictions, especially about the future.

–Yogi Berra

There is little disagreement that corruption should be eradicated from countries with weak institutional environments. However, there are a number of views as to how to achieve this goal, or whether it is an attainable goal at all, and those views are hotly debated in many corruption-ridden societies by all of the stakeholders, including active citizen groups, scholars of corruption, political parties, and policy makers. In this chapter, I will first set out an argument as to why it is necessary for the societies that are dependent upon, and ridden with, corruption to make the transition away from corruption. Second, I will review different paths for that transition.

7.1 THE NECESSITY OF THE TRANSITION: A COST–BENEFIT PERSPECTIVE

In Chapter 4, we briefly alluded to the logical conclusion that, as the scale and scope of their markets expand, relation-based economies will lose their cost competitiveness, since they will be forced to deal with strangers, and dealing with strangers is costly for people who have been relying on private relationships and have no access to reliable and efficient public information and public enforcement. This will force them to adopt and develop a rule-based governance system. Applying this framework to analyze the role and the effect of corruption in countries with weak institutional environments, we will arrive at the conclusion that the transition away from dependence

167

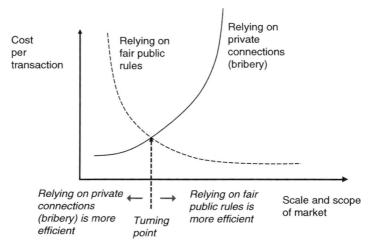

FIGURE 7.1 Cost comparison as market grows: public rules versus
private connections

on bribery and corruption is not only desirable, but, more importantly,
it is logical and, thus, inevitable.

As I explained in Chapter 4, the cost structures of relying on
private connections and relying on public rules are different. Public
rules need to be supported and enforced by both a legal infrastructure
and a public information infrastructure. The legal infrastructure
includes the legislative system, the judicial system, and the executive
system, and the public information infrastructure includes a free and
competitive media market, public rating agencies, auditing, and
accounting information services. These systems are costly to develop
and maintain. Once they are built, the costs of building them are sunk
and fixed, regardless of whether one firm uses them once or one
hundred million firms use them many times. From this perspective,
rule-based governance has high fixed costs and low incremental (marginal) costs. The more people and firms use these public systems, the
lower the average cost per transaction. As the cost line of relying on
public rules (the dotted line) shows in Figure 7.1, the more the scale

and scope of the market expand, the more efficient and competitive it is for firms and for society to rely on public rules.

In contrast, relying on private connections to conduct business and to protect business interests does not require well-established legal and information infrastructures. Societies with weak institutional environments tend to invest little in such infrastructures. Instead, people and firms rely on their private connections and on informal networks to conduct business and for protection. The easiest and most cost-effective way to develop such connections is to first rely on one's family members, since people tend to know their family members very well and trust them, which can substantially reduce transaction and enforcement costs. In other words, doing business among family members incurs low average transaction costs, as shown by the early portion of the solid cost line (relying on private connections) in Figure 7.1. As markets expand in scale and in scope, firms and government officials will run out of family members to hire or to bribe, and they need to deal with people outside of their family. They will expand their networks to include both friends and people they know from their neighborhood. When they exhaust these, they will have to expand the networks to include strangers or foreigners. Private relationships, such as bribery–corruption relationships are, by their nature, secretive, and they usually cannot be enforced by public laws. If a corrupt official does not deliver what he promises to a bribe payer, the latter cannot take the official to court. The only way to enforce a bribery–corruption agreement is by private means. As we discussed in Chapter 4, through a series of overlapping circles, one may enforce a private deal with a stranger or with foreigners (see Figure 4.5 in Chapter 4), but it will become increasingly difficult and costly as one's business expands nationally and internationally. This is why the solid cost curve in Figure 7.1 for reliance on private connections rises rapidly as the market expands.

In sum, when markets are small, relying on private connections enjoys a substantial cost advantage as compared to relying on public rules. As markets expand, the cost advantage of relying on private connections over relying on public rules keeps narrowing until it reaches the turning point (see Figure 7.1), after which relying on private connections will have an increasing cost disadvantage compared with relying on public rules. In order to be competitive, as markets expand, economies that have traditionally relied on private connections, such as the bribery–corruption relationship, to conduct and to protect businesses must shift away from such reliance to embrace the rule-based governance system, including the rule of law and checks and balances in the political system. This logical analysis can be particularly persuasive to the elites in corruption-ridden countries with weak institutional environments. These elites – powerful business people and high-level government officials – may not care about the cultural and ethical consequences of corruption; all they are concerned about is economic performance. They may be deaf to arguments about the importance of cleaning up corruption from the moral and ethical perspectives, but if they realize that, logically, the bribery–corruption method of running the country and conducting business may leave their economy behind and hinder their global competitiveness and expansion, they will be more likely to pay attention. Historically, many countries that were corruption-ridden under weak institutional environments have attempted to make this transformation in various ways. Some are more successful than others. Below, we will review some cases.

7.2 PATHS TO TRANSITION

There is little research on the paths taken in the transition from corruption-ridden to relatively corruption-free societies. Broadly speaking, we can group the attempts into two types: (1) transitions or attempted transitions triggered by a violent social upheaval such as a revolution against corruption, and (2) transitions through relatively peaceful reforms or evolutions without major social and political disruptions.

7.2.1 Hong Kong: A Success Story

Hong Kong, which historically had been a farming and fishing village and a salt production site, became a British colony in 1841 after China lost the Opium War to the United Kingdom. In the early days of the colonial era (1841–1997), Britain ruled Hong Kong, with its laissez-faire governing policy, involving minimum interference. This created a "free for-all," "anything goes" business environment that was susceptible to bribery and corruption. Due to its deep-water seaport and its strategic and convenient location in East Asia and as a gateway to China, Hong Kong had steadily prospered from trade with China and with the rest of the world under British rule, while China was embroiled in wars, famines, and turmoil. Refugees from its much bigger and more chaotic neighbor flocked to Hong Kong in large numbers, seeking safer lives and greater economic opportunities. From the 1900s to the 1970s, Hong Kong's population grew more than tenfold, from a mere 300,000 to more than four million (Wikipedia, 2018e). Such a huge influx of refugees not only brought new social problems, but also made existing issues worse, one of them being corruption (De Speville, 1997; Li, 2004).

First, due to the massive waves of immigrants, there was a severe shortage of public goods such as social services. This forced the government to put stringent controls and limits on the distribution of daily necessities: housing, water, schools, health care, and even food. The combination of the shortage of public goods and the power to distribute them provided easy opportunities for officials to ask for bribes. Furthermore, immigration officers had discretionary power to send the refugees back to China. All of these powers fueled official corruption.

Second, the immigrants brought a culture that was accustomed to corruption, therefore inadvertently contributing to the problem. China had been ruled by an absolute monarchy for centuries, and later by the authoritarian government of the Nationalists (Kuomintang). Under these dictatorial rules, officials demanding payments from people and firms was a common practice, and people, in turn, were accustomed to it. So when the refugees arrived in Hong Kong, they thought that officers there would also expect to be paid on the side. This perception on the part of the Chinese immigrants reinforced the propensity of officials in Hong Kong to accept bribes.

The third factor, which I believe was the major culprit in Hong Kong's rampant corruption problem back then, was the flawed organizational structure of the government. Before 1974, the official anticorruption agency, the Anti-Corruption Office, was under the supervision of the police department, which would have been fine if the latter had been reasonably clean. Unfortunately, this was not the case: the police department was totally corrupt, from the very top down. The Anti-Corruption Office was commonly viewed as useless in Hong Kong back then, and people joked that asking the police to catch corrupt officials was like asking the fox to guard the chickens. Almost no one would report bribery and corruption cases to the police, because the police would ignore them or sometimes would even retaliate against the informants (De Speville, 1997; Li, 2004).

Economically, the British ruled Hong Kong's economy using the philosophy that was used at home, namely, that the government was to be the rule-setter and the referee of the market, but not a player. This essentially left the market free. Since it was not involved in big, government-sponsored projects, grand corruption involving top leaders in return for lucrative deals were rare. Most bribery–corruption cases involve petty corruption (see Chapter 3 for grand and petty corruptions), what the locals called "tea money" paid by citizens or firms to officials to secure public services or to speed things up. An often-cited extreme case of corruption was that an on-duty firefighter would not turn on his hoses until demands for "tea money" were met (De Speville, 1997; Li, 2004, 11–19).

Left unchecked, by the early 1970s, the corruption in Hong Kong was running wild, especially in the disciplinary services such as the police department. Corrupt police officers protected illegal operations such as gambling and prostitution and received "protection fees." The corruption was so bad that the government became very concerned and decided that it must do something. Bertrand de Speville, a former head of the ICAC, described the corruption in Hong Kong prior to the establishment of the ICAC as "deeply rooted, widespread, generally tolerated, and, in some sectors, highly organized" (De Speville, 1997, p. 11).

The big obstacle to the cleanup was the police force. They controlled the Anti-Corruption Office, and they took bribes. Eventually, the Hong Kong residents, many of whom were Chinese immigrants who were obedient and were accustomed to being bullied by government officials back in China, could not take it any longer. Thousands of students and citizens took to the streets to demand that the corruption be eradicated. Under mounting public pressure, the government began to investigate some high-level police officers for corruption. But the senior police officials, who were British expatriates, felt that they were above the law. In 1973, the government ordered a senior police officer, Peter Godber, to explain how he amassed the equivalent of nearly 4.4 million Hong Kong Dollars (about $600,000) in bank accounts located in various places including Canada, Australia, Singapore, the USA, England, and Hong Kong. Defying the order, Godber fled to England, and was confident that his government would not extradite him back to the colony. This incident greatly enraged the people of Hong Kong and triggered a governance crisis. All eyes were on the government to see how it would react to the demand that corruption be eradicated and Godber brought back to face justice (De Speville, 1997; Li, 2004).

In 1974, Governor Sir Murray MacLehose took the bold step of setting up the Independent Commission Against Corruption (ICAC), outside of the police department. This was viewed as a huge loss of face for the police, who had previously been in charge of fighting corruption (De Speville, 1997; Li, 2004; Miners, 1998).

Considering Hong Kong's circumstances and the experience of other countries, MacLehose wanted the ICAC to be independent and highly powerful – both legally and organizationally – and yet subject to certain checks and balances. As a result, the newly formed ICAC had the following key features: (1) it was established by law, not by administrative order, giving it high legal status; (2) the commissioner of the ICAC reported directly to the governor and had the authority to investigate anyone – except the governor – for corruption; (3) the commissioner prepared the ICAC's budget estimates and the governor approved them; (4) its budget was audited by the director of audits; and (5) the commissioner prepared an annual report which the governor was required to present to the Legislative Council of the Hong Kong government (De Speville 1997). This structure gave the ICAC the greatest authority and resources to fight corruption (see points (1) to (3) above), while keeping its power in check (see points (4) and (5) above) (Li, 2004).

Citizens and firms welcomed this, and had high expectations of the ICAC. However, the first test as to whether the government's resolve to clean up corruption was for real was what it would do about the runaway corruption suspect, Peter Godber. In April 1974, Godber was arrested in the UK. However, bringing a citizen of the colonial power to the colony to face trial was not easy. The Hong Kong government and the ICAC fought hard and succeeded. In January 1975, they brought Godber from England to Hong Kong to face trial. This success quickly boosted people's confidence in the ICAC and in the government's intention to fight corruption. Since then, the ICAC's efforts to root out bribery and corruption in Hong Kong have been very successful (De Speville, 1997; Li, 2004). A common way for the ICAC to start investigating a suspected bribery– corruption case is to invite the person of interest over "for a cup of coffee." Even the possibility of such an invitation has become a deterrent to corruption. The ICAC is highly respected for its integrity and its effectiveness, and corrupt officials dread being invited over to drink the agency's "famed coffee," as a *South China Morning Post* story puts it (Lam, 2009).

Now, Hong Kong enjoys the status of being one of the most corruption-free countries in the world. In 2017, Hong Kong had a Corruption Perception Index of 77 (0 = most corrupt and 100 = least corrupt) and was ranked the thirteenth cleanest country in the world (Transparency International, 2017).

7.2.2 *South Korea: Just Walked out of the Shadows*

After the Second World War, the Republic of Korea was founded in the southern half of the Korean peninsula. In 1948, it elected its first president, Syngman Rhee. Rhee ruled the country in an authoritarian style and his tenure was marred by mismanagement and rampant corruption. According to a report on Korean corruption, "[c]orruption under Rhee took the form of payoffs from foreign aid funds and bank loans" (GlobalSecurity.org, 2018). In other words, Rhee and his cronies stole directly from the state coffers, which was a deadweight on the economy and did not facilitate economic activities. On April 19, 1960, a student-led uprising broke out against his autocratic rule and corruption. Rhee resigned a week later. The political turmoil offered a chance for parliamentary democracy, which was short-lived. In 1961, the military staged a coup and General Park Chung Hee emerged as the *de facto* leader of the country. Under pressure from the USA, Park agreed to restore civilian rule in South Korea. In 1963, a presidential election was held and Park defeated his opponent by a narrow margin of 1.5%, and became the president of the young Republic of Korea. While Park made a great effort to shake up the bureaucracy and improved the efficiency of the government in order to implement his ambitious economic development plan, he still allowed corruption to happen, but in a different style from the corruption under Rhee. According to the report by Global Security:

> In contrast [to corruption under Rhee], corruption under Park took the form of payoffs from private investment. But the payoffs took place in an economic environment more favorable to growth. Thus, the private capital – despite payoffs and the like – fed an investment boom that followed reasonably accurate market indicators of real benefits and costs for the country. Investments approved by the government, even though payoffs were extracted from them, had been tested and approved through feasibility studies and were generally consistent with Korea's economic plan.
> (GlobalSecurity.org, 2018)

The report concludes that "corruption in the 1950s was more detrimental than that in later years because of the economic policies pursued by the Rhee government" (GlobalSecurity.org, 2018).

A dominant form of bribery–corruption transaction under Park is the typical relation-based (see Chapter 4) exchange between him and the *chaebols*, the family-owned business groups. These family firms would cultivate a cozy relationship with Park and would help him achieve his objectives, and Park, in turn, would provide them with access to low-cost or free funds and special licenses to enter lucrative industries. For a *chaebol*, the effort and the cost of investing in such a relationship are sunk costs, since they cannot sell the relationship or get refunds. Once they have established such a relationship, they should use it to the full extent and get into as many industries as possible, regardless of whether they have expertise in those industries. Consequently, the major *chaebols*, with Park's blessing, all entered an array of industries, some of them seemingly unrelated. For example, Hyundai, a major *chaebol*, first entered automobile manufacturing and construction, and later added shipbuilding, cement, chemicals, and electronics to its portfolio. The Koreans, in the 1960s, nicknamed them "octopus" for extending their "tentacles" into all of the sectors of the economy (Hwang, 2010).

The way in which Park governed the *chaebols* is like a CEO of a company managing his or her subsidiaries. He would set goals for the *chaebols* and would reward them if they met the goals. Under this model, it can be argued that such an exchange of favors between Park and the *chaebols* helped Korea's economic development (see "efficiency-enhancing" corruption in Chapter 5) (Huang & O'Neil-Massaro, 2001). Scholars of corruption even argued that corruption under Park was "nationalized" (Moran, 1999; Tella, 2013), similar to the "big mafia" model in Chapter 2. During Park's rule, the Korean economy took off rapidly, achieving what is known as the "Miracle on the Han River." (Note: the Han River is the main river flowing through the capital city of Seoul.)

Park continued to win his second and third terms in 1967 and 1971, respectively. But the 1971 election was a close call against his opponent Kim Dae Jung (who eventually became president after democratization in 1998). In 1972, Park made a new constitution called the "Yushin Constitution" that essentially changed him from a *de facto* dictator to a *de jure* dictator. His rule after that was increasingly more authoritarian, which prompted more and more people, especially students, to take to the streets to protest against the Yushin Constitution and his dictatorship. The government forces and demonstrators clashed violently. On October 26, 1979, Park was shot dead by the director of the Korean Central Intelligence Agency after they had dinner together, putting a dramatic end to his long dictatorial rule.

Since the late 1980s, Korea has taken strides toward becoming a more rule-based society and toward the eradication of corruption. This effort was accelerated by two major events (Li, Park, & Bao, 2018). One is democratization in the late 1980s and early 1990s, and the other is the 1997 Asian Financial Crisis.

From 1980 to 1987, Korea embarked on a democracy movement which pushed the government to take many measures toward the implementation of a more rule-based system. These measures included reforms such as limiting presidential terms and strengthening the authority of the National Assembly. Popular protests forced the government to implement additional social reforms and to hold a presidential election in 1988. The 1992 election of President Kim Yeong Sam can be viewed as a new era of greater rule-based governance. For example, he implemented the Real-Name Financial

Transaction Act to end the relatively easy ways in which bribe money could be hidden (Koreabridge, 2012).

The 1997 Asian Financial Crisis hit South Korea extremely hard because of the vulnerability of the economy due to the cozy relationship between the *chaebols*, the government, and the banks (which had been used by the government to finance the *chaebols'* aggressive expansions). Lee Yong-Keun, chairman of the Financial Supervisory Commission said, in 2000, "[a]nachronistic activities by *chaebol* were part of what caused Korea's economic crisis and the government has the responsibility to protect the rights of the people" (Solomon, 2007). When Korea's stock market crashed, the currency dropped by more than half of its value against the US dollar (from 800 won/$1 to 1,700 won/$1), further exacerbating Korea's inability to service its foreign debt, and, as a result, the national debt-to-GDP ratio more than doubled – from approximately 13 percent to 30 percent (Wikipedia, 2015a).

Responding to the crisis, the government, led by the newly elected president, Kim Dae Jung, made sweeping structural reforms that fundamentally changed the governance environment of Korea and greatly contributed to its transition from relation-based to rule-based governance. These reforms included labor reforms that broke the relation-based, rigid employment practices; financial reforms that increased transparency, accountability, sound management, deregulation, and liberalization; corporate reforms that specifically targeted the *chaebols* with five principles of corporate restructuring, which are essentially rule-based governance, and economic liberalization (Moon & Mo, 2015). In sum, these reforms substantially changed the old bribery–corruption relationship between the government and the *chaebols*. Because of these reform measures and the resolute effort to implement them, Korea's economy has quickly bounced back, and the governance environment has been substantially improved, moving away from relying on private connections to relying on public rules.

After democratization in the late 1980s, Korea's effort to pursue and prosecute corrupt officials has been relentless and resolute. Since the mid-1990s, a slew of corruption scandals that involved current or former presidents broke. In 1995, two former presidents, Chun Doo Hwan and Rho Tae Woo, were jailed for corruption (and for other crimes). In 1997, former president Kim Yong Sam's son was arrested on the charge of receiving bribes. In 2002, two sons of former president Kim Dae Jung were arrested for bribery. In 2009, former president Roh Moo Hyun committed suicide, amid a corruption scandal and investigation. In 2018, former president Lee Myung Bak was arrested on at least 14 counts, including taking bribes valued at ten million US dollars. Among the corruption cases relating to or involving former or current presidents, the most visible case is the one involving former president Park Geun-hye, the daughter of Park Chung Hee.

In 2018, former president Park Geun-hye was accused in the Central District Court in Seoul of helping a close friend to get bribes worth millions of dollars from major corporations, among them Samsung and Lotte. The prosecutor sought a 30-year jail term for Park, along with a fine of 118,500,000,000 won ($110,579,397). A three-judge panel of the Central District Court in Seoul sentenced Park to 24 years in prison and a fine of 18,000,000,000 won ($16,798,683) (Wikipedia, 2018f).

These cases show not only that old habits die hard, but, more importantly, how determined and relentless the Korean people are in cleaning up corruption, even at the highest levels of the government. In a culture that respects authority, the Korean people's willingness to take down the most powerful and respected person – the president – is unprecedented.

Despite, or perhaps because of, the wide coverage of these high-profile corruption scandals, the corruption level in Korea has been categorically and substantially reduced since democratization, especially since the 1997 Financial Crisis. Surveys show that, for people doing business in Korea, corruption is not as major a concern as it is in other corruption-ridden countries (GAN Integrity, 2017a).

7.2.3   Tunisia: Light at the End of the Tunnel?

On the morning of December 17, 2010, in Sidi Bouzid, Tunisia, a city 300 kilometers south of the capital, Tunis, a government official confiscated an unlicensed street vendor's cart. The vendor fought back unsuccessfully and, in desperation, set himself on fire in front of the government headquarters. His dramatic protest by self-immolation triggered a revolution that eventually toppled the dictator Ben Ali, who ruled the country with an iron fist for 23 years (Wikipedia, 2018j).

By any measure, the trigger event – a government official confiscating an unlicensed vendor's cart – is a rather trivial incident with no obvious significance; it happens frequently to many of the tens of thousands of street vendors in Tunisia. Both the government officers and the vendors knew the drill: the officer would threaten to confiscate the cart, the vendor, Bouazizi, would pay a small sum, and that would be it. It could even be argued that, technically, in terms of the law, the officer did nothing wrong in confiscating the vending cart since the seller did not have a license. However, from the perspective of governance environment theory (see Chapter 4), Tunisia is a non-rule-based society in which people and officials ignore formal rules and use commonly accepted, informal ways to settle disputes, such as having the unlicensed vendor pay the officer. In this sense, Bouazizi was right: the officer breached the unwritten, but mutually agreed upon, informal way of settling matters.

To understand how such a common incident could lead to a revolution that would change the political landscape of the Arab world, we need to review the incident more closely and to consider its background in detail.

On the morning of that fateful day, Faida Hamdi, a 45-year old city employee, was enforcing the law on the street. She spotted

Bouazizi selling foods without a license, which violated the regulations. So Hamdi confiscated Bouazizi's cart and all of the produce, on which Bouazizi had spent about $200, a very large sum for him. It was not the first time that Bouazizi had been caught. So, as usual, Bouazizi tried to settle this by paying the 10-dinar "fine" (a day's wages, equivalent to $7) to get his cart back. But Hamdi seemed to disregard the informal settlement that most officers and vendors followed. It seemed that she followed the regulations to the letter. Bouazizi felt that her refusal to settle with payment violated the common practice and kept arguing with her. But Hamdi did not budge; she called over police officers, who, together with her, allegedly roughed up Bouazizi.

Bouazizi was desperate. He went to the local government for help, but was rejected. "The law is the law," he was told. By now, Bouazizi felt that his world had come to an end. In the morning, the 26-year-old had been a hard-working young man with great familial responsibilities and a dream. Not only did the entire family of eight depend on his income, but his sister's university education also relied on his support. In addition to providing for his family, he had a dream: to save money to buy a truck. Now, his cart was gone, along with the $200 worth of produce that he had purchased on credit. His dream had turned into a nightmare.

At 11:30 am, Bouazizi returned to the front of the city office, doused his body with inflammable liquid and set himself on fire. He was severely burned and was taken to a hospital. People were outraged by the incident and took to the streets to protest.

To quell the public's outcry, the then president, Zine el Abidine Ben Ali, went to the hospital on December 28 to visit Bouazizi, who later died on January 4, 2011, as anti-Ben Ali protests raged on.

To save his rule, Ben Ali announced that he would set up two independent commissions: one to investigate corruption, and the other to investigate the deaths and injuries during the protests. But it was too late. Days later, Ben Ali fled the country and resigned his presidency.

During Ben Ali's rule, from 1987 to 2011, he and his family had controlled the whole economy of Tunisia. Through taking bribes, controlling and monopolizing industries, and participating in major investments and projects, Ben Ali, his wife Leila Trabelsi, their extended families, and their friends had amassed huge wealth. Part of their ill-gotten wealth includes "550 properties, 48 boats and yachts, 40 stock portfolios, 367 bank accounts, and 400 enterprises at an estimated value of $13 billion (the equivalent of 25 percent of the 2011 Tunisian gross domestic product), as well as $28.8 million held in a Lebanese bank account by the former first lady" (Yerkes & Muasher, 2017, p. 19).

Among the causes that triggered the revolution, two stand out. The first is the rampant corruption by the ruling kleptocracy, which can be viewed as more of an economic reason. Ben Ali and his cronies had been systematically looting the country (Yerkes & Muasher, 2017). The second cause is more political. Ben Ali's ruling strategy was to have people "shut up and consume" (Goldstein, 2011). Like all dictatorships, Ben Ali's autocratic rule relied heavily on the police to suppress any challenges or dissenting views in the society (Goldstein, 2011). Once a large police force had been formed, Ben Ali faced another problem: the large police force put an unbearable burden on the already strained government budget. The salary of the police was low. According to information from Tunisia.com, it was about 700 TND ($490), which is similar to that of a secretary (600–900 TND). Whether implicitly or explicitly, Ben Ali had to allow his government officials and police to obtain extra income to supplement their meager pay. In other words, the government had to turn a blind eye to illegal acts, such as intimidation, by officials and by the police. And people were fully aware of this. So, whenever a low-ranking policeman or an official mistreated people, they would blame the government and Ben Ali, instead of regarding it as an isolated or random act by an individual public employee. In general, in a dictatorship, the main role of the armed forces (and the whole government, to a lesser extent) is to maintain stability and to silence dissent. When the objective of the police degenerates from protecting people's safety to crushing dissidents, their morality and their efficiency deteriorate. This, plus the low pay that they receive, decreases their loyalty to and their willingness to defend the state and the state leader.

While, on the surface, the omnipresence of the police and the silence of the people created an impression that the dictator's rule was invincible, it had actually been undermined by the anger of the silent majority (Goldstein, 2011) and by a corrupt and disloyal armed force. The regime was consequently vulnerable – if an anti-government action broke out, the police would not fight for the regime with their lives; instead, they joined the protesters. Goldstein, a human rights worker who worked in Tunisia, referring to the unexpected collapse of the regime, wrote: "My Tunisian friends were right: A police state looks stable only until the day it is not" (Goldstein, 2011).

And as one might expect, as soon as the old regime had fallen and the new government had formed, it set the eradication of corruption as its main governing goal. However, it has turned out that the move away from corruption has not been smooth. In the early stage of the transition, the government was in a chaotic state and was highly fragmented. With the exit of Ben Ali, grand corruption has been substantially reduced, but petty corruption has emerged and has even flourished. According to a report by the Carnegie Endowment for International Peace, even ordinary citizens engage in and benefit from corrupt practices. This observation and other evidence seem to confirm and support the argument about the challenge facing the transition, or infant democracy, during which the state capacity is weak, and dukedom ("many small mafias") tends to emerge to replace the dictator ("the big mafia"– see Chapter 2). Our hope, of course, is that Tunisia can overcome the weaknesses associated with infant democracies and win the war on corruption.

From the institution-building perspective, Tunisia has made great strides, although some issues remain. From January 2011 to September 2017, the government has taken 22 measures to eradicate corruption, including making new laws, holding trials, establishing new agencies, and promoting cultural changes and other social and civil development. Seventeen of the 22 measures can be viewed as more ad hoc, such as a law made for a specific purpose, or the initiation of a task force to deal with an important or urgent issue of the time. Five of them are more institution-building in nature. They are (1) to create a "good governance cell" "in every public institution, administration, and ministry to promote integrity and fight corruption"; (2) to start a "National Dialogue on Transitional Justice"; (3) to join the "Open Government Partnership"; (4) to pass a law regarding access to information; and (5) to pass a law regarding reporting corruption cases and protecting whistle-blowers (Yerkes & Muasher, 2017).

Based on various studies, I think that there are two areas in Tunisia's effort to eradicate corruption that need to be improved. The first is that the anticorruption authorities must be relatively independent, especially of the executive branch. This is the experience of Hong Kong. The executive branch tends to be more prone to petty corruption as compared to the legislative and judiciary branches. Second, the anticorruption agencies must be adequately funded (Yerkes & Muasher, 2017).

Finally, it should be noted that a factor, to some degree external to the existing domestic issues that complicate and adversely affect the progress of the transition in Tunisia, is terrorist attacks and the instability of its neighboring countries.

7.2.4   *China: Still in the Authoritarian Trap*

While the three cases that we just viewed either have completed the transition or are in the middle of the transition, China, in a strict sense, has not yet begun the transition, since it is still under a dictatorship. I include China because it has been commonly recognized by scholars of corruption that it faces a serious corruption problem (Gong, 2002; Pei, 2016; Pei, 2017; Sun, 2004; Wedeman, 2012) and because the sheer size of its economy makes the issue global. Our discussion on the possible paths that China may take in fighting corruption and possible transition will enhance our understanding of this issue.

Today's China in many senses is at a crossroads. After decades of rapid economic growth, which has benefited from relying on relation-based governance, the very mode of governance now seems to be an obstacle to further growth. It is impossible to cultivate cozy, private relationships with all of the firms in all of countries with which the Chinese government and firms want to do business. If the Chinese government and Chinese firms want to extend their activities beyond the country and globalize, which they very much do, they must shift away from the relation-based way of governing and doing business and begin to embrace the public rules that are used by all advanced economies (see Chapter 4).

On the anticorruption front, China is also at a crossroads. The vested interest groups, including the Communist Party and the business elites, have benefited tremendously from their privilege to engage in corruption and, thanks to the thick and extensive informal networks, corruption has been relatively efficiency-enhancing (Chapter 5). With large-scale and rampant corruption, the Chinese economy has enjoyed nearly double-digit growth for a number of years. But now, the economy has begun to show signs of fatigue, and ordinary people are fed up with the inside dealings and nepotism, from which they are excluded. If corruption was tolerated when the total economic pie was rapidly expanding, now it is unconditionally hated by the populace. However, the elites who have invested so much in the corrupt system will not give it up easily. So, parallel to the challenge that China (its government and firms) faces regarding whether (and how) to transition from a relation-based system to a rule-based system, the Chinese government seems to be unsure about what to do with the corruption problem.

There is little dispute that corruption in China is widespread, deeply rooted, and large in scale, and that it occurs across all levels and sections of the government, including not only the agencies that control the economic resources, but also the functional departments that appear to be far from the economic activities, such as the propaganda sector and the education sector.

Comprehensive and accurate statistics on corruption in China are not available. Below are some of the statistics reported by official sources and academic research. (See Zh.wikipedia.org (2014) for a summary of statistics and sources.)

- The total number of officials who were punished for corruption from 1982 to 2017 is about 6.3 million. Most were caught in recent years and the trend has been rising: 3.5 million were apprehended from 1982 to 2007; 660,000 were disciplined between 2007 and 2012; and 2.08 million officials were investigated and processed for corruption from 2012 to 2017 (Epoch Times, 2017).
- China's Public Security Ministry issued a report in 2004 that at least 500 corrupt officials, whose embezzlements amounted to RMB 70 billion ($12 billion), had fled China and were in hiding. As of June 2008, 16,000–18,000 corrupt officials have fled China, taking with them about RMB 800 billion ($130 billion).
- In 2004, the total embezzled by corrupt officials was estimated to be between RMB 409 billion and RMB 683 billion ($68 billion to $114 billion).
- According to a 2016 report by the CCTV, the official television station, the government recovered 20.1 billion yuan ($3.09 billion) from corrupt officials (CCTV, 2016).
- In 2014, anticorruption agents raided a place owned by Wei Pengyuan, former associate director of the coal section of China's Energy Bureau, and discovered a large amount of cash in Chinese and foreign currency. It took more than ten agents, using five cash-counting machines, 14 hours to count, with one of the machines burning out due to non-stop counting. The total amount was about 200 million yuan ($31 million), setting a record (Sina. com, 2016). In 2018, Wei's record was broken by Lai Xiaomin, a former CEO of a large state-owned company, who stowed away "270 million yuan ($39 million) worth of Chinese and foreign currency . . . at several residences" (Choi, 2018).
- A 2012, a *New York Times* story reported that Wen Jiabo, a former premier of China, and his family and relatives controlled assets worth at least $2.7 billion (Barboza, 2012).

- Various media reported in 2012 that the family of Xi Jinping, the then incoming president of China had "wealth of hundreds of millions" (Bloomberg News, 2012; Moore, 2012).

After Xi Jinping assumed power in the 18th Party Congress in November 2012, he waged a new war on corruption. Xi seems to be very determined and has said that "the corruption is getting worse and worse and will ultimately destroy the party and the state." Ordinary Chinese and policy analysts, as well as corrupt Chinese officials, all took his intentions seriously. In less than two years since the 18th Party Congress, 48 officials at province/ministry level or higher have been investigated for corruption, almost five times the average over the past 25 years (SinovisionNet, 2014). The case that has shocked the world was Xi's investigation of Zhou Yongkang, the former state security czar and a politburo standing member, who had, until his fall, been viewed as having immunity from any criminal investigations. On the basis of evidence and analyses, Xi has the following objectives for his anticorruption campaign:

1. Unlike his predecessor Hu Jintao, Xi is confident and is convinced that he can save the party by eradicating corruption. He wants a clean party that will be able to rule forever and a market economy under the party's absolute control. In this sense, his campaign is for real, based on his confidence and conviction. However, his concerns about corruption seem hypocritical in the sense that he is fully aware that corruption is inevitable under one-party rule and, thus, he has to tolerate reasonable corruption. We may surmise that, to him, the current level of corruption is not reasonable.
2. Xi's anticorruption campaign is a political move that will earn him political capital. Waging an anticorruption campaign is the action most calculated to increase his popularity among China's ordinary people, who are very angry at the corrupt officials.
3. The campaign is a convenient way for Xi to get rid of his political enemies. Xi's anticorruption campaign is a political movement, not a legal action (Wedeman, 2017). There is strong evidence that his campaign is selective. For example, there are no officials of "second generation red" (princelings) being investigated or arrested for corruption (World News Net, 2014).

It is widely believed that, through his selective purge, Xi has made so many enemies that he was afraid of stepping down at the end of two terms, as specified in the constitution. At the March 2018 meeting of the People's Congress, he successfully eliminated the term limit for the presidency.

What is the effect of Xi's campaign so far? Xi's anticorruption campaign has brought down a large number of high-level officials. These officials may have exhibited more greed than their peers and may have grabbed substantially more than the unwritten rules allow for their ranks, and they are, thus, hated by their peers. Therefore, bringing them down is justified in Xi's eyes and enables him to earn political capital and popular support.

Xi has promised that "there is no limit as far as investigating corruption is concerned." However, carrying on the anticorruption campaign will ultimately destroy the party and will paralyze the government. Thus, this anticorruption campaign, despite being carried out on a broader scale and reaching higher levels in the hierarchy, will be only temporary in effect. It can only clean up some of the most egregious corruption cases and, thus, reduce corruption for a short period of time. The system (the party) is similar to an obese person who has made a new year's resolution to exercise but does not curb his access to and his appetite for junk food. The newly intensified exercise will help him to shed some pounds, but his ability to grab food, and his unabated appetite for it will ensure that he regains his weight. As long as the Chinese Communist Party monopolizes the governance of China, the unbalanced and unchecked power of the officials will enable them to find new ways to benefit themselves. Corruption will be a constant feature in China. When the corruption level is so high that it causes the masses to complain, the party will prosecute a few people to make the masses feel better.

Furthermore, due to the absence of well-developed legal institutions, the campaign relies on KGB-style secret investigations and arrests that all end in show trials and convictions in court. In the meantime, Xi has consolidated his power and has promoted a new generation of officials who are loyal to him. Unfortunately, their loyalty is ultimately based on the opportunity to grab on the job. As the anticorruption campaign will fade away, and as the newly promoted officials learn how to (ab)use their power, there is no reason to believe that this new generation of party elites will stay clean and will not grab. And then the cycle repeats itself: a new anticorruption campaign must be waged, which may work like injecting a drug into the ordinary Chinese people to temporarily make them forget about the pain inflicted upon them by corrupt officials.

For the government, an outcome of the anticorruption campaign will be the establishment of more rigid policies and regulations to reduce the opportunities for officials to enrich themselves. These new rules, which are based on the Chinese Communist Party's lack of trust in its own officials, will demoralize government employees and will reduce the operational efficiency of the government. Thus, if the anticorruption measures are too effective, they will substantially hinder economic performance. Furthermore, attempting to eradicate corruption in the absence of the rule of law risks a return to Mao's communism, which is not in the best interests of the government either, since the government relies on the capitalist measures to keep the economy humming. Trapped in this corruption – anticorruption cycle, China will likely experience slow economic growth, or even stagnation, in the foreseeable future.

7.3 TRANSITION ISSUES

7.3.1 *Different Experiences of Transition*

The above cases present several typical situations. Hong Kong's transition was peaceful and successful. There are several factors that stand out in Hong Kong's experience. First, the government's ruling philosophy was hands-off and it did not get involved in economic activities. This substantially reduced the opportunities for officials to engage in corruption. Second, a key prerequisite for the success of its war on corruption was that the top leader of the colony, the governor, must not be corrupt. This was safeguarded by two assumptions: since the ruler of the colony, the British government, is a mature democracy and one of the cleanest governments, it could monitor the governor to make sure that he stayed clean. Another assumption is that, since the remuneration of the governor (his salary, benefits, and retirement package) was very generous and attractive (De Speville, 1997; Li, 2004), the incentive to take bribes was extremely low (in other words, the opportunity cost of being corrupt was very high). Third, Hong Kong's success can also be attributed to the independence of the anticorruption agency. It had to be separate from other, corruption-ridden parts of the government (in Hong Kong's case, the police department). The Hong Kong experience also shows that a corrupt culture can be changed quickly in both society and government.

South Korea's transition was full of dramas, with assassinations, uprisings, and government crackdowns (the 1980 democratic uprising in Gwangju ended in more than one hundred people being killed). But it did not involve large-scale and prolonged civil wars, and opposition existed even during the long dictatorial rule of Park Chung Hee. The watershed event in the transition was the assassination of Park in 1979. Overall, the transition was completed within the existing political system, through democratic and legal methods, in a continuous fashion. There was no large-scale purge of Park's officials after his demise.

In comparison to the case of South Korea, the transition in Tunisia was more like a regime change, or a revolution. The then-president was ousted by the people through mass demonstrations and violent confrontations with the forces loyal to the president. He and his family hastily fled the country moments before the airport was closed by the army under pressure from the people. Many of his relatives who wanted to flee were stopped. Thousands of prisoners were released. Battles broke out between Ben Ali's loyalists and the military that had turned against him. Years after the revolution, the government is still working on reconciliation, cleaning up remnants of Ben Ali's influence in the government, and recovering the loot taken by Ben Ali and his associates. Tunisia's transition is a typical case of democratic transition. It seems that the country is encountering many of the issues that face infant democracies (Alon et al., 2016).

Unlike the three cases above, China is still under a dictatorship and has not started its transition, in a strict sense. The question that we should consider here is: what can China learn from the experiences of the above cases in its (future) transition? With Yogi Berra's warning about making predictions in mind, this exercise is not to predict when a transition will occur in China, but, rather, to understand the conditions and factors that are necessary for, or conducive to, a successful transition.

Of the three cases, Hong Kong's is the most appealing to China: it has been smooth and peaceful, and Hong Kong is closely related to China culturally and geopolitically. So it is natural and logical for China to want to learn from Hong Kong's experience of fighting corruption. In fact, China has been learning from Hong Kong. In 2001, the Chinese government sent eleven official delegations, including a total of 168 cadres, to Hong Kong to learn from the experience of the ICAC. Also, the ICAC held 224 seminars for a total of 6,743 Chinese officials on fighting corruption, at the request of the Chinese government (ICAC, 2002). While the Chinese government may learn tactics and field experience from the ICAC, fundamentally, it cannot achieve the success of the ICAC, due to its political and economic systems. First, the Chinese government controls vast economic resources and participates in business operations. This makes its officials very susceptible to bribery and corruption. Second, unlike Hong Kong's political system, that was checked and monitored by the British government, there are no checks on the Chinese Communist Party or on its top leader, which makes the Hong Kong model not applicable. Third, the Hong Kong model requires the anticorruption agency to be independent of all other government agencies, and especially to be separate from the part of government that is corrupt. This, for China, would mean that the anticorruption agency must be outside of the Chinese Communist Party, which is not an option, given the current political system (Li, 2004). In sum, China would have to undergo more fundamental political changes in order to learn from Hong Kong's experience in fighting corruption.

In terms of fundamental political changes, the experiences of South Korea and Tunisia are, however, relevant. South Korea seized the opportunity provided by the death of the long-time dictatorial ruler Park Chung Hee to push for the transition. In China, a comparable event would have been the death in 1976 of the dictator Mao Zedong, who had ruled China for 27 years. The leaders of the Chinese Communist Party ended Mao's purge and initiated an economic reform, but they have failed to fundamentally change the political system.

The cases of South Korea and Tunisia have the following factors in common. First, the basic principle of their constitutions was, intrinsically, parliamentary democracy – or at least their constitutions did not explicitly designate a single party as the only legitimate ruling party. Second, oppositions existed and, to some degree, were organized under the dictatorship. They held seats in the parliament, and even had viable candidates for presidential elections. Neither of these situations exists in China. The constitution designates the Chinese Communist Party as the only ruling party, and no organized opposition is allowed to exist.

In pre-revolution Tunisia, the state could not afford to adequately pay its police, forcing them to take bribes. This is less the case in China. The state is well-funded and the police force, so far, is adequately paid and well-treated by the state. The local police offices receive extra funds for monitoring dissidents in their territory.

The case of the death of Lei Yang can further illustrate the contrast between China and Tunisia. In 2016, Lei Yang, an environmental worker, was arrested by the police on the suspicion of having bought sex services from a prostitute. Lei was taken into a van by the police, who beat him to death. This caused a national outrage in China. But, due to tight and effective control by the government, there were no organized protests on the streets. Angry discussions on the internet exploded at first, but then quickly disappeared after the government cracked down on them. The victim's family first demanded that the officers responsible be brought to justice, but later became silent under pressure from the government. The government paid an undisclosed amount to Lei's family. The police officers responsible for Lei's death were never charged (Wikipedia, 2017).

These occurrences suggest that the conditions that would propel China to take the path of South Korea or of Tunisia would have to be much more severe and unbearable. The logical conclusion is that China will be trapped in the corruption – anticorruption cycle, with precarious stability, for the foreseeable future.

7.3.2 The Danger of a Governance Vacuum during the Transition[1]

During the transition from reliance on private relations (including bribery–corruption relations) to reliance on public rules, the old relation-based way declines. Realizing this, people and firms begin to reduce their investment in establishing new (bribery–corruption) relationships and try to get as much from old relationships as possible, since the investment in them is sunk. This encourages opportunistic behaviors, such as officials taking bribes but not delivering the goods. At the same time, newly established public rules and laws may not be functioning well. For any law or public regulation to be effectively and efficiently enforced, there must be a stronger moral code, along with a legal culture that respects the law and encourages self-discipline, for without such a culture, laws and regulations are nothing more than ink on paper. For example, according to the report by the Carnegie Endowment for International Peace, the ineffectiveness of the new government in Tunisia's effort to fight corruption has resulted not so much from the lack of anticorruption laws as from failure to observe and enforce the laws (Yerkes & Muasher, 2017).

The combination of the decline of the relation-based way and the ineffective infancy of a rule-based system may create a governance vacuum that makes the society unstable and business activities vulnerable to organized crime. Furthermore, businesses may suffer from a worsening of bureaucracy, resulting from the mushrooming of the number of independent regulatory agencies when a dictatorship collapses (Shleifer & Vishny, 1993). For example, after the fall of the dictator Suharto in Indonesia, corruption got worse, because there was no one to keep a rein on the government bureaucracy to make sure that the demand for bribes by each government department was optimized, so that the dictator could maximize his total bribe income and deliver the public goods that the briber was asking for. After Suharto's departure, many semi-independent politicians emerged who acted like dukes, controlling one segment of the government bureaucracy and demanding much higher amounts in bribes (Kuncoro, 2008). A similar situation is also occurring now in Tunisia (Yerkes & Muasher, 2017).

7.3.3   The Tendency to Over-Regulate during the Transition[2]

An intriguing phenomenon in societies undergoing rapid transition from reliance on private relations, such as bribery–corruption relations, to rule-based governance is that transitioning societies tend to implement and enforce more formal rules, to an even greater extent than rule-based countries. Two examples from Taiwan, a society undergoing a rapid transition from a relation-based to a rule-based governance environment, vividly illustrate this tendency.

The first example concerns the changes in Taiwan's primary and secondary education. Before Taiwan's democratization, the hiring of teachers was done by school principals. Although certain rules were used, such as the requirement for new teachers to hold a degree from an accredited teacher's college, the process tended to be influenced by powerful politicians. During the democratization process (which was, essentially, an effort to transform from a relation-based to a rule-based governance system), reformers tried to eliminate the corruption in the teacher-hiring process. In doing so, the reformers seem to have over-done it: they effectively took the power to hire away from the princi-pals, and made the hiring solely dependent on a very clearly defined, easily measured, and strictly enforced rule: a nationwide teachers' test. Anyone who scored high enough on the test would be hired. Needless to say, the ones with the highest scores were not necessarily the best candidates for the job.

Another example concerns the tenure and promotion process at the universities in Taiwan. In order to eliminate corruption and poli-tical influence, the reformers instituted a points system that allows professors to accumulate points based on teaching, research, and ser-vice. In so doing, they essentially made qualified administrators (the president, provost, dean, and chairs of each university) powerless to influence the process. Similar issues exist in South Korea (Li et al., 2018).

These two examples suggest that, during the transition from a traditionally relation-based governance system to a new rule-based way of governance, a society tends to go overboard, nullifying all human authorities, out of the fear that the people at the top will abuse their power, just as they did in the old relation-based system. The main reason for such an overreaction and such a limiting of authorities' discretion (in favor of strict formal rules) is the long dura-tion of authoritarian rule in which power had been abused for personal gains. This kind of abuse has left a deep, indelible scar on the society, and on the people, such that they would rather take away any discre-tionary power from the authorities and rely completely on formal, objective rules. A lack of trust in the government, public officials, or anyone in power is the fundamental cause of this overregulation.

While such measures may successfully curtail the abuse of power common in the old relation-based setting, the cost of doing so for the society and for business can be quite high. The discretion of the authorities to make decisions is necessary in any organization or society. Indeed, if formal rules can take care of every contingency, then officials and managers are not necessary. There must be a certain amount of trust in the people who are in power, in order for an organization or society to run efficiently. The challenge to societies undergoing the transition from relying on private connections such as bribery and corruption to a rule-based governance environment is for them to learn how to nurture and establish public trust in general, and confidence in the government in particular.

NOTES

1. This section is adopted from pp. 113–114, Li, S. 2009. *Managing International Business in Relation-Based versus Rule-Based Countries.* New York: Business Expert Press.
2. This section is adopted from pp. 114–115, Li, S. 2009. *Managing International Business in Relation-Based versus Rule-Based Countries.* New York: Business Expert Press.

8 The Globalization of Corruption by Countries with Weak Institutional Environments

Geneva—Inside the cement compound housing the World Trade Organization lies a colorful Chinese garden of cultivated rocks, arches and calligraphy. The gift from the Chinese commerce ministry symbolizes "world prosperity through cross-cultural fertilization," according to a marble plaque.

–"How China Swallowed the WTO," *The Wall Street Journal*[1]

8.1 GLOBALIZATION AND COUNTRIES WITH WEAK INSTITUTIONAL ENVIRONMENTS

In the past quarter of a century or so, the world has witnessed a rapid globalization of trade, investment, consumption, and technologies, as well as an increase in the mobility of people. While globalization has brought many good things to many countries, such as the availability and affordability of goods and services and the dissemination and fusion of ideas, it has also enabled and accelerated the spread of bribery and corruption, especially from countries with weak institutional environments. In this chapter, we will examine how countries with weak institutional environments export bribery and corruption to the world not only in scope and in scale, but also in new forms.

What is globalization? A typical international business textbook definition of globalization is "the shift toward a more integrated and interdependent world economy ... including the globalization of markets and the globalization of production" (Hill & Hult, 2019, p. 6). Globalization makes the flow of goods and services across countries easier and more efficient, thereby lowering the costs of doing business and the cost of living for the participating countries. Less visible to the common people, but equally important, is the increased mobility of capital, which, by its nature, always seeks the highest return wherever its destination may be, provided that the destination country can provide a reasonable guarantee of its safety. This is in accordance with the argument of comparative advantage heralded by one of the founding economists of comparative advantage theory, David Ricardo: the free flow of productive resources, such as capital, can make their allocation more efficient; therefore, it can increase the total output for the world, with the same amount of resources, achieving a win-win for everyone (Ricardo, 1967, 1817). Since the early 1990s, when the communist block collapsed and when China accelerated its opening up, many countries that had been off-limits to trade and investment have embraced globalization, greatly increasing the flow of cross-border capital investment. And, as the theory of comparative advantage had predicted, capital did flow from rich countries with abundant capital and a low investment return, such as the West European nations, the USA, and other developed nations, to less developed countries with capital shortages and a plentiful low-cost labor supply, such as China, India, Vietnam, and others. Indeed, this globalization has increased global output and has improved the welfare of many people in the participating countries, both as consumers and as producers.

However, this globalization did not happen in an ideal world free of political and legal issues, as Ricardo had assumed when he developed his model. Along with the benefits of globalization, there are costs. In addition to the costs that are highlighted in virtually all of the elections in mature democracies (which are also mature market economies), such as the loss of domestic manufacturing industries, there is another cost that has been largely overlooked: the spread of bribery and corruption that, as I will argue, mostly originates from the less developed or emerging countries: those with weak institutional environments.

As I mentioned earlier, investors will go to any country as long as the expected profit is high, provided that their investment will be reasonably safe there. Unfortunately, most of the countries with a capital shortage and an ample supply of low-cost laborers tend not to have a strong rule of law, which is vital for the protection of investments. But that does not deter the profit seekers. As the trade unionist T. J. Dunning once said (famously quoted by Karl Marx in his *Das Kapital*):

> Capital eschews no profit, or very small profit, just as Nature was formerly said to abhor a vacuum. With adequate profit, capital is very bold. A certain 10 percent will ensure its employment anywhere; 20 percent certain will produce eagerness; 50 percent, positive audacity; 100 percent will make it ready to trample on all human laws; 300 percent, and there is not a crime at which it will scruple, nor a risk it will not run, even to the chance of its owner being hanged. (Dunning, 1860, quoted from Marx, 2007 (1867), p. 834)

Indeed, capital is powerful and it drives its owner to be creative. If the host country is not rule-based, investors tend to rely on private connections for protection, which means that formal laws and regulations can be circumvented (since they are not fair and since the officials who make and enforce them tend to be corrupt), as we discussed in Chapter 4. When investing in these countries, the first thing the investor would do is cultivate and invest in private relationships with people who have power and who can make things happen in the country: the dictator, powerful politicians, or officials. They would wine and dine, play golf, and go to the sauna together, and, once mutual trust was built, they would help each other by exchanging favors: big favors. The foreign investor would get the blessing of the powerful in the form of exclusive licenses, land, clients, and private protection. The powerful would get cash (usually in their foreign accounts – the powerful, including the dictator, usually do not like to park their money in the bank of the country they rule) or real estate in foreign countries, scholarships at foreign elite schools, or shares in the investor's projects. As Gideon Rachman observed:

> The globalization of business and finance opened up opportunities to make corrupt profits in fast-growing emerging economies. Industries that often need official involvement, such as natural resources and infrastructure, are particularly lucrative targets. There are contracts to be awarded and development projects that need official approval. And the money for bribes can always be deposited offshore. (Rachman, 2018)

Through the investor, the powerful people in the host country are introduced to investors and the powerful people in the home country of the investor, and in other countries in which the investor does business, and likewise, the powerful people of the host country may also introduce their foreign investor friends to other heads of state that are equally corrupt. In the process, a vast network of private relations between multinational corporations and politicians is being built, and bribery and corruption are spreading worldwide.

Empirical data of global patterns of foreign investment show that investors do not shun countries with a poor rule of law. Instead, they go in with a mode of investment that allows them to protect their assets and interests. There are two modes of foreign investment: direct investment and indirect investment (commonly known as portfolio investment) (Hill & Hult, 2019; Li & Filer, 2007). In foreign direct investment, the investor not only invests capital to gain full or partial ownership, but also has substantial control over how the investment is managed, or manages it directly. For example, a Japanese investor goes to Vietnam, invests, and then manages a restaurant. She would be an "insider" in the sense that she would decide how the restaurant is run; she would determine how the capital is used and recorded on the books; and she would deal with the local officials regarding the affairs of the restaurant. If her restaurant were involved in a dispute with the government or a competitor, she would have all the inside information about the restaurant and thus could decide how to deal with it: either by relying on her private connections to settle the dispute or by relying on the public laws to settle it. If the host country's laws were opaque and judges were corrupt, she would, instead, use her private connections to seek a favorable outcome.

An example of foreign indirect investment, or foreign portfolio investment, can be seen when a Russian investor buys a few shares of a Kenyan company listed in the Nairobi Securities Exchange. The investor has only a small percentage of ownership of the company and, therefore, cannot directly influence or control how the company is run. As compared to direct investment, he is an "outsider" who must rely on publicly released, second-hand information, such as the company's annual report, to learn how his investment is performing. In other words, if the "insiders" of the company, such as the CFO, cook the financial data of the company, he would not be able to participate or to interfere to protect his investment. Usually, by the time that he learned of it, it would be too late. In countries with poor-quality public information and a weak legal system, making a portfolio investment is inherently dangerous, due primarily to corruption in the country (Li & Filer, 2007).

In a study on governance environment and mode of investment, my coauthor and I show that, in non-rule-based societies, foreign investments tend to be in the form of direct investment as opposed to indirect, portfolio investment (see Figure 8.1).

8.2 COUNTRIES WITH WEAK INSTITUTIONAL ENVIRONMENTS AS THE HUB OF CORRUPTION

Anecdotal evidence and recent corruption cases also support the argument that countries with weak institutional environments tend to be hubs for the bribery–corruption wheels of the world. Below are some examples.

8.2.1 Brazil's "Operation Car Wash"

In March 2014, a Brazilian police team raided a car wash shop that was thought to be a money laundering operation. During the investigation, the police found that the money launderer paid for a car for an official of Petrobras, a big oil company owned by the Brazilian government. Petrobras had many lucrative construction

FIGURE 8.1 Rule of law and FDI
FDI/FI = (foreign direct investment)/(total foreign investment)
Number of countries: 58 (21 in low, 18 in medium, and 18 in high
category)
Source: (Li & Filer, 2007)

projects to be handed out. Its executives would accept bribes from
construction firms and would award projects to them with inflated
prices. One of the major construction firms was Odebrecht.
It would, in turn, use the profits from these deals to bribe politicians. "Operation Car Wash" was big: the law enforcement authorities determined that the amount of misappropriated funds was
about $1 billion, and the total amount that they are trying to
recover is about $11.3 billion.

From Petrobras and Odebrecht, the investigation team discovered that the bribery–corruption activities extended to many high-
level politicians in Brazil, including the former presidents Luiz
Inácio Lula da Silva and Dilma Rousseff. But it did not stop there; the
bribery–corruption case eventually spread beyond Brazil, to involve
many businesses and government officials in at least twelve countries,
including Panama, Argentina, Mexico, Peru, Venezuela, Ecuador, and
Angola. The US Department of Justice was involved in the

investigation, and Swiss banks held accounts belonging to Odebrecht (Valle, 2018; Wikipedia, 2016a).

8.2.2 Malaysia Development Berhad (1MDB)

Founded in 2009, 1MDB is a Malaysian strategic development company that is wholly owned by the Minister of Finance. Below is how Wikipedia describes 1MDB (the company's own website seems no longer to be working):

> 1MDB was established to drive strategic initiatives for long-term economic development for the country by forging global partnerships and promoting foreign direct investment. 1MDB focuses on strategic development projects in the areas of energy, real estate, tourism and agribusiness. 1MDB is currently involved in several high-profile projects such as the Tun Razak Exchange, Tun Razak Exchange's sister project Bandar Malaysia, and the acquisition of three independent power producers. (Wikipedia, 2018a)

Since 2015, 1MBD has been in the spotlight of the international media for its suspicious financial transactions and for anecdotal evidence that suggests the presence of money laundering and possible corrupt activities. It was widely believed that the former prime minister, Najib Razak, who controlled the fund, had directed money and other benefits from the fund to himself and to his family members and friends.

It was first reported by the news media that a Penang-based financier with ties to Najib's stepson took $700 million from a joint venture project between 1MDB and PetreSaudi International. It was further discovered that Najib approved a $1 billion loan to the same financier. As the negative reaction by the public to these allegations grew, the Malaysian Anti-Corruption Commission (which was under Najib back then) investigated the allegation of the $700 million transfer and subsequently (in August 2015) cleared 1MDB of the any wrongdoing.

However, these obvious cover-ups by the Malaysian government under Najib did not quell the public's discontent and, in the 2018 general election, Najib's ruling party, the Barisan National Party, lost its majority for the first time in Malaysia's history (since the founding of the country in 1957). Najib accepted the results of the election and promised to help facilitate a smooth transition of power. Subsequently, under the new government, he was charged with abuse of power and a criminal breach of trust for actions during his time as the prime minister.

After the election, the new prime minister, Mahathir Mohamad, started to investigate the 1MDB scandal and the involvement of former prime minister Najib. Najib and his wife were barred from leaving the country. In May 2018, police searched the residence of Najib, two condominium units owned by him, and his former office. They seized 72 bags containing jewelry, 284 boxes of luxury handbags (reportedly a favorite collection item for his wife), and luxury wristwatches. As of June 2018, the total assets seized from Najib and his family were valued about $270 million, which includes 12,000 pieces of jewelry, 423 luxury wristwatches, 234 pairs of luxury sunglasses, 567 luxury handbags from 72 brands, and $29 million in over 26 different currencies.

The repercussions of the 1MDB corruption scandal are truly international. As of July 2018, the following countries or foreign entities were known to have been affected: Switzerland (especially Swiss banks), Hong Kong, Scotland, the United States (including several major financial institutions and a film studio), Singapore, Luxembourg, the United Arab Emirates, the Seychelles, China, and Australia (Wikipedia, 2018a).

8.2.3   Corruption Spreads Like Disease, Literally

A bizarre case of corruption in a remote small town in China shows how quickly corruption may spread, with a scope and scale that are difficult to gauge and to contain. It is a domestic case, but it spread in the same way as corruption spreads globally from the countries where it originates, which tend to have weak institutional environments.

On August 14, 2011, Mr. Yang Changming, a deputy county clerk at Sanhui County, Miao-Tong Autonomous Zhou, Guizhou Province, was detained on corruption charges. Later, he was found to have the AIDS virus. This finding caused consternation in the small town of some ten thousand people (*Vision Times*, 2018). It is well-known that sex bribes are common in China, according to the report in *Vision Times*. Junior officials wanting promotions send their wives to their superiors as bribes. Yang confessed that he had had sexual relationships with more than 30 women. If what he had were an ordinary sexually transmitted disease, victims might have dealt with it quietly without seeking outside help. However, AIDS can be life-threatening, and most people have little knowledge about it. As soon as the news of his carrying the AIDS virus broke out, many teachers and government workers, both female and male, rushed to the AIDS prevention center demanding to be tested. According to staff at the center, Yang's having the virus did not affect only his mistresses; his mistresses might give it to their husbands and to other male partners, and these males, in turn, might infect their other female partners (*Vision Times*, 2018).

8.3   THE (CORRUPT) ALLIANCE OF MULTINATIONAL CORPORATIONS AND POLITICIANS OF NON-RULE-BASED COUNTRIES

As we briefly discussed above, in order to access the untapped markets of labor and consumers in countries with weak institutional environments, multinational corporations and investors from rule-based countries must deal with the rulers (politicians) in these countries, who dictate the terms of entry for them. These terms are usually not based on fair and open public rules; rather, they tend to be secretive and private agreements where the executives of the multinational corporations provide private benefits to the rulers of the host countries, who, in turn, allow them to enter the markets. This pattern of investment and trade flows in the globalization of the last 25 years or so has led to an alliance of executives of multinational corporations and politicians of countries with weak institutional environments, facilitated and cemented by the bribery–corruption relationship.[2]

Such a corrupt alliance has also helped to bring about a new divide in the world, from the perspective of the winners and losers in globalization since the 1990s. The biggest winners in globalization are multinational corporations (mostly from developed, rule-based countries) and the politicians of non-rule-based countries (mostly those under dictatorships). They have won at the expense of various segments of their trading partners. The major losers have been the workers and industries in advanced economies (mostly rule-based countries). The natural environments of the host countries (the less developed countries under dictatorships) have fared worse when polluting industries from advanced economies have moved there. Workers from the less developed countries have gained, in the sense that investment by multinational corporations has created more job opportunities (although most of them work long hours in poor conditions). A hidden cost of the alliance has been the spread of the culture and practice of bribery and corruption to rule-based countries.

An interesting and worrisome phenomenon is that multinational corporations from mature democracies side with the dictatorships of the countries in which they do business. For example, Apple, Inc., a highly respected multinational corporation that champions all of the values commonly protected by the governments of mature democracies, (where Apple itself is based), apparently has double standards at home and abroad.

On February 16, 2016, Judge Sheri Pym of the Central California District Court required Apple, Inc. to bypass security functions on the cellphone used by Syed Rizwan Farook. Along with his wife Tashfeen Malik, Farook, inspired by the terrorist organization ISIS, opened fire at a pre-Christmas lunch for employees of the San Bernardino health department where he worked, killing fourteen. Both of the assailants were, themselves, killed later by police. Apple refused to comply with the court order to crack the code of the iPhone used by the terrorist.

According to Apple, it defied US law enforcement in order to protect individual privacy and human rights (Zetter, 2016).

In July 2017, at the request of the Chinese government, Apple removed anti-censorship tools from its China app store. The tools had been popular with Chinese users because they allowed them to circumvent what is commonly referred to as "the Great Firewall of China," a vast system of internet filters set up by the Chinese government to prevent its citizens from accessing political information about democracy and human rights. "Shame on Apple!" was a sentiment voiced on social media by some who felt that Apple was placing its commercial interests above the people's need to access information. Apple's response this time, contrary to its earlier response to the US government, was that it did so in order to meet China's regulatory requirements (Morris, 2017).

In 2018, the US government imposed tariffs on exports from China because the Chinese government had been using unfair and illegal practices related to trade in order to gain advantages from the U.S., such as market barriers for US firms entering China, high tariffs on US goods, the forcing of US firms to share technology, and stealing technologies and trade secrets from US companies. In an attempt to influence the US policies, the Chinese government called on the US firms doing business in China to complain and to put pressure on their home government on behalf of the Chinese government. Many of the US firms in China agreed to the call (CBS/AP, 2018).

To multinationals from mature democracies, siding with the dictator of their host country instead of the democratic government of their home country is a carefully calculated move: it is perfectly alright, and even fashionable, to criticize or oppose your own democratic government's policies, because in a mature democracy with sound rule of law, the democratic government cannot retaliate against a firm for criticizing or opposing its policies. But voicing concerns about any policies or any aspects of the government in a dictatorship is a big no-no, and all executives from mature democracies working in countries under dictatorships know this very well. If an executive thinks that a policy is unfair to his or her firm and voices this, both the executive and the firm will be treated more unfairly, and may even be kicked out of the country (Rosenberg, 2002).

8.4   THE EFFORT BY LARGE COUNTRIES TO BRIBE AND CORRUPT THE WORLD

So far, our discussion of the bribery–corruption relationship has been limited to non-government entities, such as people's and firms' bribing of government officials. However, such a limitation has ignored a new form of the bribery–corruption relationship that poses a challenge to the world with unprecedented scale and scope: the bribery of the world by the dictatorial government of a nation, especially of a large nation with a big and strong economy.

A key difference between dictatorships and democracies is that the former can use disproportionately more resources to achieve their goals. For example, the dictatorial government of a poor country may outspend the government of a rich democratic country in international aid, and, more ironically, the recipient country of the aid may have a much higher income level than that of the donor country. In spending money globally to buy influence and other advantages, no government in the world can match the Chinese government. Below is some anecdotal evidence.

8.4.1   Hanban/Confucius Institutes

Hanban is the colloquial abbreviation for a Chinese government agency called "the Office of the Chinese Language Council International." It was established in around 2004, with the following mission, according to its official website:

> Hanban/Confucius Institute Headquarters, as a public institution affiliated with the Chinese Ministry of Education, is committed to providing Chinese language and cultural teaching resources and services worldwide, it goes all out in meeting the demands of foreign Chinese learners and contributing to the development of multiculturalism and the building of a harmonious world.

According to a 2006 BBC report, the Chinese government initially committed $10 billion for operating the Confucius Institute program (BBC, 2006 cited from Wikipedia, 2015b). The operating cost for a Confucius Institute ranges from $100,000 to as much as $400,000. According to an article in *The Economist*, the Hanban's spending on Confucius Institutes is "considerable, and growing rapidly." In 2013, it was $278 million, more than six times as much as in 2006 (*The Economist*, 2014; Wikipedia, 2015b).

As of 2017, there are 525 Confucius Institutes and 1,113 Confucius Classrooms in 146 countries (Hanban, 2014).

There are a number of ironies associated with the Confucius Institutes. First, as Peter Wood, president of the National Association of Scholars in the USA, points out, "The philosopher's name is a smoke screen. These institutes have nothing to do with Confucius; they are instruments of China's statecraft" (Wood, 2018).

Second, while China's government has spent hundreds of millions in setting up Confucius Institutes in foreign countries, many of the host countries have much higher income levels than China. In the rural areas of China, millions of children do not have adequate education resources. Furthermore, "the Chinese Communist Party, which organizes and funds the Confucius Institutes through a state agency, the Hanban, is not known for altruistic cultural outreach" (Wood, 2018). According to an article in *Foreign Policy*, many Chinese view the spending on Confucius Institutes as a waste of money, and believe that that money would be better spent on building schools in poor rural areas of China (cited from Wikipedia, 2015b).

Perhaps the biggest irony is that the Chinese Communist Party was founded on an anti-Confucius platform in 1921. Its mobilizing slogan to start the party was "down with the shop of Confucius!" Since then, the Chinese Communist Party has labelled him the mastermind of all counter-revolutionary and anti-communist forces, and has waged many movements to eradicate his influence. Now, suddenly, and without any logical explanation, while still upholding its Marxism and Mao Zedong Thought (which is inherently anti-Confucius), the party appears to have embraced the old adversary as a dear friend. Even today, the conflicts between Confucius' philosophy and the ideology and practice of the Chinese Communist Party are many and can be seen in the Confucius Institutes. For example, Confucius says, "Teaching should not discriminate," but the Confucius Institutes discriminate against certain religious beliefs in hiring; bar people who are critical of the Chinese Communist Party from the Institutes' activities; and ban topics that the Chinese Communist Party does not like, such as Taiwan, Tibet, the 1989 Tiananmen Democracy Movement, and current affairs in China.

What is the reason for the about-face? Why does the party throw hundreds of millions of dollars around the world in the name of its old enemy? Perhaps we can get some clues from the speeches by the Chinese officials in charge of ideology and propaganda.

In 2010, Liu Yunshan, then the minister of propaganda of the Chinese Communist Party, made it quite clear: "We should actively carry out international propaganda battles on issues such as Tibet, Xinjiang, Taiwan, human rights, and Falun Gong. Our strategy is to proactively take our culture abroad ... We should do well in establishing and operating overseas cultural centers and Confucius Institutes" (quoted from Sahlins, 2015, p. 6).

In 2011, Li Changchun, the Chinese Communist Party leader in charge of ideology and propaganda at the time, explained that "The Confucius Institute is an appealing brand for extending our culture abroad. It has made an important contribution toward improving our soft power. The 'Confucius' brand has a natural attractiveness. Using the excuse of teaching Chinese language, everything looks reasonable and logical" (quoted from Sahlins, 2015, p. 1).

Ironically, both Liu Yunshan and Li Changchun are old enough to have witnessed the party's condemnation campaign against

Confucius during the Cultural Revolution. It is hard to believe that their 180-degree turn in their attitude toward Confucius is genuine.

So what do Confucius Institutes do in their host countries? According to a study on Confucius Institutes by the National Association of Scholars, "the institutes stifle academic freedom, censor teachers, engage in unlawful religious discrimination, disseminate Chinese propaganda, and violate norms of transparency" (Wood, 2018). The operations of the Confucius Institutes and Hanban's terms with the American hosting schools are not for the public to know. They are secret and off-limits (Peterson, 2017).

Why do some foreign universities want to host these institutes? According to Wood:

> First, colleges receive substantial financial support for hosting the institutes. Second, key academic administrators find themselves suddenly in demand as speakers in China. Third, the administrators discover that China tightly controls the number of Chinese students permitted to enroll at a particular American college. And fourth, China frequently offers the additional enticement to the college of opening an overseas program in China.
>
> Confucius Institutes, in short, become the first thread of a silk cocoon. For a relatively modest price, the Chinese government gains enormous influence over major American colleges and universities. And it gets privileged access to American campuses, from which it exercises other kinds of influence. (Wood, 2018)

8.4.2   Train Future Foreign Leaders in China

The Chinese government also sets aside quotas, scholarships and housing in universities in China for foreign applicants. It was reported that, in 2018, the Chinese government set aside $5.1 billion for scholarships for foreign students studying in China. For example, a foreign undergraduate student could get $9,108–$10,185 per year, while a foreign doctoral student could get as much as $15,353 per year (Radio Free Asia, 2018).

This takes educational resources away from Chinese students and is unfair. In 2018, many Chinese believed that the policy was unfair and were not happy about it. A group of rights lawyers wrote an open letter asking the government to reconsider the policy, and hundreds of parents who want their children to have a fair chance to compete for good colleges signed the letter. However, there is no sign that the government will reverse the policy anytime soon (Radio Free Asia, 2018).

In her article, "Beijing is cultivating the next generation of African elites by training them in China," Lily Kuo (2017) observed:

> China is particularly interested in the next generation of African elites. Last year [2016], Beijing announced it would invite 1,000 young African politicians for trainings in China, after hosting more than 200 between 2011 and 2015. Thousands of African students are pursuing undergraduate and graduate degrees in China on scholarship programs funded by Beijing. As of this year, more Anglophone African students study in China than the United States or the United Kingdom, their traditional destinations of choice.

To make sure such a strategic intention does not raise any suspicion, "Chinese officials are quick to say these scholarships and trainings are not an attempt to remake Africa in its own image" (Kuo, 2017).

8.4.3 Influence the Influencers

Citing a report by *Foreign Policy*, Josh Rogin, a *Washington Post* journalist, commented on "how former Hong Kong chief executive Tung Chee-hwa has spent money through his China-United States Exchange Foundation (CUSEF), funding research at the Johns Hopkins University School of Advanced International Studies, the Brookings Institution and elsewhere" (Rogin, 2017). (As vice chair-men of the Chinese People's Political Consultative Conference, Tung is a very high-level official in the Chinese government.) Rogin commented:

... as China exploits these [American academic] institutes' need for cash, examples of self-censorship mount. Researchers understand that their access to China depends on not ruffling feathers. Publishers agree to erase critical articles from journals to gain access to the Chinese markets.

By influencing the influencers, China gets Americans to carry its message to other Americans. (Rogin, 2017)

Glenn Tiffert, a visiting fellow at the Hoover Institute, agreed: "That's much more effective than having Chinese officials deliver those messages" (quoted from Rogin, 2017).

8.4.4 Thousand Talents Program

In 2008, the Chinese Government started a "Thousand Talents Program" to recruit leading international experts in scientific research, innovation, and entrepreneurship to work in China. The program was later, in 2010, elevated to become the top-level award given through China's National Talent Development Plan. The program gives the invitees two options: either working in China on a permanent basis, or short-term appointments. The short-term program "typically target[s] international experts who have full-time employment at a leading international university or research laboratory" (Wikipedia, 2018h). OODA Loop, an intelligence and security analyses website, reports that the US government is concerned about the program:

[The National Intelligence Council's] analysis of China's "Thousand Talents" program has named it a project to "facilitate the legal and illicit transfer of US technology, intellectual property and know-how" to China as part of the country's aggressive "toolkit for foreign technology acquisition." The program began in 2008 and is likely the largest and best funded of its kind in China. 44% of the program's 2,629 recruits specialize in medicine, life or health sciences, with 22% in applied industrial technologies, 8% in computer sciences and 6% in aviation/aerospace. The remainder have acquired economics, finance, and math specialties from the US. (OODA Analyst, 2018)

I interviewed a participant in the "Thousand Talents Program" who is a faculty member at a university in the USA. The interviewee told me that the Chinese hosting agency allows him to keep his job in the USA, while working in China. His Chinese hosting agency even pays his home university in the USA to buy his teaching time out, so that he does not have to teach at the US university during regular semesters and, thus, can work in China. In essence, the Chinese government, through the hosting agency in China, bribes the American faculty member (so that he can keep his regular job in the US and receive another salary in China) and his university (by giving the American university a grant to buy him time out from teaching).

8.4.5 Blue-Gold-Yellow

"Blue-Gold-Yellow" is a term introduced by Guo Wengui to describe the "bribe and corrupt" efforts by the Chinese government in the United States. Guo is a Chinese businessman in exile who claims to have had close ties with the Chinese government and to have worked for the government intelligence agency. In a news report about how the Chinese Communist Party targets the USA, *The Washington Beacon* cited him on the effort:

> ... China is engaged in a three-pronged campaign of subversion in the United States he labeled "Blue-Gold-Yellow," with each color standing for a different line of attack.
>
> Blue represents large-scale Chinese cyber and internet operations while gold represents China's use of money and financial power. The yellow is part of a plan to use sex to undermine American society. (Gertz, 2017)

If what Guo said is true, then the last two tactics, gold and yellow, are clearly bribery and corruption attempts.

8.4.6 Belt and Road

In 2013, the Chinese government initiated a very ambitious plan called the "One Belt and One Road Initiative" to help countries build their infrastructures. Later, the word "One" was dropped from the name to make it more universal. So it is now known as the "Belt and Road Initiative." It is estimated that the Belt and Road framework would provide up to $1 trillion in Chinese support for participating countries to help them develop their infrastructures. "[S]ome estimates list the Belt and Road Initiative as one of the largest infrastructure and investment projects in history, covering more than 68 countries, including 65% of the world's population and 40% of the global GDP as of 2017" (Wikipedia, 2018c).

The basic financial and economic arrangements for the initiative are that China will fund the infrastructure construction by loans, which will be paid back by the recipient country, and are secured by land or other valuable assets or rights in the recipient country. Some analysts believe that China does it "out of political motivation rather than real demand for infrastructure" (Wikipedia, 2018c). They feel that the initiative is "a way to extend Chinese influence" (Wikipedia, 2018c).

8.4.7 Foreign Aid

From 2000 to 2014, China provided aid in various forms, totaling $350 billion, to 140 countries and territories. During the same period, the USA spent about $395 billion in international aid, just slightly more than China. From 2009 onwards, China increased its aid. From 2009 to 2014, China's aid spend surpassed that of the USA, to become the highest in the world (AIDDATA, 2017). Though 2009–2014 is a short period, the trend is clear: there is little question that China is poised to become the largest aid-giving country in the world.

While the Chinese economy has been growing rapidly, China is still a low-income country, when measured on a per capita basis. In 2007, the mid-point of the period 2000–2014, per capita income in the USA was $48,061, whereas in China, that number is $2,695, one-eighteenth of the US income (World Bank, 2018). Data on poverty levels in China vary widely; depending on the definition of poverty and the data sources, the number of people below the poverty line (defined by the World Bank as $1.9/day) ranges from a low estimate of 27 million to a high of over 100 million. At any rate, China itself still faces the daunting task of lifting many people out of poverty. This is why global generosity by the Chinese government raises suspicion in the world and angers many people in China. The Chinese people have coined a term for this generous giving of money by the leadership of China: "da sa bi." Its literal meaning is "greatly throwing money," but it sounds like the Beijing colloquial term "da sha bi," which means "a great fool."

Why has the Chinese government embarked on a worldwide giving spree in recent years? What is it trying to achieve? A closer look at the breakdown of the aid may give us some clue. In the aid database compiled by a research team at the College of William and Mary, aid is classified as ODA, OOF, and Vague OF. ODA is "primarily intended for development and welfare," or commonly known as "aid." OOF is "primarily intended for commercial and representational purposes," and Vague OF is the type with "insufficient information" (AIDDATA, 2017).

For the USA, the majority of its foreign aid is ODA for development and welfare purposes, accounting for 85 percent of its total aid. In the case of China, that category only accounts for 23 percent. The bulk of the aid from China is classified as OOF, 61 percent, with the purpose of commerce and representation in the recipient country. Of the Chinese aid, there is $81 billion whose purpose is unknown (in the Vague OF category). If we assume that it is likely also to be used for commerce and representation, then OOF would account for 84 percent of the total Chinese aid. At any rate, we can safely conclude that aid by the Chinese government is not primarily for development and welfare, but for commercial and representational purposes.

In her article in *The Financial Times*, "China's globalisation paradox," Emily Feng observed:

> China exports its authoritarian model. There are already signs of this as Chinese companies test powerful commercial surveillance technologies and the country increases pressure on regional allies to extradite individuals back to China on the grounds of security and anti-corruption. Beijing's global-facing strategy will only amplify its ability to use economic might to muzzle freedom of speech and advocacy with its trade partners. (Feng, 2018)

8.5 EFFECTS OF CHINA'S BRIBE AND CORRUPT EFFORT

8.5.1 *Victims of China's Effort*

Who are the victims of China's bribery behavior? There seem to be no immediate and visible victims on the receiving end of the bribes. The countries, politicians, officials of international agencies, academics, etc. are all happy about the windfalls of funding and gifts. In most cases, the requirements seem harmless, at least to the recipient: vote along with China in international organizations such as the United Nations on issues such as Taiwan, human rights, or North Korea; and do not openly criticize the Chinese Communist Party or the Chinese government, which is synonymous with the party. Some requirements may cause a bit more concern, such as steering policies in favor of the Chinese government, or collecting information for or sharing technologies with the Chinese government. But, in general, there is no concrete victim, such as individuals or even organizations in the recipient country and in many cases, the bribees, the people or organizations that directly receive the funds, are benefiting from them, at least in the short run.

The adverse effect of this bribe and corrupt strategy is long-term. According to experts on China, the Chinese Communist Party is well known for its patience and its long-term orientation in its effort to achieve world dominance (Pillsbury, 2015; Wise, 2011). Unlike the

Russian government, whose strategy tends to be short-term and specific, such as interfering in an election with the goal of affecting specifically targeted candidates, the Chinese Communist Party does not, usually, have any specific goals in its effort to bribe and corrupt foreign countries. Rather, it aims to change the culture of the world. It invests, long-term, to nurture a positive attitude toward the party around the world. One of its objectives is to tell the world that the Chinese Communist Party and its government are equivalent to China. If someone criticizes the party or the government, then that person is anti-China and, therefore, must be denounced and shunned.

In fact, it does not take much for the Chinese government to buy off foreigners with power, skills, or influence. A card game that I use in my strategy class (introduced by Adam Brandenburger and Barry Nalebuff (1997)) can illustrate this point. I hold the 26 black cards and I hand out the 26 red cards to 26 students. A deal (a pairing) between a black card and a red card will be worth $100, and an unmatched card will be worthless. Accordingly, each student comes to me to make a deal on how we can split the $100. Since an unmatched card is worthless for the student as well as for me, the students have the same bargaining power as I do. Furthermore, it would be logical to assume that the students and I would split the $100 equally. However, I then publicly throw away two cards and begin the negotiation. Realizing that two of them will have no match, they are desperate to make any deals with me. In many deals, I only agree to give the student $1, keeping the lion's share for myself!

This is what the Chinese government is doing to Apple, and to the other influential people and entities, including to foreign governments. There are many firms and foreign governments eager to get opportunities or payments from China, but there is only one China, which is the equivalent of my openly discarding several cards from my hand in the card game. All foreign politicians and CEOs compete to please the Chinese government, in order to get their share. As a result, in this bribery–corruption game, the Chinese party-state is holding the whole country hostage, in order to play the foreign academics, politicians, governments, firms, and members of international organizations off against each other.

8.5.2 Can One Country Buy the World Off?

According to *The World Facts Book* of the CIA (CIA, 2018), in 2017, the size of the world's economy was $127 trillion, of which China (with $23 trillion) alone accounted for 18 percent, making China the world's largest economy in terms of purchasing power parity, surpassing the United States' $19 trillion. Unlike the USA, which is a mature democracy with strong checks and balances in government spending, the Chinese Communist Party has unchecked power and can mobilize the whole country's resources to achieve its goals. In other words, the extent to which the Chinese Communist Party can leverage its $23 trillion economy to buy and influence the world is much higher than the extent to which governments in mature democracies such as the United States or European countries can mobilize their economies to defend themselves, let alone the other smaller countries.

8.5.3 The USA versus China in Attempting to Influence the World

One could argue that the USA has also used its resources to "buy off" the whole world since the end of Second World War. However, there are several key differences between the USA and China in using their own resources in other countries.

First and most fundamentally, the two countries have categorically different political and economic systems, which define their different ways of funding foreign aid. The United States is a mature democracy. One of the most important principles of allocating government resources is that the branch of the government that approves the budget, such as the congress (or parliament), is separated from the branch that spends it, such as the executive branch. Not only do the two branches keep a close check on each other, but they must also both be accountable to the taxpayers whose votes determine their fates. If the taxpayers/voters believe that their taxes are being used to bribe foreign nations, they can voice their opposition and can ultimately change the practice. Thus, in the long run, bribery of the world by their government can be effectively corrected by the political mechanism built into a mature democracy (such as the United States). Furthermore, in a mature democracy with a free market such as the United States, the line between the government and the economy is reasonably clear: the government cannot take resources from firms to bribe foreign nations. Neither can it ask firms to bribe foreign nations on its behalf.

In China, in contrast, the Chinese Communist Party has total control over all of the branches of the government, including the legislative, the judiciary, and the executive branches. Frank Dikötter, a scholar of the Chinese Communist Party, calls such a political system a "Leninist one-party state" (Dikötter, cited from Hamilton, 2018, p. 276), which I will call the "party-state." The party-state makes, approves, and spends the budget single-handedly. Since it controls all of the state-owned firms such as the giant oil firms, the telecom firms, and the banks, the party can use its resources for whatever purpose it sees fit, including bribing foreign nations. Furthermore, it can even ask private firms to carry out its bribery activities, since the survival of the private firms (and even the personal fates of their CEOs, to a large extent) depends on the party-state.

Second, the USA and China have different ideologies. The official ideology of American governments (federal, state, and local governments) is to respect universal human rights and to obey the rule of law. This ideology is best manifested in the American Declaration of Independence:

> We hold these truths to be self-evident, that all men are created equal, that they are endowed by their creator with certain inalienable Rights, that among these are Life, Liberty and the pursuit of Happiness. (United States Declaration of Independence, 1776)

This is not only the official ideology, but it is also the ideology of the American people. The government is merely created by the people in order to safeguard their rights. Projecting this ideology internationally, the United States, either explicitly or implicitly, expects or prefers that other nations, including the recipients of aid, respect universal human rights and the rule of law.

In contrast, the official ideology of the Chinese Communist Party is Marxism, Leninism, Mao Zedong Thought, and now Xi Jinping Thought. The Chinese constitution repeatedly states the following, in various versions:

> Under the leadership of the Communist Party of China and the guidance of Marxism-Leninism, Mao Zedong Thought, Deng Xiaoping Theory, the important thought of Three Represents, the Scientific Outlook on Development, and the Xi Jinping Thought on Socialism with Chinese Characteristics for a New Era, the Chinese people of all nationalities will continue to adhere to the people's democratic dictatorship and the socialist road. (Chinese Government, 2018)

The basic premise of this ideology is that communism/socialism is the ideal state of human societies. The second premise is that the Communist Party is the only party that can lead the world to realize the ideal. Given its mission, it must impose a dictatorship on society. Everyone must obey the party's rule without dissent. Since 2013, under the leadership of Xi Jinping, the Chinese Communist Party has made it very clear that it rejects universal values such as respecting human rights and the rule of law, and it will not democratize. Under this ideology, the party has made China a police state in which the people have no freedom of expression and cannot criticize the party. Projecting this ideology internationally, the Chinese Communist Party wants other nations to follow its view of "global governance" and to support its agenda, and it silences any criticism about its ideology or practices.

In terms of its track record in international affairs, even though the United States has given the most international aid and has played the largest role in international conflicts since the Second World War, it has never taken or occupied other countries, nor has it unilaterally claimed any international land or sea. China (the party-state) has only become powerful recently, so its track record is short, but we have already seen its expansion into international waters such as the South China Sea. This has caused concerns globally, and especially among China's neighbors such as the Philippines, Vietnam, and Japan.

In conclusion, the intent to bribe and the practice of bribery and corruption of the world by the party-state of China is categorically different from the USA's aid program. Currently, most countries in the world are in various forms of democracies, with ideologies that are in fundamental conflict with the ideology of the Chinese Communist Party. If the Chinese Communist Party's goal is using the initiatives and efforts reviewed above to persuade the world to accept, or at least to be acquiescent to, its ideology and its way of governing, this would be a major concern for the world.

NOTES

1. Schlesinger, J. 2017. How China swallowed the WTO. *Wall Street Journal*, November 1 (www.wsj.com/articles/how-china-swallowed-the-wto-1509 551308): Accessed Aug 13, 2018.
2. In general, when firms from non-rule-based countries enter rule-based countries, they do not need to bribe the politicians of the country they want to enter, as the terms of market entry are publicly stipulated and are consistently and fairly applied to everyone.

9　Conclusion: Challenges and
　Hopes in Fighting Corruption
　Globally

> In August 2018, "Argentine police raided two homes of ex-President
> Cristina Kirchner, in the latest graft probe involving a former Latin
> American president as a sweeping anticorruption movement takes hold in
> the region . . . The probe is the latest example of the reckoning that was
> unthinkable in Latin America just a few years ago: More than a dozen
> powerful ex-presidents from across the political spectrum are under
> criminal scrutiny or already in jail for corruption." Starting with
> "Operation Car Wash" four years ago, two ex-presidents, Dilma Rousseff
> and Luiz Inacio Lula da Silva, fell in Brazil. Recently, Panama's ex-
> president Ricardo Martinelli was extradited from the U.S. to face charges
> of corruption. El Salvador sentenced ex-president Tony Saca for 10 years
> for embezzlement, and is seeking the extradition of another ex-president
> Mauricio Funes for stealing millions of state funds. In Guatemala, ex-
> president Alvaro Colom "is barred from leaving the country" for fraud
> investigation, while another ex-president Otto Perez is already in jail.
> In Peru, four ex-presidents are investigated. In July 2018, Ecuador is
> investigating ex-president Rafael Correa and has convicted his vice pre-
> sident for corruption. In Colombia, ex-president Alvaro Uribe is under
> investigation for corruption. According to experts in the U.S. and Latin
> Americans, "[t]he crackdown has been enabled by better-trained and more
> independent prosecutors, as well as legal changes." All these are signs of
> maturing democracy in the region.
>
> –"Argentine Ex-President's Homes Raided in Graft Probe," *The Wall
> Street Journal*[1]

Seventy years ago, in his political novel, *1984*, George Orwell painted
the grim picture of a society in which the dictator can systematically
cover up the corrupt activities committed by him and by his cronies to
ensure that corruption will go on forever: "He who controls the past
controls the future. He who controls the present controls the past"
(Orwell, 1949). As we have discussed in this book, his concern was not
unfounded: a powerful dictatorial regime is not only capable of

corrupting the country that it controls, but it is also capable of corrupting the world, if it goes unchecked.

Fortunately, there is hope. As we can see from the sweeping anticorruption movement in Latin America, the maturing of democracy and the rule of law is enabling countries to establish and to strengthen their anticorruption ability and their ability to hold the powerful accountable. In my concluding remarks, I will first summarize the key points discussed in the book, with a reminder that the new trend in the globalization of corruption makes Orwell's worry more relevant than ever. Next, I will discuss our hope in fighting the globalization of corruption.

9.1 KEY POINTS DISCUSSED IN THE BOOK

9.1.1 Bribe Takers and Givers

In order to provide the necessary background for the main arguments of the book, in its early chapters (Chapters 2 and 3), we considered the general concept of "corruption" and examined it from both the briber's and the bribee's perspectives. A dissection and examination followed the theoretical underpinnings that the most fundamental reason for corruption to exist is the power and control of the government over the economy and social life. More specifically, if we want to pinpoint the cause (or the exogenous variable), and the result (or the endogenous variable) between the bribe givers and the bribe takers in the bribery–corruption relationship, the answer is straightforward, from the theoretical underpinnings: it is the bribe taker who is the cause of corruption. Based on this logic, we first discussed the bribe takers, and then, the bribe givers.

Before we delved into the bribe takers and givers, we provided an overview on the bribery–corruption relationship in terms of winners and losers. Interestingly, while the bribe takers are always the winners, the bribe payers are not always the losers (see Table 2.1). There are at least three types of relationship: (1) corruption without theft; (2) corruption with theft; and (3) corruption without victims.

In corruption without theft, corrupt officials do not steal directly from the state coffers. Instead, they impose an extra charge on the briber. The briber, forced to pay a bit extra, is the loser and, therefore, is naturally angry at the corrupt official. The logical conclusion is that the briber will turn the official in, if the opportunity arises. In the second and third types, the bribers are winners and, thus, they have little incentive to denounce the corrupt official, making cleaning up corruption more difficult. Furthermore, in the third type, corruption without victims, even the society at large is not a loser, at least in an economic sense. In terms of the political system and culture, corruption without victims stifles social mobility by favoring people with powerful connections; undermines fairness and confidence in the government; and nurtures a culture that tolerates bribery and corruption.

Reviewing the types of corruption in various political-economic systems, we discussed three models from the industrial organization perspective: (1) the big mafia model; (2) the many small mafias model; and (3) the competitive model. We also discussed the way in which the tenure of the bribe taker and the types of political systems affect economic growth (see Chapter 2). These discussions provided the necessary background for our discussion on the bribe payers.

In Chapter 3, we first discussed the motivations of the bribe payers: why do they bribe? We distinguished two types of bribery. The first is the type in which people and firms engage in it out of necessity. This tends to correspond to the "corruption without theft" that we reviewed in Chapter 2. Bribery out of necessity is also termed "petty corruption." The second type is bribery for profit. This type can be described as "grand corruption." While bribery out of necessity tends to be forced, bribery for profit tends to be voluntary. Ultimately, the propensity of people and firms to pay bribes is determined by the macro environment of a society. In a society in which officials are mostly corrupt, refusing to pay bribes is not a viable option, in the long run. However, the collective efforts by people and firms to refrain from bribing can make a difference (Li & Ouyang, 2007; Yadav & Mukherjee, 2016).

Together, Chapters 2 and 3 examined the mechanisms of bribery and corruption and provided the background for the main arguments of the book that appear in its later chapters.

9.1.2 The Importance of the Governance Environment in Shaping the Forms and Outcomes of Corruption

In Chapter 4, we introduced the concept of the governance environment, which is the set of political, legal, and social institutions prevalent in a society that collectively facilitate or constrain the choice of governance mechanism by people or by firms. On the basis of the degree to which public rules are developed in a society, we distinguished two types of governance environment: the rule-based governance environment and the non-rule-based governance environment (or the weak institutional environment). Among the non-rule-based environments, we further distinguished relation-based governance and clan-based governance. This distinction has important implications for the economic outcomes of corruption. A key feature of relation-based governance is that, when the scale and scope of the economic activities are small, it can be more efficient than rule-based governance. Our analysis of the governance environment lays a foundation that allows us to address a key argument of our book: why some countries thrive despite corruption.

9.1.3 Why Do Some Countries Thrive despite Corruption?

In Chapter 5, we addressed a major puzzle in the study of corruption, that is: among the corruption-ridden societies, while many experience slow or negative economic growth, why do some achieve rapid economic growth?

Scholars of corruption have long speculated that corruption might be efficiency-enhancing where a government bureaucracy is stifling and its officials shirk. In such an environment, people and firms (are forced to) pay bribes to officials to speed up their work –

the so-called "greasing the bureaucratic wheel" argument. This argument may partially explain the motivation for petty corruption, but it fails to explain, theoretically, why some countries achieve remarkable economic development and rapid GDP growth under rampant corruption.

Based on our discussion of relation-based versus clan-based governance in the preceding chapter, in Chapter 5, we argued that the extensive and overlapping private networks, which essentially act like trust, enable corruption to be more efficiency-enhancing in relation-based societies. In contrast, the lack of trust beyond the family in clan-based societies has made corruption more predatory, dragging down economic performance.

9.1.4   The Symbiotic Relationship between Corruption and Anticorruption in Dictatorships

An important regime type in non-rule-based countries is the dictatorship, in which corruption is a major feature. In Chapter 6, we argued that corruption and periodic anticorruption campaigns are two important institutional arrangements necessary for the survival of dictatorial regimes.

The political system of dictatorship relies on three types of controls: bureaucratic, ideological, and military controls (MacFarquhar, 2016). In order to motivate its officials in both the bureaucracy and the armed forces to work for the regime, the dictator must pay them well. However, reliance on a lofty ideology (such as the communist ideology) prohibits the regime from formally and publicly rewarding its officials with high salaries and generous benefits. Instead, the dictator, either implicitly or explicitly, allows the officials to use their powers to enrich themselves, which means that corruption is institutionalized in, and is a necessary part of, dictatorial rule. Unfortunately, the corrupt officials' insatiable appetite for wealth tends to drive the level of corruption out of control, causing massive discontent in the society, which in turn threatens the survival of the regime.

To pacify the people and to strengthen the regime's legitimacy, the dictator must periodically launch anticorruption campaigns to bring down some highly visible corrupt officials. But these anticorruption campaigns cannot and will not eradicate corruption, for without the privilege of enriching themselves on the job, the bureaucracy and the armed forces will not work effectively and efficiently for the dictator. Furthermore, without the rule of law, anticorruption campaigns under dictatorships tend to be arbitrary in nature, and inevitably are political purges and become tools for internal power struggles. As a result, the cycle of corruption and anticorruption campaigns is institutionalized. But such symbiotic relationships are, by their nature, intrinsically inefficient and unstable. A regime can maintain the fragile balance between the waves of corruption and the anticorruption campaigns, but the economy tends to suffer between booms (associated with corruption) and busts (associated with anticorruption crackdowns). Furthermore, as the 2011 revolution in Tunisia shows, once the symbiotic relationship is off balance, the regime can be toppled.

9.1.5   The Inevitability of the Transition from a Highly Corrupt to a Clean Society

According to governance environment theory, the cost advantage of relation-based governance will decrease as the scope and scale of the economic activities increase, from local, to national, to international. In order to be competitive in the global marketplace, relation-based societies must move away from a reliance on personal connections to an embracing of public rules. Following this logic, the transition from relation-based governance to rule-based governance is inevitable. Bribery and corruption, which are an intrinsic part of relation-based governance, will have to be eradicated once a society adopts public rules to govern socioeconomic activities because, by their nature, public rules are transparent and fair to everyone, leaving no room for opaque, private deals that only people with personal connections with power can obtain. In Chapter 7, we discussed the inevitability of and the possible paths toward transition, as well as the issues associated with transition.

A main challenge to the transition is the governance vacuum created by the fall of the "big mafia" in the old regime and the lack of power and experience in the new government. The governance vacuum allows many politicians to seize control over a local area or an industry and extort more bribes. Furthermore, due to the lack of a centralized authority and the lack of coordination among the independent politicians, the bribe payers may not receive the promised public goods. This is why, in many transitioning countries, corruption becomes worse than it had been before under the dictator.

Another, less known, challenge for the transition is the tendency to establish too many new rules. Under the dictatorship, people suffered so much abuse of power that they lost their trust in authorities. Once the dictator is gone, and the opportunity to reform or recreate the governing system arises, they want to constrain the power of officials as much as possible. The experience of some transitioning societies shows that people prefer a governance system in which the personal discretion of officials is completely eliminated and in which every decision is based on impersonal public rules. However, creating too many rules, and overreliance on them with little flexibility, may stifle efficiency and effectiveness in governance. As transitioning societies proceed to build their governance systems, they need to nurture public trust. Good public rules cannot function well without basic trust.

9.1.6 The Globalization of Corruption by Countries with Weak Institutional Environments

The world is facing unprecedented challenges posed by countries with institutional environments that are weak in fighting corruption. First, through increasingly globalized investment and trade, corruption spreads from its hubs, which tend to be in countries with weak institutional environments.

The second issue is relatively new and presents a challenge that is unprecedented and can be far-reaching: the Chinese party-state, which controls the largest economy (based on purchasing power parity) with a weak institutional environment, is leveraging the enormous economic resources of China to bribe the world to advance its ideology and interests globally. It is in this book that we first identify this new form of corruption in which a government of a country uses the country's resources to bribe the rest of the world. This poses several important questions, not only to the scholars of corruption, but to the entire international community. Why is China doing it? What are the consequences of such corruption for the world? While addressing these questions thoroughly is beyond the scope of this book, I would like to offer my preliminary thoughts on why China is doing it.

The ideology and the political control of the Chinese Communist Party are in fundamental conflict with the ideology of democracy; this is well known, and there is nothing new about it. In the past seventy years or so, since the Chinese Communist Party took over China in 1949, the divergent forces have lived alongside each other in the world relatively peacefully, with the Communist Party ruling China under communism and the developed world (mostly Western Europe, the USA, and other mature democracies) adhering to democracy and the rule of law. The reason that they have coexisted in peace is because China has not only been weak economically and militarily, but also because the party-state shut China off from the outside world.

Now, after more than three decades of rapid economic growth, China has become the largest economy in the world (measured in purchasing power parity), thanks to its open-door policy and its effort to go global. Most scholars and leaders of international communities had predicted that, with economic prosperity, China would democratize. However, contrary to their expectations, the Chinese Communist Party has not allowed China to democratize, and continues to subject the country to its anti-democracy, anti-rule of law, and anti-universal human rights ideology. In order to maintain its ideology and, therefore, its rule, the party does what Orwell predicted: it erases the atrocities committed by the party in history, controls what people say, and paints a portrait of a glorious future (the "China dream").

The problem of maintaining control is that, with its involvement with international business and its reliance on the internet, China is no longer closed. Foreign ideas and cultures have come to China, and vice versa. The leaders of the Chinese Communist Party clearly realize that their ideology has little appeal worldwide. Thus, if it allows foreign ideologies to freely enter China to compete with the party's ideology, the result will be the demise of its ideology and then, logically, of the party's rule. On the other hand, shielding the country from the invasion of foreign ideologies is becoming increasingly unfeasible, since China depends on international interactions more than ever for its economic survival and prosperity. This leaves only one option, given that the Chinese Communist Party does not want to give up its ideology: make the outside ideologies favorable to it. Using money, rather than (or along with) guns, to make the world adhere to or at least respect its ideology is very appealing. The sheer size of the Chinese economy and the party's virtually total control of it allow the party to mobilize disproportionally large amount of resources to buy off foreign entities: governments, international organizations, multinational corporations, academics, and even ordinary people. If the above logical analysis holds, we will see more efforts by the party-state to use China's economic resources to influence the world, especially for ideological reasons. Scholars of corruption should pay more attention to this type of corruption and should study its effects and the corresponding policies that may be undertaken by other countries.

9.2 HOPES IN THE GLOBAL FIGHT AGAINST THE GLOBALIZATION OF CORRUPTION

In releasing its most recent Corruption Perception Index in 2017, Transparency International warned the world that "[t]his year's

Corruption Perceptions Index highlights that the majority of countries are making little or no progress in ending corruption ... more than two-thirds of countries score below 50, with an average score of 43" (100 = least corrupt, 0 = most corrupt (Transparency International, 2017). Not surprisingly, almost all of these countries have weak institutional environments (Freedom House, 1972–2018; Transparency International, 2017).

Despite the grim picture of corruption, there are hopes for fighting corruption globally, aided by efforts and policy recommendations by governments, volunteer groups, journalists, and international organizations such as Transparency International. In concluding the book, and based on our discussions in the book, I would like to highlight a few measures that may help to fight corruption in countries with weak institutional environments.

9.2.1 The Power of Information

Rulers of non-rule-based countries maintain their rule by monopolizing the flow of information. They deliberately manipulate and distort public information in order to cover up their corrupt acts. Publicly, they project an image of a clean government working hard for the people, while privately, they loot the country. Once their corrupt acts are exposed, people are outraged, not only by their greed and crimes, but, perhaps to a greater degree, by their hypocrisy. This is why dictators view the free flow of information as a grave threat to them.

In its press release on the 2017 Corruption Perception Index, Transparency International highlighted the alarming fact that "[e]very week at least one journalist is killed in a country that is highly corrupt," and "of all journalists who were killed in the last six years, more than 9 out of 10 were killed in countries that score 45 or less on the index" (Transparency International, 2017).

All of these situations suggest that what dictators are most afraid of is also the most effective weapon in fighting corruption.

In 2015, some 11.5 million secret documents created by the Panamanian law firm and corporate service provider Mossack

Fonseca for wealthy individuals (including politicians in many countries) were leaked by an anonymous source. The leaked documents (known as "the Panama papers") shocked the world by exposing shady financial transactions and ownerships in secret companies held by current and former presidents, prime ministers, and kings and their families, across many countries. For example, the documents exposed at least five incumbent state or government leaders, two former state heads, five former prime ministers, and 51 families related to state heads, prime ministers, and kings. The exposure has caused a political earthquake and governance crisis that has rocked the cabinets and parliaments in many countries and has caused several state leaders to resign or to be investigated (Wikipedia, 2016b). This case shows the power of the free flow of information in exposing and fighting corruption.

Transparency International made five recommendations for governments and businesses to strengthen the free flow of information to fight corruption, including: (1) encourage free speech, independent media, political dissent, and a civil society; (2) minimize regulations on media; (3) promote laws that protect free access of information; (4) leverage international organizations' efforts to increase the free flow of information, and (5) increase disclosure by governments and businesses (Transparency International, 2017).

9.2.2   *What Businesses Can Do: Organize*

In Chapter 3, we introduced a mathematical model that depicts the roles of firms and the governance environment, their interactions, and their effect on the overall corruption level in a society. We showed that the effect of firms resisting the paying of bribes is multiplicative: if many firms collectively refuse to pay bribes, their effect is more powerful than being merely additive. Together, they exert an effect that is larger than an arithmetic sum, because first, if a firm knows that its competitors are on its side in fighting corruption and will do the same as it does, the firm will be more confident and more willing to say no to bribery. Second, if firms organize as an association, the collective voice of the organization carries more weight and, therefore, is more effective.

In a Transparency International study entitled "The role of business associations and chambers of commerce in the fight against corruption," author Maira Martini commented that "Companies are more likely to behave ethically and act against corruption if they are confident that their competitors also adhere to the same ethical standards. Business associations and chambers of commerce can potentially offer a good platform for companies operating in a given sector to collectively engage in the fight against corruption and level the playing field between competitors" (Martini, 2013, p. 1). The author listed several ways in which these organizations can help firms refuse to pay bribes, including facilitating collective action, advocating for reforms in the governments to improve transparency and accountability, and helping firms that adopt the best practices in corporate integrity (Martini, 2013).

In a study on how to reduce corruption in dictatorships, authors Yadav and Mukherjee argue that national business associations "organized by and representing private-sector small- and medium-scale firms" can play an effective role in curbing corruption in societies ruled by dictators (Yadav & Mukherjee, 2016).

9.2.3 The Transition from Non-Rule-Based to Rule-Based (Democratic) Governance: A Necessary Step toward a Clean Society

For countries with weak institutional environments, the ultimate solution to the corruption problem is to embrace the rule-based way. An effective way to achieve it is through democratization, despite the fact that corruption may worsen during the transition.

The phenomenal economic performance of some non-rule-based countries with rampant corruption, such as China, versus the virtual economic chaos in some democratizing countries has challenged our faith in democracy's ability to deliver economic prosperity and has forced us to rethink the effect of corruption on economic development.

In Chapters 4 and 5, using our theory of the governance environment, we showed that it is the extensive and overlapping private networks that have made corruption more efficiency-enhancing. We also showed that, as the scale and scope of a relation-based economy expand, reliance on private connections will be increasingly less competitive cost-wise, and thus, the relation-based economy must make the transition to rule-based governance.

In our study on the relationship between corruption, regime type, and economic growth that we briefly reviewed in Chapters 2 and 6, my coauthors and I examined the corruption level of three types of country: countries under dictatorship, countries in (democratic) transition, and mature democracies (Alon et al., 2016). We found that the levels of corruption in dictatorships, transitioning countries, and mature democracies are 0.41, 0.66, and –0.21, respectively (a high, positive number means high corruption). This finding shows that corruption has been found to be worse during the transition than it was under the dictatorship. However, this finding also suggests that as the democratic system of the transitioning country matures, corruption will decrease. The empirical evidence strongly supports the view that democracy and the rule of law, or the rule-based governance system, are the ultimate solution to the corruption problem. Keep in mind that this does not mean that corruption does not exist in mature democracies. Rather, mature democracies have a corruption level that is substantially lower than the corruption level in countries with weak institutional environments, and mature democracies have fair, transparent, and efficient rules to systematically clean up corruption.

9.3   POLICY AND STRATEGIC CONSIDERATIONS DURING THE TRANSITION

While we are fully aware that each business situation is different, and that the application of what we have discussed in this book has to be made by business executives in specific situations, I will highlight several general points below that may help both business executives and policy makers in dealing with relation-based societies and with the transition from relation-based to rule-based governance.

For countries with weak institutional environments, the transition to rule-based governance is hard and dangerous. Governments of mature democracies can help them to achieve it. Policy makers in mature democracies, as well as international agencies, should promote democratization and, at the same time, they should help those countries undergoing transition to limit the period of chaos. In addition, the policy makers in countries undergoing transition should make efforts to curb corruption in fledgling democracies and to restructure their bureaucracies to minimize dukedom (i.e., the "many small mafias" situation) that tends to increase corruption by multiple independent government agencies.

9.3.1 Relying on Private Relationships Can Be a Double-Edged Sword[2]

It is vital for a foreign player entering into a non-rule-based market to invest in establishing reliable relationships in the local market. In doing so, the foreign player should consider two caveats. First, using relations to circumvent formal rules may be illegal, even in a relation-based society. Second, when the foreign player uses relations to gain advantage in the local market, its partners and competitors may also use relations to try to outcompete it. And local partners or competitors may have stronger relationships within the power circle. In the early 1990s, McDonald's obtained a prime location in Beijing through guanxi, only to find that a Hong Kong businessman, Li Ka-shing, who had a stronger guanxi, had McDonald's evicted in favor of his own real estate development project (Chew, 1994).

9.3.2 Beware of the Governance Vacuum during the Transition

The vacuum created by the transition (see Chapter 7, section 7.3.2.) is especially dangerous for foreign investors and firms. As outsiders, they see new investment and business opportunities created by the newly promulgated laws and regulations and so rush in to do business, without realizing that the laws and regulations are routinely ignored and that the insiders see the vacuum created by the transition as an opportunity to loot (Li, 1999).

9.3.3 Beware of Rigid and Many Formal Rules during the Transition

Firms that enter a transition country that has recently established many new rigid formal rules must make a strategic choice on how to operate in the market. Broadly speaking, they have two options.

The first option is to be patient and follow the (many) new rules. At the same time, the firm may try to persuade the government to reduce some of the rules that are unnecessary and that stifle business activities. The firm should also ask its association, such as the chamber of commerce, to persuade the government to reduce these inefficient rules. As the transition deepens, and as public trust increases, the government should streamline its bureaucracy to make it more flexible and efficient.

The second option may be more effective and efficient but, at the time, it may also be less ethical (or even illegal) from a rule-based perspective. If the firm's executives hold the view that "when in Rome, do as the Romans do" (see the "relativist approach" in Chapter 3), they should make an effort to establish relationships with well-connected local players, as we showed in Chapters 4 and 5. Once the foreign firm becomes a new insider through a series of overlapping private networks, it should quickly learn the hidden informal rules of the game in order to overcome the obstacles erected by the formal rules. In this regard, local partners or consultants are very useful in helping to navigate through the maze of bureaucracy.

Every firm must evaluate the environment, its strategic goals, and its operating philosophy to decide which option to use.

9.3.4 The Role of Government in the Transition[3]

The role of the government in a society undergoing the transition from relation-based to rule-based governance environment is severalfold.

First, assuming that the government is actively pushing through the transition, it should effectively and efficiently deal with the resistant forces, which are the vested interest groups that hold deeply entrenched positions in the private relational networks. The government must be able to design and implement incentives for them to support the transition. In other words, the government needs to use its power and resources to compensate the vested interest groups, so that they can part with their sunk capital in the established relations without strong resistance.

Second, the government should make a great effort to minimize the social disruption associated with the transition. A radical transition that dismantles the old relation-based way almost overnight tends to cause great social upheaval and a dislocation of social groups and segments and tends to make the government unable to effectively and efficiently manage the society. However, there is always a trade-off between the speed of the transition and the stability during the transition.

The Russian model of transforming from communism (a non-rule-based system) toward a more rule-based system was characterized by a revolutionary change, or what is commonly known as the "big bang" approach, or "shock therapy." The intent was to give the old communism a powerful electric shock to knock it out; then, when the society woke up, it was under capitalism!

By contrast, institutional change in China is slow and is focused on the economic dimension only, with the political dictatorship being preserved, prompting some scholars to question whether it is actually a transition toward a rule-based system (see review in Li, 2014). The most important feature of the Chinese "transition" is that it is under the absolute control of the Communist Party, which calls its strategy "feeling the stones when crossing the river," or "gradualism."

The verdict is still out on which approach is better, and there are not even any commonly agreed upon criteria to use to evaluate them. While there is little dispute that China's economic growth has been

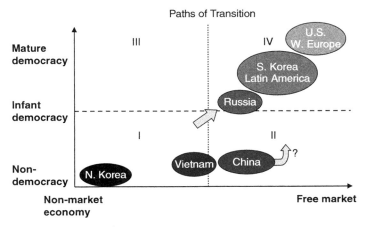

FIGURE 9.1 Paths of transition

faster than Russia's, in terms of institutional development in the
political and economic systems, Russia is slightly ahead of China.

The Russian political system is in the early stage of democracy,
with an aggregate political freedom score of 20 (0 = least free, 100 =
most free), while China is still under the communist dictatorship,
with an aggregate political freedom score of 14 (Freedom House,
1972–2018). In Red Square, in the center of Moscow, several actors
impersonating Putin, Lenin, Stalin, and one of the tsars compete for
audiences, and aspiring politicians give speeches. In Tiananmen
Square, in the center of Beijing, hundreds of police and security personnel in uniforms or in plain clothes patrol the area. Anyone who
attempts to give a speech is subdued and is put into a van at lightning
speed.

Figure 9. 1. provides a map of the major types of political and
economic systems in the world, as well as paths toward transition.
Quadrant I includes countries that are politically nondemocratic and
that economically follow a state central planning system that bans
private ownership. All of the former communist countries (Russia,
Central and Eastern European countries, China, Vietnam, etc.) once

belonged to Quadrant I, but there are not many countries left there. Today, probably only North Korea and Cuba still belong there. Countries in Quadrant II are those in which the government maintains nondemocratic rule (mostly authoritarian or totalitarian) but permits private ownership and markets, such as China and Vietnam. There are no countries that fit Quadrant III, since mature democracies with checks and balances cannot ban private ownership and centralize all economic activities. The most developed, rule-based countries are in Quadrant IV, which is also the goal for most transitioning economies. Based on the theory of governance environment presented in this book, the transition is inevitable because, as their markets expand from local to international, the non-rule-based countries will lose their cost advantage and thus will not be able to compete with rule-based countries. In conclusion, the question is not *whether* they will move to Quadrant IV, but *when* and *how* they will get there.

NOTES

1. Dube, R. 2018. Argentine ex-president's homes raided in graft probe. *The Wall Street Journal*, August 24.
2. Taken from Li, S. 2009. *Managing International Business in Relation-Based versus Rule-Based Countries*. New York: Business Expert Press.
3. Taken from Li, S. (2009).

References

AIDDATA. 2017. China's Global Development Footprint. College of William and Mary (www.aiddata.org/china). Accessed July 21, 2018.

Alon, I., Li, S., & Wu, J. 2016. Corruption, regime type, and economic growth. *Public Finance and Management*, 16(4): 332–361.

Anderson, J., & Narus, J. A. 1990. A model of distributor firm and manufacturer firm working partnership. *Journal of Marketing*, 54(1): 42–58.

Arrow, K. 1972. Gifts and exchanges. *Philosophy and Public Affairs*, 1(4): 343–362.

Baike. 2016. The 2014 group corruption of Shenzhen Custom. Baidu Baike (https://baike.baidu.com/item/2014年深圳海关腐败窝案). Accessed July 10, 2018.

Barboza, D. 2012. Billions in hidden riches for family of Chinese leader. *The New York Times*, October 25.

Barro, R. 1997. *Determinants of Economic Growth: A Cross-Country Empirical Study*. Cambridge MA: The MIT Press.

Barro, R., & Lee, J. 2000. International data on educational attainment updates and implications. NBER Working Paper Series, No. 7911.

BBC. 2012. India's bureaucracy is 'worst in Asia'. BBC News, January 12 (www.bbc.com/news/world-asia-india-16523672). Accessed July 1, 2018.

BBC. 2018a. Brazil corruption scandals: All you need to know. BBC News, April 8 (www.bbc.com/news/world-latin-america-35810578). Accessed October 25, 2018.

BBC. 2018b. Malaysia 1MDB: Ex-PM Najib arrested by anti-corruption officials. BBC News, July 3 (www.bbc.com/news/world-asia-44693275). Accessed July 9, 2018.

BBC. 2018c. Argentina notebook scandal: Driver details 'decade of bribes'. BBC, August 2 (www.bbc.com/news/world-latin-america-45049064). Accessed August 26, 2018.

Becker, G. S. 1968. Crime and punishment: An economic approach. *Journal of Political Economy*, 76(2): 169–217.

Berlinger, J. 2012. Why China should study Singapore's Anti-Corruption Strategy. *Business Insider*, December 6.

Bhargava, V., & Bolongaita, E. 2004. *Challenging Corruption in Asia: Case Studies and Framework for Action*. Washington, DC: The World Bank.

Bjørnskov, C. 2006. Determinants of generalized trust: A cross-country comparison. *Public Choice*, 130(1): 1–21.

Bloomberg News. 2012. Xi Jinping Millionaire relations reveal fortunes of Elite. Bloomberg News, June 29 (www.bloomberg.com/news/articles/2012-06-29/xi-jinping-millionaire-relations-reveal-fortunes-of-elite). Accessed August 12, 2018.

Bradsher, R. 2004. Informal lenders in China pose risks to banking system, *The New York Times*, November 9.

Brandenburger, A., & Nalebuff, B. 1997. *Co-opetition*. New York: Doubleday.

Bueno de Mesquita, B., Smith, A., Siverson, R. M., & Morrow, J. D. 2003. *Logic of Political Survival*. Cambridge: MIT Press.

CBS/AP. 2018. China urges U.S. companies to lobby Washington on trade. CBS News, July 12 (www.cbsnews.com/news/china-urges-u-s-companies-to-lobby-washington-on-trade/). Accessed July 20, 2018.

CCTV. 2016. Anticorruption: 20.1 Billion Yuan: What to do with money recovered from corrupt officials? China Central Televison, November 17 (http://m.news.cctv.com/2016/11/17/ARTIVqCYcS3jo5mTy2sdUYOt161117_2.shtml). Accessed July 15, 2018.

Cheung, Y. L., Rau, P. R., & Stouraitis, A. 2012. How much do firms pay as bribes and what benefits do they get? Evidence from corruption cases worldwide. NBER Working Paper Series.

Chew, A. 1994. McDonald's seeks meeting on Beijing eviction. *South China Morning Post*, November 29 (www.scmp.com/article/97722/mcdonalds-seeks-meeting-beijing-eviction). Accessed July 29, 2018.

Child, J. 2001. Trust – the fundamental bond in global collaboration. *Organizational Dynamics*, 29(4): 274–288.

Chinaaffairs.org. 2007. Section of 'Corruption of the Chinese Communist Party'. Chinaaffairs.org (www.chinaaffairs.org/gb/forum-step1.asp?categoryID=55 (2001–2007). Accessed May 25, 2007.

Chinese Education Online. 2014. Civil Service job admission rate in past 5 years. Chinese Education Online, September 17 (http://gongwuyuan.eol.cn/gkz x_12120/20140917/t20140917_1176740.shtml). Accessed July 7, 2018.

Chinese Government. 2018. Constitution of People's Republic of China (https://n pcobserver.com/2018/03/11/translation-2018-amendment-to-the-p-r-c-consti tution/). Accessed October 26, 2018.

Choi, C. 2018. Chinese corruption inquiry finds US$39 million in cash at homes of ex-boss of Huarong Asset Management. South China Morning Post, August 10 (www.scmp.com/news/china/policies-politics/article/2159221/chinese-cor ruption-inquiry-finds-us39-million-cash). Accessed August 12, 2018.

Choi, J. P., & Thum, M. 1998. Market structure and the timing of technology adoption with network externalities. *European Economic Review*, 42(2): 225–244.

CIA. 2018. *The World Factbook* (www.cia.gov).

Clague, C., Keefer, P., Knack, S., & Olson, M. 1996. Property and contract rights in autocracies and democracies. *Journal of Economic Growth*, 1(2): 243–276.

Corruption Watch. 2012. Report 1. Corruption watch, November 27 (www.corrup tionwatch.org.za/these-are-your-stories). Accessed August 4, 2018.

De Speville, B. 1997. *Hong Kong Policy Initiatives against Corruption*. Paris: Development Centre of the OECD.

Dehghan, S. K. 2016. Fury erupts in Iran over vast salaries paid to government officials. The Guardian, June 17 (www.theguardian.com/world/2016/jun/17/f ury-iran-salaries-government-officials). Accessed September 10, 2018.

Deloitte. "Use of IFRS by Jurisdiction" (www.iasplus.com/en/resources/ifrs-topic s/use-of-ifrs#Note14). Accessed June 14, 2018.

Dixit, A. 2004. *Lawlessness and Economics: Alternative Modes of Governance*. Princeton: Princeton University Press.

Dube, R. 2018. Argentine ex-president's homes raided in graft probe. *The Wall Street Journal*, August 24: A7.

Duowei. 2013. Housing allowance for high-level officials exposed: 220 square meters for ministers. BackChina.com, June 26 (www.rosechina.net/jd/szrd/2 015–05-04/6669.html). Accessed July 10, 2018.

Dwyer, F. R., & LaGace, R. R. 1986. On the nature and role of buyer-seller trust. In Shimp, T. A. and Sharma S. et al. (Eds.), AMA Summer Educators Conference Proceedings: 40–45. American Marketing Association.

Epoch Times. 2017. Over two million cadres disciplined in less than five years. *Epoch Times*, October 9 (www.epochtimes.com/gb/17/10/8/n9712920.htm). Accessed July 9, 2018.

Fa, D. J. 2016. The unbelievable benefits of retired high-level officials BackChina. com, February 2, 2017 (www.backchina.com/forum/20160217/info-1353274-1-1 .html). Accessed November 30, 2018.

Fang, Q. 2017. Xi Jinping's Anticorruption Campaign in a Historical Perspective. *Modern China Studies*, 24(2): 112–138.

Feng, E. 2018. China's globalisation paradox. *The Financial Times*, July 13.

Fishman, R., & Golden, M. A. 2017. *Corruption: What Everyone Needs to Know*. New York: Oxford University Press.

Freedom House. 1972–2018. Freedom in the world survey. Freedom House, www .freedomhouse.org.

Fukuyama, F. 1995. *Trust, the social virtues and the creation of prosperity*. New York: Free Press.

Fxtop. 2018. Currency conversion in the past. Fxtop (http://fxtop.com/en/currency-converter-past.php). Accessed July 7, 2018.

Gallup. 2016. Corruption continues to plague Indonesia. Gallup News (https://news.gallup.com/poll/157073/corruption-continues-plague-indonesia.aspx). Accessed July 2, 2018.

Gambetta, D. 1993. *The Sicilian Mafia: The Business of Private Protection*. Cambridge: Harvard University Press.

GAN Integrity. 2016. Peru corruption report. GAN Business Anti-Corruption Portal (www.business-anti-corruption.com/country-profiles/peru/). Accessed July 2, 2018.

GAN Integrity. 2017a. South Korea corruption report. GAN Business Anti-Corruption Portal (www.business-anti-corruption.com/country-profiles/south-korea/). Accessed July 12, 2018.

GAN Integrity. 2017b. Vietnam: Vietnam corruption report. GAN Business Anti-Corruption Portal (www.business-anti-corruption.com/) Accessed July 6, 2018.

GAN Integrity. 2017c. Thailand corruption report. GAN Business Anti-Corruption Portal, (www.business-anti-corruption.com/country-profiles/thailand/). Accessed July 1, 2018.

Gertz, B. 2017. Dissident reveals secret Chinese Intelligence Plans targeting U.S. *The Washington Beacon*, October 9 (https://freebeacon.com/national-security/dissident-reveals-secret-chinese-intelligence-plans-targeting-u-s/). Accessed July 20, 2018.

GlobalSecurity.org. 2018. Korean corruption. Global Security (www.globalsecurity.org/military/world/rok/corruption.htm). Accessed July 12, 2018.

Goldstein, E. 2011. A middle-class revolution. *Foreign Policy*, January 18 (https://foreignpolicy.com/2011/01/18/a-middle-class-revolution-2/). Accessed July 15, 2018.

Gong, T. 2002. Dangerous collusion: Corruption as a collective venture in contemporary China. *Communist and Post-Communist Studies*, 35(1): 85–103.

Gutmann, E. 2004. *Losing the New China: A Story of American Commerce, Desire and Betrayal*. San Francisco: Encounter Books.

Gwartney, J., & Lawson, R. 2012. *Economic Freedom of the World: 2012 Annual Report*. Toronto, Canada: The Fraser Institute.

Hamilton, C. 2018. *Silent Invasion*. London: Hardie Grant Books.

Hanban. 2014. Hanban (http://english.hanban.org/node_7719.htm). Accessed July 20, 2018.

Hardin, G. 1968. The Tragedy of the Commons. *Science*, 162 (3859): 1243–1248.

Hays, J. 2015. Indonesia under Suharto. Facts and details (http://factsanddetails.com/indonesia/History_and_Religion/sub6_1c/entry-3960.html) (2008 updated 2015). Accessed July 7, 2018.

Hewison, K., & Thongyou, M. 2000. Developing provincial capitalism: A profile of the economic and political roles of a new generation in Khon Kaen, Thailand. In R. McVey (Ed.), *Money and Power in Provincial Thailand*: 195–220. Honolulu: Hawaii University Press.

Hiebert, M. 1996. *Chasing the Tigers: A Portrait of the New Vietnam*. New York: Kodansha International.

Hill, C. L., & Hult, G. T. M. 2019. *International Business: Competing in the Global Marketplace* (12th edn.). New York: McGraw Hill.

Hirsch, M. W., & Smale, S. 1974. *Differential Equations, Dynamical Systems, and Linear Algebra*. New York: Academic Press.

Holmes, L. 1993. *The End of Communist Power: Anti-Corruption Campaigns and Legitimation Crisis*. New York: Oxford University Press.

Holmes, L. 2015. *Corruption: A Very Short Introduction*. New York: Oxford University Press.

Hough, D. 2013. *Corruption, Anti-Corruption and Governance*. New York: Palgrave Macmillan.

Hu, S. J. 2006. China's innovations in corruption. Radio Free Asia, November 24 (www.rfa.org/cantonese/commentaries/hsj/commentary_hu-20061124.html?encoding=simplified). Accessed May 25, 2007.

Huang, Y., & O'Neil-Massaro, K. J. 2001. Case study: Korea First Bank (A) and (B): *Harvard Business Review*.

Hughes, H. 1999. Crony capitalism and the East Asian currency and financial 'crises'. *Policy: A Journal of Public Policy and Ideas*, 15(3): 6.

Hwang, K. M. 2010. *A History of Korea*. London: Macmillan.

ICAC. 2002. *Annual Report 2001*. Independent Commission Against Corruption (www.icac.org.hk). Accessed July 15, 2018.

Inglehart, R. 1995–2005. *World Values Survey*. Ann Arbor: Institute for Social Research, University of Michigan.

Jain, A. K. 2001. Corruption: A review. *Journal of Economic Survey*, 15(1): 71–121.

Kalathil, S., & Boas, T. 2003. Open networks, closed regimes: The impact of the Internet on authoritarian rule. Washington, DC: Carnegie Endowment for International Peace.

Kamnuansilpa, P. 2015. PM must seize chance to shake up police. Bangkok Post, June 1 (www.bangkokpost.com/opinion/opinion/578363/pm-must-seize-chance-to-shake-up-police).

Karpoff, J. M., Lee, D. S., & Martin, G. S. 2010. Bribery: Business as usual? Working Paper of University of Washington.

Kaufmann, D., & Wei, S. J. 2000. Does 'grease money' speed up the wheels of commerce? NEBR Working Paper, No. 7093.

Kennedy, P. 2003. A Guide to Econometrics, Cambridge, MA: The MIT Press.

Kim, A. M. 2008. *Learning to Be Capitalists*. Oxford: Oxford University Press.

Koreabridge. 2012. A quick history of the Democratization of South Korea. Koreabridge (http://koreabridge.net/post/quick-history-democratization-sout h-korea-uncloudedhope). December 18.

Kreps, D., Milgrom, P., Roberts, J., & Wilson, R. 1982. Rational cooperation in the finitely repeated prisoner's dilemma. *Journal of Economic Theory*, 27(2): 245–252.

Krugman, P. 1998. THE CAPITALIST; I Told You So. *New York Times* Magazine.

Kuncoro, A. 2008. Corruption Inc, Inside Indonesia, 25 May (www.insideindonesia.org).

Kuo, L. 2017. Beijing is cultivating the next generation of African elites by training them in China. Quartz, December 14 (https://qz.com/1119447/china-is-train ing-africas-next-generation-of-leaders/). Accessed July 20, 2018.

La Porta, R., Lopez-de-Silanes, F., Shleifer, A., & Vishny, R. 1997. Trust in large organizations. *American Economic Review*, 87(2): 333–338.

Lam, A. 2009. ICAC invites visitors, not suspects, for 'cup of coffee' at its headquarters. South China Morning Post, February 9 (www.scmp.com/arti cle/669339/icac-invites-visitors-not-suspects-cup-coffee-its-headquarters). Accessed August 12, 2018.

Lambsdorff, J. G. 2002. How confidence facilitates illegal transactions. *American Journal of Economics and Sociology*, 61(4): 829–854.

Lee, S., Oh, K., & Eden, L. 2010. Why do firms bribe? Insights from residual control theory into firms' exposure and vulnerability to corruption. *Management International Review*, 50(6): 775–796.

Leff, N. H. 1964. Economic development through bureaucratic corruption. *The American Behavioral Scientist*, 8(3): 8–14.

Li, S. 1999. Relation-based versus rule-based governance: An explanation of the East Asian miracle and Asian crisis. Paper presented at the American Economic Association Annual Meeting in New York, January. Reprinted in *Review of International Economics*, 2003, 11(4): 651–673.

Li, S. 2004. Can China learn from Hong Kong's experience in fighting corruption? *Global Economic Review*, 33(1): 1–9.

Li, S. 2009. *Managing International Business in Relation-Based versus Rule-Based Countries*. New York: Business Expert Press.

Li, S. 2014. The inevitable and difficult transition from relation-based to rule-based governance in China. *Corporate Governance: An International Review*, 21(1): 145–172.

Li, S. 2015. Assessment of and outlook on China's corruption: Stagnation in the authoritarian trap? Chapter for the project "China in 2030" at Cambridge University.

Li, S. 2016. *East Asian Business in the New World: Helping Old Economies Revitalize*. New York: Elsevier.

Li, S. 2017. Assessment of and outlook on China's corruption and anticorruption campaigns: Stagnation in the authoritarian trap. *Modern China Studies*, 24 (2): 18.

Li, S., Alon, I., & Wu, J. 2017. Corruption may worsen in democratizing economies: But don't let it erode our faith in democracy. *Modern China Studies*, 24(2): 184–188.

Li, S., & Filer, L. 2007. The effects of the governance environment on the choice of investment mode and the strategic implications. *Journal of World Business*, 42 (1): 80–98.

Li, S., & Ouyang, M. 2007. A dynamic model to explain the bribery behavior of firms. *International Journal of Management*, 25(3): 605–618.

Li, S., & Park, S. H. 2006. Determinants of locations of foreign direct investment in China. *Management and Organization Review*, 2(1): 95–119.

Li, S., Park, S. H., & Bao, R. 2018. The transition from relation-based to rule-based governance in East Asia: Theories, evidence, and challenges. *International Journal of Emerging Markets*, In press: 27.

Li, S., Park, S. H., & Li, S. 2004. The great leap forward: The transition from relation-based governance to rule-based governance. *Organizational Dynamics*, 33(1): 63–78.

Li, S., Selover, D., & Stein, M. 2011. "Keep silent and make money": The institutional pattern of earnings manipulation in China. *Journal of Asian Economics*, 22(5): 369–382.

Li, S., & Wu, J. 2007. Why China thrives despite corruption. *Far Eastern Economic Review* (April): 24–28.

Li, S., & Wu, J. 2010. Why some countries thrive despite corruption: The role of trust in the corruption–efficiency relationship. *Review of International Political Economy*, 17(1): 129–154.

Lui, F. 1985. An equilibrium queuing model of bribery. *Journal of Political Economy*, 93(4): 760–781.

Luo, L. 2015. Chinese government employees get raises, 60 percent bump up for President Xi. BBC News, January 20 (www.bbc.com/zhongwen/simp/china/2 015/01/150120_china_xi_salary). Accessed July 7, 2018.

MacFarquhar, R. 2016. The trauma from the Great Proletarian Cultural Revolution: Can the Iron Triangle Be Saved? *Modern China Studies*, 23(2): 13–18.

Mao, Z. 1986. *Select Readings of Mao Zedong Works*. Beijing: People's Press.

Marson, J., & Grove, T. 2018. In Russia, corporate raiders can be cops. *The Wall Street Journal*, August 8 (A8).

Martini, M. 2013. The role of business associations and chambers of commerce in the fight against corruption. U4, No. 394 (October 9) Transparency International : www.u4.no/publications/the-role-of-busi ness-associations-and-chambers-of-commerce-in-the-fight-against-corrup tion.pdf.

Marx, K. 1875. Critique of the Gotha program. Letter.

Marx, K. 2007 (1867). *Capital: A Critique of Political Economy*. New York: Cosimo Classics.

McGuire, M. C., & Olson, M. 1996. The economics of autocracy and majority rule: The invisible hand and the use of force. *Journal of Economic Literature*, 34(1): 72–96.

Merriam-Webster. 2018a. *Authoritarian* (www.merriam-webster.com/diction ary/authoritarian). Accessed August 11, 2018.

Merriam-Webster. 2018b. *Democracy* (www.merriam-webster.com/diction ary/democracy). Accessed August 11, 2018.

Merriam-Webster. 2018c. *Totalitarianism* (www.merriam-webster.com/diction ary/totalitarianism). Accessed August 11, 2018.

Merton, R. K. 1968. *Social Theory and Social Structure*. New York: Free Press.

Miners, N. 1998. *The Government and Politics of Hong Kong*. New York: Oxford University Press.

Moon, C.-I., & Mo, J. 2015. *Economic Crisis and Structural Reforms in South Korea*. Washington: Economic Strategy Institute.

Moore, M. 2012. China's incoming President Xi Jinping's family "has wealth of hundreds of millions." The Telegraph, June 29 (www.telegraph.co.uk/news/ worldnews/asia/china/9365099/Chinas-incoming-president-Xi-Jinpings-famil y-has-wealth-of-hundreds-of-millions.html). Accessed August 12, 2018.

Moorman, C., Deshpande, R., & Zaltman, G. 1993. Factors affecting trust and market research relationships. *Journal of Marketing*, 57 (1): 81–101.

Moran, J. 1999. Patterns of corruption and development in East Asia. *Third World Quarterly*, 20(3): 569–587.

Moreorless. 2018. Soharto Moreorless (www.moreorless.net.au/killers/suharto.ht ml). Accessed October 25, 2018.

Morgan, R. M., & Hunt, S. D. 1994. The commitment-trust theory of relationship marketing. *Journal of Marketing*, 58(3): 20–39.

Morris, C. 2010. India's bureaucracy is "the most stifling in the world." BBC News, June 3 (www.bbc.com/news/10227680). Accessed October 25, 2018.

Morris, D. Z. 2017. Apple has pulled anti-censorship apps from China's app store. Fortune, July 29 (http://fortune.com/2017/07/29/apple-censorship-apps-chin a/). Accessed July 20, 2018.

Murphy, K. M., Shleifer, A., & Vishny, R. W. 1993. The allocation of talent: Implications for growth. *The Quarterly Journal of Economics*, 106(2): 503–530.

Nguyen, T., Weinstein, M., & Meyer, A. D. 2005. Development of trust: A study of interfirm relationships in Vietnam. *Asia Pacific Journal of Management*, 22(3): 211–235.

North, D. 1990. *Institutions, Institutional Change, and Economic Performance.* Cambridge: Cambridge University Press.

Nwabuzor, A. 2005. Corruption and development: New initiatives in economic openness and strengthened rule of law. *Journal of Business Ethics*, 59(1–2): 121–138.

Olson, M. 1993. Dictatorship, democracy, and development. American Political Science Review (September).

OODA Analyst. 2018. Pentagon: China's 'Thousand Talents' program labeled a national security threat. OODA Loop, June 26 (www.oodaloop.com/briefs/20 18/06/25/pentagon-chinas-thousand-talents-program-labeled-a-national-secur ity-threat/). Accessed September 1, 2018.

Orwell, G. 1949. *1984.* New York: Houghton Mifflin Harcourt Publishing Co.

Otto, B., & Ngui, Y. 2018. Malaysia's Najib posts bail in 1MDB corruption case. *The Wall Street Journal*, July 5 (A16).

Page, J. M. 1994. The East Asian Miracle: An Introduction. *World Development*, 22 (4): 612–625.

Park, S. H., & Luo, Y. 2001. Guanxi and organizational dynamics: Organizational networking in Chinese firms. *Strategic Management Journal*, 22(5): 455–477.

PayScale. 2018. Average salary in Riyadh, Saudi Arabia. PayScale (www.payscale .com/research/SA/Location=Riyadh/Salary). Accessed July 6, 2018.

Pedigo, K. L., & Marshall, V. 2008. Bribery: Australian managers' experiences and responses when operating in international markets. *Journal of Business Ethics*, 87(1): 59–74.

Pei, M. 2016. *China's Crony Capitalism: The Dynamics of Regime Decay.* Cambridge: Harvard University Press.

Pei, M. 2017. Assessing Xi Jinping's anti-corruption fight: Views from five scholars. *Modern China Studies*, 24(2): 5–13.

Peterson, R. 2017. *Outsourced to China: Confucius Institutes and Soft Power in American Higher Education*. National Association of Scholars.

Phongpaichit, P., & Baker, C. 2000. Chao Sua, Chao Pho, Chao Thi: Lords of Thailand's Transition. In R. McVey (Ed.), *Money and Power in Provincial Thailand*: 30–52. Honolulu: University of Hawaii Press.

Pillsbury, M. 2015. *The Hundred-Year Marathon: China's Secret Strategy to Replace America as the Global Superpower*. New York: St. Martin's Press.

Platteau, J. 1994. Behind the market stage where real societies exist – Parts I and II: The rule of public and private order institutions. *Journal of Development Studies*, 30(3): 533–577 and 753–817.

Przeworski, A., Alvarez, M., Cheibub, J., & Limongi, F. 2000. *Democracy and Development: Political Institutions and Well-Being in the World, 1950–1990*. Cambridge: Cambridge University Press.

Putnam, R. 1993. *Making Democracy Work: Civic Traditions in Modern Italy*. Princeton, NJ: Princeton University Press.

Quah, J. S. T. 2017. Singapore's success in combating corruption: Lessons for policy makers. *Asian Education and Development Studies*, 6(3): 263–274.

Quora. 2018. What is the average salary in Iran? Quora (www.quora.com/What-is-the-average-salary-in-Iran). Accessed October 25, 2018.

Rachman, G. 2018. Corruption thrives in a globalised world. *The Financial Times*, June 18 (www.ft.com/content/2bd5c9a4-72cf-11e8-b6ad-3823e4384287). Accessed July 20, 2018.

Radio Free Asia. 2018. Government spends a large sum to support foreign students with, people are upset. Radio Free Asia, July 18 (www.rfa.org/mandarin/yatai baodao/jingmao/yf1-07182018100345.html/). Accessed July 20, 2018.

Rahman, K. 2017. Somalia: Overview of corruption and anti-corruption. Transparency International, December 7 (https://knowledgehub.transpar ency.org/assets/uploads/helpdesk/Somalia_2017.pdf). Accessed October 25, 2018.

Reddit. 2018. In the former U.S.S.R., how much more were "professionals" (e.g. doctors, lawyers) paid than blue-collar workers (e.g. janitors)? Reddit: AskHistorians (www.reddit.com/r/AskHistorians/comments/2byhns/in_the_ former_ussr_how_much_more_were/). Accessed July 6, 2018. Reporters without Borders https://rsf.org/en/ranking_table.

Ricardo, D. 1967 (1817). *The Principles of Political Economy and Taxation*. Homewood, IL: Irwin.

Rodriguez, P., Siegel, D. S., Hillman, A., & Eden, L. 2006. Three lenses on the multinational enterprise: Politics, corruption, and corporate social responsibility. *Journal of International Business Studies*, 37(6): 733–746.

Rogin, J. 2017. China's foreign influence operations are causing alarm in Washington. Washington Post, December 10 (www.washingtonpost.com/opi nions/global-opinions/chinas-foreign-influencers-are-causing-alarm-in-washi ngton/2017/12/10/98227264-dc58-11e7-b859-fb0995360725_story.html?nore direct=on&utm_term=.67fd6fa6d83e). Accessed July 20, 2018.

Rose-Ackerman, S. 1978. *Corruption: A Study in Political Economy*. New York: Academic Press.

Rose-Ackerman, S., & Palifka, R. J. 2016. *Corruption and Government: Causes, Consequences, and Reform* (2nd edn.). New York: Cambridge University Press.

Rosenberg, T. 2002. John Kamm's third way. *New York Times* (Chinese edition), March 2 (www.nytimes.com/2002/03/03/magazine/john-kamm-s-third-way .html). Accessed July 20, 2018.

Rotter, J. B. 1967. A new scale for the measurement of interpersonal trust. *Journal of Personality*, 35(4): 651–665.

Sahlins, M. 2015. *Confucius Institutes: Academic Malware*. Chicago: Prickly Paradigm Press.

Said, S., & Faucon, B. 2018. Saudi oil-production data sow confusion. *The Wall Street Journal*, August 10 (B1).

Sandbrook, J. 2016. The 10 most corrupt World Leaders of recent history. Integritas360, June 20 (http://integritas360.org/2016/07/10-most-corrupt-wor ld-leaders/). Accessed July 10, 2018.

Sartor, M. A., & Beamish, P. W. 2018. Host market government corruption and the equity-based foreign entry strategies of multinational enterprises. *Journal of International Business Studies*, 49(3): 346–370.

Saudi Gazette. 2018. Govt spends SR163bn on salaries of civilian employees in 2017 Saudi Gazette, January 6 (http://saudigazette.com.sa/article/525660/SA UDI-ARABIA/Govt-spends-SR163bn-on-salaries-of-civilian-employees-in-20 17). Accessed July 6, 2018.

Scheck, J., & Hope, B. 2018. Airbus deal powered Saudi royal family's wealth. *The Wall Street Journal*, May 17(A1).

Schlesinger, J. 2017. How China swallowed the WTO. *Wall Street Journal*, November 1 (www.wsj.com/articles/how-china-swallowed-the-wto-1509551 308). Accessed August 13, 2018.

Shleifer, A., & Vishny, R. 1993. Corruption. *Quarterly Journal of Economics*, 108 (3): 599–617.

Siaw, L. K. L. 1983. *Chinese Society in Rural Malaysia*. Oxford: Oxford University Press.

Sina.com. 2016. Wei Pengyuan searched, 200 million yuan cash scattered on ground. Sina.com, October 20 (http://finance.sina.com.cn/china/2016-10-20/doc-ifxwztrs9892467.shtml?cref=cj). Accessed August 12, 2018.

Sing Tao Daily. 2018. "Please help me, we are all Chinese": Chinese male indicted for attempting to bribe LAX official. Sing Tao Daily, July 17 (www.singtaousa.com/la/453-南加新聞/1008810-「幫幫忙％EF％BC％8C都是中國人」+華男涉賄LAX官員被起訴/). Accessed August 7, 2018.

SinovisionNet. 2014. 28 years of anti-corruption in China: 181 senior officials caught, two climaxes in ten years. SinovisionNet (http://news.sinovision.net/politics/201409/00310740.htm).

Smith, H. 1984 (Revised edn.). *The Russians*. New York: Ballantine Books.

Sohu Finance. 2014. Why people envy government employees. Sohu Finance, April 28 (http://business.sohu.com/20140428/n398916657.shtml). Accessed July 7, 2018.

Solomon, J. 2007. *Corporate Governance and Responsibility*: 221. Chichester: John Wiley and Sons.

Solow, R. 1956. A contribution to the theory of economic growth. *Quarterly Journal of Economics*, 70 (1): (65–94).

Stancati, M., & Said, S. 2018a. Saudi crown prince suppresses dissent in bid to control change. *The Wall Street Journal*, June 6 (A18).

Stancati, M., & Said, S. 2018b. Saudis still hold dozens in crackdown. *The Wall Street Journal*, July 5 (A6).

Steiner, A. 2018. Corruption in an anticorruption state? East Germany under communist rule. In R. Kroeze & A. Vitoria (Eds.) Anticorruption in History: From Antiquity to the Modern Era: 296. New York: Oxford University Press.

Sun, Y. 2004. *Corruption and Market in Contemporary China*. Ithaca, NY: Cornell University Press.

Svensson, J. 2003. Who must pay bribes and how much? Evidence from a cross-section of firms. *Quarterly Journal of Economics*, 118 (1): 207–230.

Svensson, J. 2005. Eight questions about corruption. *Journal of Economic Perspectives*, 19(3): 19–42.

Tang, W. 2005. *Public Opinion and Political Change in China*. Redwood City, CA: Stanford University Press.

Tanzi, V. 1998. Corruption around the world: Causes, consequences, scope, and cures. IMF Working Paper. Washington DC: IMF.

Taylor, J. 2011. *The Generalissimo: Chiang Kai-shek and the Struggle for Modern China*: Cambridge, MA: Harvard University Press.

Tella, O. 2013. Corruption and economic development: Africa and East Asia in comparative perspective. *Ubuntu: Journal of Conflict and Social Transformation*, 2(1 & 2): 47–67.

The Economist. 2014. Confucius says – soft power. *The Economist*, September 13.

Transparency International. 2011. Bribe Payers Index 2011: Transparency International. November 2.

Transparency International. 2017. Corruption Perceptions Index 2017: Transparency International. 25 January (www.transparency.org/news/fea ture/corruption_perceptions_index_2017). Accessed October 25, 2018.

Ueda, Y. 2000. The entrepreneurs of Khorat. In R. McVey (Ed.), *Money and Power in Provincial Thailand*: 154–194. Honolulu: Hawaii University Press.

United States. 1776. United States Declaration of Independence.

Uslaner, E. M. 2002. *The Moral Foundations of Trust*. New York: Cambridge University Press.

Uslaner, E. M. 2004. Trust and corruption. In J. G. Lambsdort, M. Taube, & M. Schramm (Eds.), *Corruption and the New Institutional Economics*: 76–92. London: Routledge.

Valle, L. del. 2018. Exporting corruption: Beyond Brazil's Car Wash scandal. alja zeera.com, March 10 (www.aljazeera.com/blogs/americas/2018/03/exporting-c orruption-brazil-car-wash-scandal-180307110441253.html). Accessed July 20, 2018.

Vietnam Online. 2018. Average salary. Vietnam Online, February 4 (www.vietna monline.com/az/average-salary.html).

Vision Times. 2018. Explosive: Guizhou official has AIDS, many officials – female and male – are rushing to hospitals. *Vision Times*, July 11 (www.secretchina .com/news/gb/2018/07/11/864248.html). Accessed July 20, 2018.

Vn Express International. 2017. Vietnam's corruption crackdown at all-time high: Party chief. *Vn Express International*, December 28 (https://e.vnexpress.net/ news/news/vietnam-s-corruption-crackdown-at-all-time-high-party-chief-36 91342.html). Accessed July 9, 2018.

Vn Express International. 2018. 50 high-profile officials disciplined in Vietnam's escalating corruption crackdown. *Vn Express International*, June 26 (https://e.vnexpress.net/news/news/50-high-profile-officials-disci plined-in-vietnam-s-escalating-corruption-crackdown-3768692.html). Accessed July 9, 2018.

Voice of America. 2018. Vietnam widens anti-corruption campaign by cleaning the ruling party. Voice of America, May 14 (www.voanews.com/a/vietnam-antic orruption/4392671.html). Accessed July 9, 2018.

Walker, J. 2013. Norfolk prosecutor assigned to Va. mansion chef case. *The Virginian-Pilot*, May 3 (https://pilotonline.com/news/government/politics/article_58b1057b-7f71-551a-8f49-16483eaf2769.html). Accessed August 2, 2018.

Wang, Q. 2016. Report at the 6th Plenary Session of the 18th Central Party Disciplinary Committee. Baidu Baike, January 12 (https://baike.baidu.com/item/十八届中央纪委第六次全会工作报告). Accessed July 10, 2018.

Wedeman, A. 1997. Looters, rent-scrapers, and dividend-collectors: Corruption and growth in Zaire, South Korea, and the Philippines. *Journal of Developing Areas*, 31(4): 457–478.

Wedeman, A. 2002. Development and corruption: The East Asian paradox. In E. D. Gomez (Ed.), *Political Business in East Asia*: 35–61. London: Routledge.

Wedeman, A. 2012. *Double Paradox: Rapid Growth and Rising Corruption in China*. Ithaca: Cornell University Press

Wedeman, A. 2017. Xi Jinping's tiger hunt: Anti-corruption campaign or factional purge?. *Modern China Studies*, 24(2): 35–94.

wikiHow. 2018a. How to form an LLC in Virginia. wikiHow (www.wikihow.com/Form-an-LLC-in-Virginia). Accessed September 1, 2018.

wikiHow. 2018b. How to register a company in India. wikiHow (www.wikihow.com/wikiHow/Register-a-Company-in-India). Accessed September 1, 2018.

Wikipedia. 2015a. 1997 Asian financial crisis. Wikipedia (https://en.wikipedia.org/wiki/1997_Asian_financial_crisis#;South_Korea). Accessed September 1, 2018.

Wikipedia. 2015b. Confucius Institute. Wikipedia (https://en.wikipedia.org/wiki/Confucius_Institute). Accessed July 20, 2018.

Wikipedia. 2016a. Operation car wash. Wikipedia (https://en.wikipedia.org/wiki/Operation_Car_Wash). Accessed July 20, 2018.

Wikipedia. 2016b. Panama papers. Wikipedia (https://en.wikipedia.org/wiki/Panama_Papers). Accessed July 29, 2018.

Wikipedia. 2017. Death of Lei Yang. Wikipedia (https://en.wikipedia.org/wiki/Death_of_Lei_Yang). Accessed July 15, 2018.

Wikipedia. 2018a. 1Malaysia Development Berhad scandal. Wikipedia (https://en.wikipedia.org/wiki/1Malaysia_Development_Berhad_scandal). Accessed July 20, 2018.

Wikipedia. 2018b. Authoritarianism. Wikipedia (https://en.wikipedia.org/wiki/Authoritarianism). Accessed July 5, 2018.

Wikipedia. 2018c. Belt and road initiative. Wikipedia (https://en.wikipedia.org/wiki/Belt_and_Road_Initiative). Accessed July 20, 2018.

Wikipedia. 2018d. Democracy. Wikipedia (https://en.wikipedia.org/wiki/Democracy). Accessed July 5, 2018.

Wikipedia. 2018e. Demographics of Hong Kong. Wikipedia (https://en.wikipedia .org/wiki/Demographics_of_Hong_Kong). Accessed September 3, 2018.

Wikipedia. 2018f. Park Geun-hye. Wikipedia (https://en.wikipedia.org/wiki/Park_ Geun-hye). Accessed July 12, 2018.

Wikipedia. 2018g. Suharto. Wikipedia (https://en.wikipedia.org/wiki/Suharto#So cio-economic_progress_and_growing_corruption). Accessed July 8, 2018.

Wikipedia. 2018h. Thousand talents program (China). Wikipedia (https://en.wiki pedia.org/wiki/Thousand_Talents_Program_(China)). Accessed July 20, 2018.

Wikipedia. 2018i. Totalitarianism. Wikipedia (https://en.wikipedia.org/wiki/Tota litarianism). Accessed July 5, 2018.

Wikipedia. 2018j. Tunisian Revolution. Wikipedia (https://en.wikipedia.org/wiki/ Tunisian_Revolution). Accessed July 15, 2018.

Wise, D. 2011. *Tiger Trap*. New York: Houghton Mifflin Harcourt.

Wood, P. 2018. China's Pernicious Presence on American Campuses. *The Chronicle of Higher Education*, Accessed July 19, 2018.

Woodridge, J. 2003. *Introductory Econometrics: A Modern Approach*. Mason, Ohio: South-Western College.

World Bank. 2018. World Development Indicators. Washington, DC: World Bank.

World News Net. 2014. Xi's anticorruption campaign exempts the princelings. *China Affairs*, October 26 (Chinaaffairs.org).

World Values Survey. 2005–2014. World Values Survey: World Values Survey Association (www.worldvaluessurvey.org/).

Wu, X. 2008. *China: The Era of Grabbing Wealth: Business History, 1993–2008*. Taipei: Yuanliu.

Xin, K., & Pearce, J. L. 1996. Guanxi: Connections as substitutes for formal institutional support. *Academy of Management Journal*, 39(6): 1641–1658.

Yadav, V., & Mukherjee, B. 2016. *The Politics of Corruption in Dictatorships*. New York: Cambridge University Press.

Yang, M. 2002. The resilience of guanxi and its new deployments: A critique of some new guanxi scholarship. China Quarterly, 170: 459–476.

Yang, X. 2016. The curse on the latecomer. Economists' Circle, September 20 (htt ps://mp.weixin.qq.com/s/m341JTx3vlbI1J9CSPVGzA). Accessed July 6, 2018.

Yerkes, S., & Muasher, M. 2017. *Tunisia's Corruption Contagion: A Transition at Risk*. Washington, DC: Carnegie Endowment for International Peace.

Yu, J. 2006. What kind of department is the propaganda department? Independent Chinese Pen Center, August (https://blog.boxun.com/hero/2007/yujie/444_1. shtml).

Zetter, K. 2016. Magistrate Orders Apple to Help FBI Hack San Bernardino Shooter's Phone. Wired, February 16 (www.wired.com/2016/02/magistrate-or

ders-apple-to-help-fbi-hack-phone-of-san-bernardino-shooter/). Accessed July 20, 2018.

Zhu, Z. 2007. Youquanbushi guoqizuofei, *blog.sina.com.cn*, October 23 (http://bl og.sina.com.cn/s/blog_4de7afca01000cgp.html). Accessed November 30, 2018.

Zh.wikipedia.org. 2014. Tabulating corruption cases of the PRC. www.google.com/ search?q=%E4%B8%AD%E8%8F%AF%E4%BA%BA%E6%B0%91%E5%8 5%B1%E5%92%8C%E5%9C%8B%E8%85%90%E6%95%97%E6%A1%88 %E4%BB%B6%E5%88%97%E8%A1%A8¡utf-8œutf-8&aq=t&rls=org.mozill a:en-US:official&client=firefox-a&channel=sb.

Index